2nd Edition

IT MATTERS

Englisch für IT-Berufe

von

Ken Thomson

und

Wolfgang Towara

In Zusammenarbeit mit der Verlagsredaktion

Cornelsen

Verfasser: Ken Thomson, Berlin; Wolfgang Towara, Würzburg
Berater: Antje Baehr, Velbert; Uwe Schlenger, Berlin

Verlagsredaktion: Kari-ann Seamark
Redaktionelle Mitarbeit: Kieran Breen, Oliver Busch (Wörterverzeichnisse), Christiane Grosskopf, Oliver Kenny
Layout und technische Umsetzung: Sabine Theuring, Berlin
Bildredaktion: Kieran Breen
Umschlaggestaltung: Sabine Theuring, Berlin
Titelfoto: Getty Images / R and R Images
Illustrationen: Oxford Designers & Illustrators

Erhältlich sind auch:
Handreichungen zum Unterricht + Lehrer-CD + Audio-CD
ISBN 978-3-06-520507-8

www.cornelsen.de

1. Auflage, 1. Druck 2011

Alle Drucke dieser Auflage sind inhaltlich unverändert und können im Unterricht nebeneinander verwendet werden.

Druck: CS-Druck CornelsenStürtz, Berlin

ISBN 978-3-06-520505-4

Inhalt gedruckt auf säurefreiem Papier aus nachhaltiger Forstwirtschaft.

Vorwort

IT Matters 2nd Edition ist die aktualisierte Neubearbeitung des bewährten Lehrwerks für IT-Berufe, das für die Ausbildung in Berufsschulen sowie innerbetriebliche Aus- und Weiterbildung geeignet ist. Das einbändige Lehrwerk setzt Englischkenntnisse voraus, die der Stufe B1 des Europäischen Referenzrahmens *(Common European Framework of Reference)* entsprechen und kann zur gezielten Vorbereitung auf die KMK-Zertifikatsprüfung benutzt werden.

IT Matters enthält 10 Units, in denen handlungsorientiert und praxisbezogen alltägliche Gegebenheiten und aktuelle Themen aus den wesentlichen Bereichen der gewerblich-technischen und kaufmännischen IT-Berufen aufgegriffen werden. Der Schwerpunkt liegt auf dem dialogischen Austausch in typischen Berufssituationen. Dabei werden das nötige Fachvokabular und entscheidende Redewendungen anhand von abwechslungsreichen Übungen bearbeitet und gefestigt, um sie später handlungsorientiert (Rollenspiele) anwenden zu können. Als weitere Unterstutzung finden Sie *Useful language boxes* im Anhang zum Nachschlagen.

Zusätzlich wird selbstorganisiertes und binnendifferenziertes Lernen gefördert, indem jede Unit ein Webcode und eine *Refresh your knowledge box*, sowie zumindest eine *Extra material*-Seite anbietet. Die Webcodes festigen oder entwickeln ein Thema der Unit weiter und können selbstständig zu Hause auf der Webseite www.cornelsen.de/cbb bearbeitet werden. Bei den *Refresh your knowledge*-Teilen bekommen Sie die Möglichkeit, das Gelernte nochmal schnell zu überprüfen sowie nützliche Vokabeln und Redewendungen zur Weiternutzung zu sammeln. Fortgeschrittene Lernende bekommen auf den *Extra material*-Seiten anspruchsvollere Texte und Aufgaben mit höherem Schwierigkeitsgrad geboten.

Die Grammatik in *IT Matters* ist auf das Wesentliche begrenzt. Grundlegende Strukturen werden in den Units im situativen Kontext vermittelt. Weitaus wichtiger ist jedoch die Erweiterung des berufsrelevanten Wortschatzes und das Erlernen feststehender Redewendungen, die als Rüstzeug für eine flüssige, effektive berufliche Kommunikation dienen.

Im Anhang finden Sie außerdem Vorlagen für Partnerübungen und Rollenspiele, die Transkripte der Hörverständnistexte sowie nützliche Redewendungen. Abgerundet wird das Lehrwerk mit chronologischen und alphabetischen Wörterverzeichnissen sowie einer Grundwortschatzliste, die etwa 900 Wörter enthält, die für die Arbeit mit *IT Matters* als bekannt vorausgesetzt werden.

Der Verlag, der Autor und die Berater wünschen Ihnen viel Erfolg und Freude bei der Arbeit mit *IT Matters 2nd Edition*.

Symbolerklärungen:

Track 00 Hörverständnistext auf die Audio-CD

Webcode

Hinweis auf *Useful language* im Anhang

IT Matters im Internet

Webcode:
ITMU0101

Auf den Seiten Ihres Kursbuches finden Sie für jede Unit einen so genannten „Webcode“. Wenn Sie den entsprechenden Code auf der Webseite www.cornelsen.de/cbb im Feld „Webcode“ oben rechts eingeben, gelangen Sie zu weiterführenden Übungen, die speziell auf ein Thema der jeweiligen Unit abgestimmt sind. Sie können damit selbstständig zu Hause arbeiten. Einen Überblick der Themen finden Sie hier:

Unit 1, nach Übung 6	Talking to a visitor
Unit 2, nach Übung 10	Building a PC
Unit 3, nach Übung 5	On the telephone
Unit 4, nach Übung 11	If sentences types 1 & 2
Unit 5, nach Übung 9	Hotlines & flow charts
Unit 6, nach Übung 13	AUPs
Unit 7, nach Übung 4	Comparatives & superlatives
Unit 8, nach Übung 16	Complaining
Unit 9, nach Übung 8	Talking about projects
Unit 10, nach Übung 15	Talking about your training / Simple past & present perfect

Exploring an IT company

1

- looking at company profiles
- welcoming a visitor
- describing jobs & departments

1 Start up

Discuss your company and what it does with a partner. Include the following information.

1 What kind of work does your company do?

We design/assemble/repair/sell ...

2 What type of customers does it have?

We have mainly private/commercial/industrial ...

3 What are your company's main business activities?

We specialize in ...

4 How many people work for your company?

We have ... IT specialists, ... software designers and ...

5 Where is your company located?

My company is located in ... / 100 km from ... / between ... and .... / near ...

2 IT International

Read IT International's company profile and answer the FAQs.

I.T. International

http://www.itinternational.com/

IT International

IT International – A Multinational Telecommunications and Information Technology Company

IT International is a multinational telecommunications and information technology company. Although the headquarters are in Munich, over 50 per cent of our revenue is generated outside Germany. We have an international focus and subsidiaries in 30 countries, including Asia (several in China as the fastest growing market), Africa, the United States and some European countries. More than half of our 180,650 employees work abroad.

We supply network access, communication services, fixed and mobile networks and telephones, including smart phones. We also focus on services and IT solutions for the energy, health care and automotive sectors.

Our business activities are determined by the principle of providing our customers with excellent products and services at a fair price.

FAQs

1. What is IT International?
2. Where is IT International located?
3. Where are the company's subsidiaries?
4. What is special about China?
5. How many people work for IT International?
6. What are the company's business activities?
7. What is IT International's business philosophy?

3 Working with words

a Copy the grid below and then match the words (a–h) to the correct explanation (1–10) to make a vocabulary list. There are two explanations too many.

Vocabulary	Explanation
multinational	international

a headquarters
b revenue
c subsidiary
d employee
e access
f focus on
g determine
h provide

1 a person who works for a company
2 to concentrate on
3 the total annual income of a company
4 to offer
5 a company which is owned by a larger company
6 a way into something
7 to be concerned with motor vehicles
8 in or to a foreign country
9 to decide something firmly
10 a place from which something is controlled

b **Now find the words in the text which match the two remaining explanations.**

c **Complete the table with other words from the text which you did not know. Use a dictionary to help with the explanations.**

Grammar | **The present tenses**

1 IT International **generates** most of its revenue abroad.
2 It **doesn't offer** electricity.
3 **Does** IT International **have** subsidiaries in other countries? Yes, it **does**.
4 **Is** the company **recruiting** staff at the moment?
5 IT International **is expanding** rapidly and **needs** more staff.

- Das *simple present* wird für regelmäßige, wiederholte Handlungen und Zustände verwendet (1–3). Es steht oft in Verbindung mit Signalwörtern wie *regularly, usually, always*, etc.
- In der 3. Person Einzahl (*he, she, it, the company*, etc.) wird ein *–(e)s* an die Grundform angefügt (1). Frage und Verneinung werden mit einer Form von *do* (*do/does, don't/doesn't* + Grundform) gebildet (2, 3).
- Das *present progressive* wird für eine nur vorübergehend andauernde Handlung verwendet, die im Augenblick des Sprechens geschieht (4, 5). Es steht oft in Verbindung mit Signalwörtern wie *at the moment, now*, etc.
- Das *present progressive* wird mit *is/am/are* und der *-ing* Form gebildet (4, 5).

4 Practice

Complete the sentences using the simple present or present progressive of the verbs in brackets.

1 At the moment our company ... quickly. (grow)
2 That is why we ... new staff right now. (recruit)
3 We ... subsidiaries in many countries. (have)
4 Peter ... in technical support. (work)
5 He ... when customers ... problems. (help, have)
6 Just now we ... a new software. (develop)
7 We usually ... our customers good value for money. (give)
8 Today we ... a discount of ten per cent. (offer)

5 FAQs

a **Write FAQs and answers about your company or another company you know about. You can use your company's website.**

b **Use your information to give a presentation to the class.**

6 A visitor

Track 2

a Listen to the dialogue at the reception of IT International headquarters and decide who the visitor is and why he is there.

b Complete the sentences from the dialogue. Who says them: the receptionist or the visitor?

1. How can I ... you?
2. I have an ... with Ms Wang but I'm ... I'm a few minutes early.
3. ... to Munich, Mr Matthews.
4. I'll ... Maggie ... that you're here.
5. If you could just ... a moment, I'm ... she'll be here soon.
6. I don't ... waiting.
7. Pleased to ... you.
8. I hope you ... your stay in Munich.

Webcode: ITMU0101

7 Role-play: welcoming a visitor

page 111

Work with a partner to do the role-play. Use the language from exercise 6.

Empfang

Begrüßen Sie den Besucher / die Besucherin.

Besucher/in

Stellen Sie sich vor.

Stellen Sie sich ebenfalls vor und fragen Sie, ob Sie helfen können.

Sagen Sie, dass Sie für heute einen Termin mit Frau Maggie Wang vereinbart haben. Sie sind leider eine halbe Stunde zu früh gekommen.

Bitten Sie den Besucher / die Besucherin um einen Augenblick Geduld. Sagen Sie, dass Sie Frau Wang über seine/ihre Ankunft informieren werden.

Antworten Sie, dass es für Sie kein Problem ist zu warten.

Fragen Sie den Besucher / die Besucherin nach seiner/ihrer Tätigkeit.

Antworten Sie.

Verabschieden Sie sich und stellen Sie den Besucher / die Besucherin Frau Wang vor, die gerade gekommen ist.

Bedanken Sie sich für die Hilfe.

Wünschen Sie dem Besucher / der Besucherin eine gute Zeit in Deutschland.

Skills **Wie verbessere ich meine Englischkenntnisse?**

Es gibt verschiedene Möglichkeiten (durch Lesen oder Schreiben, durch Zuhören oder Sprechen, in der Gruppe oder alleine) eine Sprache zu lernen. Hier sind einige Ideen, wie Sie Ihre Englischkenntnisse verbessern können:

- Englische Bücher lesen
- Englische Wortschatzlisten lernen
- Englischsprachige Radiosender hören
- Englische Gebrauchsanweisungen lesen
- Mit Freunden per E-Mail oder Skype auf Englisch kommunizieren
- Witze auf Englisch erzählen
- Englischsprachige Filme mit oder ohne Untertitel ansehen
- Englische Computerzeitschriften lesen
- Im Internet auf englischsprachigen (technischen) Seiten surfen
- Ins englischsprachige Ausland fahren

8 Building skills: improving your English

a English is important even when you are still in Germany, for example, when welcoming international visitors. Read the skills box above and decide which ideas work best for you when trying to improve your English.

Put them in order (1 = most helpful, 10 = least helpful) and then add any other ideas.

b In groups, identify the best English language a) technical websites, b) computer magazines or c) radio stations which can help you improve your English for work. Present your findings to the class.

9 A tour of the company

Track 3

Maggie Wang is telling the new interns what they will be doing during a tour of the company. Copy the timetable below and then listen and complete it.

Time	Tour item
9.30 – 10.00 a.m.	Company's history and ...
3.00 p.m.	

Maggie Good morning and welcome to our new interns. My name is Maggie Wang and I'm your guide for today. I will be showing you around the company to give you an idea what IT International looks like. I've divided the day into four parts.

From 9.30 to 10.00 you will get some information about the company's history and its organization here in the conference room. Then we'll have a look at the different departments, for example, order processing, marketing and customer service. We will take a look at the marketing department first, which is responsible for finding out what the consumers want. They also arrange promotional tours and organize our presence at trade fairs. Next we'll go to the order processing department, which places orders and then labels, packs and ships them. Finally we'll visit the customer service department. The staff there deal with our customers' questions, complaints and requests. The experts have to deal with all kinds of technical problems.

At twelve we will have lunch in the canteen and then at one we are going to visit the research and development department – or R & D as we call it. Here our experts will demonstrate our latest research project – innovative telecommunication applications for day-to-day use in the home. Here we are currently testing and developing state-of-the-art information and communication technology in a 'futurist' household. The results of our research will benefit all our customers in the future.

Finally, we'll meet here in the conference room again at three for a question-and-answer session. But before we start the tour, are there any questions now?

Intern Er ... yes ..., can we take photos?

Maggie I'm sorry, I'm afraid you can't. Photography is not allowed here. But you will all get a full-colour brochure with photos and information at the end of the tour.

Intern That's nice, thank you.

10 Talking about departments

Track 3

a Listen or read again and decide which of these departments are mentioned.

1 human resources
2 customer service
3 finance
4 marketing
5 research and development
6 order processing

b Now decide which of the departments these people work in.

11 Describing jobs and departments

a Sort these phrases into two categories: a) talking about responsibilities and duties and b) talking about work patterns.

1. I work in an office / a firm / a workshop / a factory / on site.
2. We work with customers / subsidiaries / suppliers / etc.
3. We install / test computers / devices / IT systems.
4. My main duties include …
5. I am sometimes on call.
6. My department is responsible for marketing / administration / customer service / etc.
7. I mostly work with …
8. We help/advise customers.
9. I work fixed hours / shifts / nights / a 37-hour week / flexitime.
10. Ms/Mrs/Mr … is in charge of the department.
11. I do lots of overtime.
12. The department specializes in organizing research / customer training / taking care of foreign visitors / etc.

b Now add any extra phrases from the dialogue in exercise 9 and the texts in exercise 10.

12 Your job

a Describe what you can see in the picture.

b Read the text and then use the information and the language from exercise 11 to write a profile of your own job.

Hi, I'm Tobi Mathews and I am an IT specialist from the subsidiary in Manchester. I'm here for a six-month placement at IT International in Munich. My role as an IT specialist may vary in England depending on the specific work environments. In my company I work from Monday to Friday. I test, install and maintain computer and IT systems, LAN and WLAN networks and troubleshoot hardware and network-related issues. In recent years my responsibilities have broadened and now include IT security problems, monitoring software programs and maintaining or repairing all peripherals and removable storage devices. I also diagnose faults and provide technical advice for customers or solve technical problems by phone or in person. I work fixed hours and have a 37-hour-week.

13 An organization chart

Track 4 **a Listen to the presentation and complete IT International's organization chart.**

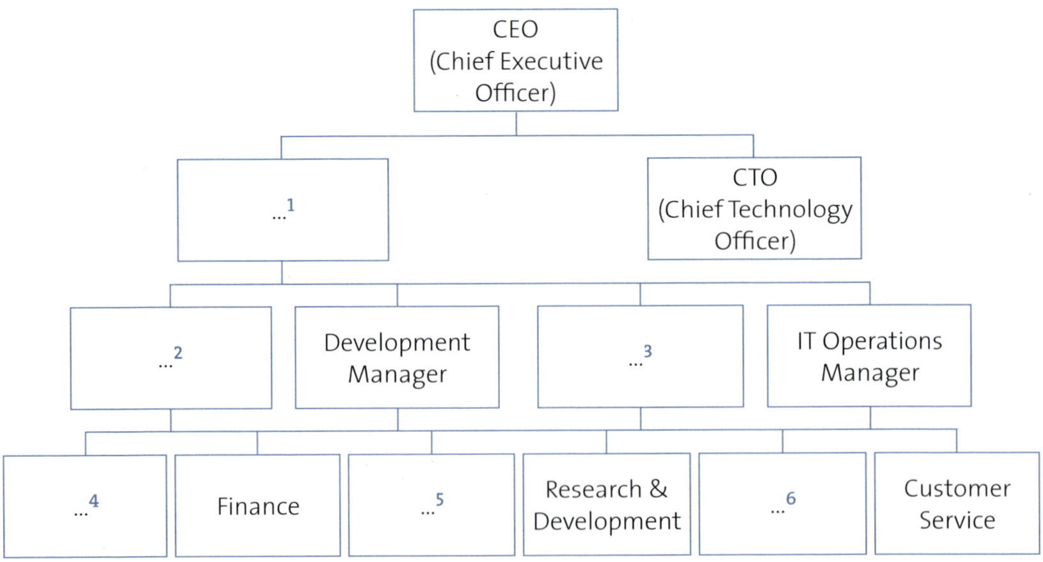

b Listen again and decide which of these phrases are used to describe the company structure.

1 ... works for ...
2 ... is in charge of ...
3 ... is responsible for ...
4 ... reports to ...
5 ... works in ... department

14 Talking about responsibilities

page 111

a Take turns to describe the organization of IT International using the information and phrases from exercise 13.

Student A: Choose a position or department from the organization chart. Do not tell your partner which one. Describe what the people in the position or department do.
Student B: Ask your partner questions about the job he/she is describing.

b Now swap roles.

Refresh your knowledge

1 Choose the correct answer.

1 What does CIO stand for?

a Central Intelligence Organization
b Chief Information Officer
c Central Information Office
d Certified Information Online

2 Which department is responsible for finding out what the consumers want?

a customer services
b human resources
c finance
d marketing

3 Where does the development of new software take place?

a in communication technology
b in purchasing
c in R & D
d in finance

2 Now draw an organization chart for your company. Write a few sentences for each of the departments explaining who works there and what they do.

IBM – A Global Information Technology Company

International Business Machines Corporation, abbreviated IBM and nicknamed "Big Blue" (because of its official corporate colour), is a multinational computer technology and consulting corporation with its headquarters in Armonk, New York, United States. The company is one of the few information technology companies with a continuous history dating back to the 19th century. IBM manufactures and sells computer hardware and software and offers infrastructure services, hosting services and consulting services in areas ranging from mainframe computers to nanotechnology.

With over 388,000 employees worldwide, IBM is the largest information technology employer in the world. Despite falling behind Hewlett Packard in total revenue in 2006, the company remains the most profitable. IBM holds more patents than any other US-based technology company. It has engineers and consultants in over 170 countries and IBM Research has eight laboratories worldwide. IBM employees have earned three Nobel Prizes, four Turing Awards, five National Medals of Technology and five National Medals of Science. As a chip maker, IBM has been among the Worldwide Top 20 Semiconductor Sales Leaders in past years, and in 2007 IBM was second in the list of largest software companies in the world.

IBM has pioneered a new operating model. It is no longer a classic 'multinational', with smaller versions of the parent company replicated in countries around the world. Instead it is a global model with one set of processes, shared services and broadly distributed decision making carried out by a highly skilled global workforce managed by a common set of values. IBM's shift to a globally integrated model allowed the company to refocus their country organizations on generating growth and serving clients.

(adapted from http://www.linkedin.com/companies/ibm)

1 True or false

Say whether the statements below are true or false. If they are wrong, say why.

1 IBM is an international machine cooperation.
2 Its history dates back to the 19th century.
3 IBM buys computers and computer services.
4 It is the largest information technology company worldwide.
5 It is less profitable than Hewlett Packard.
6 IBM employees have already earned the Nobel Prize.
7 It is a pioneer in a new operating model.
8 Now it has a globally integrated operating model.

2 Mediation

Ihr Chef möchte sich über IBM informieren. Fassen Sie den Text aus der Firmenbroschüre für ihn auf Deutsch zusammen.

Installing & configuring hardware 2

- building your own PC
- advising customers
- installing hardware safely

1 Start up

a **Copy the table below and then read the internet discussion thread. Summarize the answers to Karen_69's question in the correct column.**

Advantages and disadvantages of building your own PC

Advantages	Disadvantages

Karen_69:	I've been thinking about building my own PC. Can anyone out there advise me what the pros and cons are?
Boris_online:	It can take quite a lot of time.
Zim:	Building your own PC can make doing upgrades in the future easier.
Julie_the_only:	Yeah, but you have to buy the operating system which is quite expensive.
Pinter@work:	Right ... building can cost more in general.
Brian81:	But it's really satisfying.
Cassie:	If something goes wrong, you can't just take it back to the shop.
Pete_1:	Yeah, but you become an expert on your own system.
	...

b **Now work with a partner and think of other advantages and disadvantages. Write these as if they were points in the internet discussion thread.**

c **Discuss whether you think it is better to build a PC rather than buy a pre-built one. What would you recommend to a customer and why?**

2 Which PC components?

Track 5

Karen goes to Computerland for more advice. Decide which of the components below are mentioned and then name the ones that are not mentioned.

1

2

3

4

5

6

7

8

3 Advice from a PC specialist

Track 5

Listen again and decide whether the following statements are true or false. Correct the false statements.

1 Karen will use her PC to store a lot of music and films.
2 She's mainly going to use the PC for work.
3 The PC she has at the moment isn't powerful enough for the games she plays.
4 Karen can spend over £1,500 on her PC.
5 The salesperson recommends a processor which will let Karen work with more than one graphics package at a time.
6 The salesperson says that the video card will take up a lot of Karen's budget.

Grammar | **Question forms**

1 **Do** you **need** to run these pieces of graphic design software at the same time?
2 What **do** you want your PC to be able to do?
3 How much money **do** you **want to spend** on the PC?
4 What **would** you recommend?
5 How much memory **will** I **need**?
6 **Can** I **save** money on the hard drive?
7 Why **is** the speed of the processor so important?

- Fragen werden mit dem Hilfsverb *do* + Infinitiv des Vollverbs gebildet (1–3).
- Fragen mit Modalverben (*can, must, should*, usw.) und anderen Hilfsverben (*will, would*, usw.) werden ohne *do* gebildet (4–6).
- Fragen mit dem Verb *be* werden ebenfalls ohne *do* gebildet (7).
- Fragen mit Fragewörtern beginnen mit *when, where, how, why, who, which*, usw. (2, 3, 4, 5, 7).

4 Practice

a Put the words in the correct order to form questions.

1 advice / I / your / can / about / PC / building / a / ask / ?
2 on / want / play / to / PC / your / games / do / you / ?
3 processor / recommend / you / type / what / of / would / ?
4 I / motherboard / much / need / will / to / on / spend / the / how / ?
5 PC / want / do / with / do / you / to / your / what / ?
6 money / spend / more / card / I / the / should / video / on / ?
7 better / is / a / graphic / operating / Mac OS / why / work / system / for / ?
8 software / on / of / what / computer / you / run / sort / the / will / ?

b Now match the answers (a–h) to the questions (1–8).

a This one. It's quatro core and fast enough to handle anything you want to do.
b I'd say not less than £75.
c Just the usual stuff ... word processing and going on the internet.
d Yes, I would recommend that if you can.
e Some people think it provides a more stable environment.
f Not really. It's mostly for working on.
g Sure. What would you like to know?
h Two or three DTP packages and PhotoFix.

5 Giving advice

Track 5

How does the salesperson express his advice to Karen? Listen to the dialogue from exercise 2 again and choose between a, b or c.

1 a You shouldn't really think about ...
b You should really think about ...
c You should certainly think about ...

2 a I advise you to...
b My advice to you ...
c I'd advise you to ...

3 a You're going to need a ...
b You'll need a ...
c You need a ...

4 a In my opinion ...
b The better option would be ...
c Your best option would be ...

5 a If I were in your position, I would ...
b If I were you, I would...
c If I were buying the computer, I would ...

6 a My advice is to ...
b I'd advise that ...
c My advice would be to ...

Tip a piece of advice BUT to advise

6 Role-play: advice about building a PC

page 111

Work with a partner to do the role-play. Use the language from exercise 5.

Customer

Sagen Sie, dass Sie sich einen PC zusammenstellen möchten. Fragen Sie den Fachmann / die Fachfrau, was er/sie Ihnen raten würde.

PC specialist

Fragen Sie den Kunden / die Kundin, wofür er/sie den Computer nutzen möchte.

Sagen Sie, dass Sie den Computer für Ihre Arbeit benötigen. Darüber hinaus werden Sie persönliche Bilder und Musik darauf speichern.

Fragen Sie den Kunden / die Kundin, wie viel Geld er/sie für den Computer ausgeben möchte.

Sagen Sie, dass Sie nicht mehr als 1100€ ausgeben möchten, obwohl Sie mehr zur Verfügung haben.

Fragen Sie den Kunden / die Kundin, welche Software er/sie für seine Arbeit benutzt.

Sagen Sie, dass Sie Grafik- und Video-Software parallel verwenden werden.

Machen Sie den Kunden / die Kundin darauf aufmerksam, dass er/sie mehr investieren muss – ca. 1300 € –, um einen PC zusammen zu stellen, der stabil läuft und für diese Nutzung geeignet ist.

Nehmen Sie den Rat an. Fragen Sie den Fachmann / die Fachfrau, welchen Prozessor er/sie empfehlen kann.

Schlagen Sie den Terra Quatro Core 9000F vor. Sagen Sie dem Kunden / der Kundin, dass er sehr schnell ist.

Fragen Sie, welche Grafikkarte Sie benötigen.

Machen Sie den Kunden / die Kundin darauf aufmerksam, dass die beste Wahl die Cyclon 4839 HD wäre. Sie ist leistungsstark und das Preis-Leistungsverhältnis stimmt.

Fragen Sie, wie viel Arbeitsspeicher Sie benötigen würden.

Empfehlen Sie dem Kunden / der Kundin, ein Minimum von 8 GB Speicher.

Fragen Sie, welche Festplatte die beste Wahl wäre.

Raten Sie dem Kunden / der Kundin, in eine SolidBase 4378 mit 500 GB Speicherkapazität zu investieren.

7 Safety advice for PC builders

a Karen has decided to build her own PC and has found the article below. Look at the first part and decide which mistakes the people in the cartoons are making.

Tips to keep you – and your computer – safe when installing parts

General tips

- Make sure you have the right tools for the job. You're not going to need many but you will need two types of screwdriver – Phillips and flat-head – as well as pliers.
- PC components are often extremely delicate. Handle them with care and try to pick them up by their edges to avoid damage.
- Beware of sharp edges inside the PC case and the small solder pins on boards. The edge of a case can look harmless but can be as sharp as a knife. This can cause cuts if not handled with care.
- Cable connectors are generally designed with an alignment system to prevent incorrect connection. Line the cable connector up properly and use firm, even pressure. Excessive force can cause damage of sensitive parts such as signal pins.
- If dust gets onto any of your components, do not attempt to clean them with liquid detergent or a cloth: use a can of compressed air to do this.

b Read the first part of the article again and find words which have the same meaning as the German expressions below.

1 Werkzeuge
2 Schraubendreher
3 Zange
4 Kanten
5 Kabelstecker
6 Reinigungsmittel

c Use the words in the box to complete the second part of the text. The form of some of the words will need to be altered.

avoid | ensure | dismantle | install | remove

Tips about electricity

- Never work on the inside of your PC with the power turned on. Before you start working, ensure that the power supply is disconnected from the mains. Always make sure that all network cables are disconnected.
- You should only switch on the power to your PC when the housing is on.
- You should never try to ...[1] the PSU as it contains very dangerous mains voltages, even when not connected to the power supply.

Tips about static

- Always wear an antistatic wrist band when ...[2] parts to your PC.
- ...[3] against damage to sensitive components by not ...[4] them from their antistatic bags until you are ready to install them.
- When installing PC parts, ...[5] carpeted areas, where there is often a lot of static. Don't wear synthetic clothing as this also creates static.

8 Further safety tips

What other safety tips can you think of? Discuss these with a partner and put them into a table like the one below.

Ensure ...	*Avoid ...*

Skills **Wie lese ich einen schwierigen (Fach-)Text?**

Wenn Sie längere, schwierige (technische) Texte lesen, ist es wichtig zu wissen, worauf Sie Wert legen. Wählen Sie die Lesetechnik, die Sie am besten ans Ziel bringt.

1 **Vorwissen abklären als Vorbereitung auf das Lesen**
Bevor Sie einen Text lesen, sollten Sie sich vergegenwärtigen, was Sie bereits zur Thematik wissen. Dies hilft Ihnen, den Text besser zu verstehen.

2 **Schnelles Lesen zum Erfassen des allgemeinen Textverständnisses**
Verschaffen Sie sich einen ersten Eindruck, indem Sie sich die Überschrift, Zeichnungen und Bilder ansehen und dann den Text überfliegen. (*skim reading*)

3 **Selektives Lesen zum Erfassen wichtiger Textabschnitte**
Nach dem ersten Lesen merkt man oft, dass nur ein Teil des Textes wichtig ist. Suchen Sie den Text nun nur nach den Fakten ab, die Sie interessieren. (*scan reading*)

4 **Verarbeitendes Lesen zum Erfassen des Detailverständnisses**
Wollen Sie den Zusammenhang, Fakten oder einzelne Wörter genau verstehen, müssen Sie den Text oder die entsprechenden Textabschnitte langsam, Satz für Satz lesen. Ein Wörterbuch sollte nur dann zu Rate gezogen werden, wenn Sie alle sprachlichen Differenzierungen verstehen müssen. (*close reading*)

5 **Umgang mit unbekannten Wörten**
Schlagen Sie nur dann unbekannte Wörter nach, wenn das Wort aus dem Satzzusammenhang nicht erschlossen werden kann und für das Textverständnis unabdingbar ist. Auch bei schwierigen Texten ist es oft nicht notwendig, jedes Wort genau zu verstehen, um alle wichtigen Informationen entnehmen zu können.

9 Building skills: reading

Read the skills box about reading strategies and then complete the following tasks.

a Skim read the text on page 24 to find alternative expressions for these PC components.

1 processor   2 motherboard   3 case

b Scan the text again to match the illustrations to the highlighted words.

1

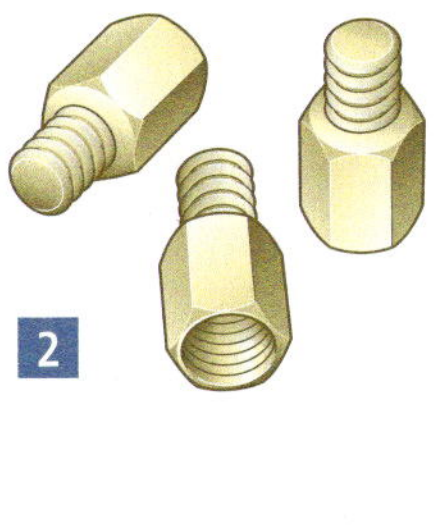
2

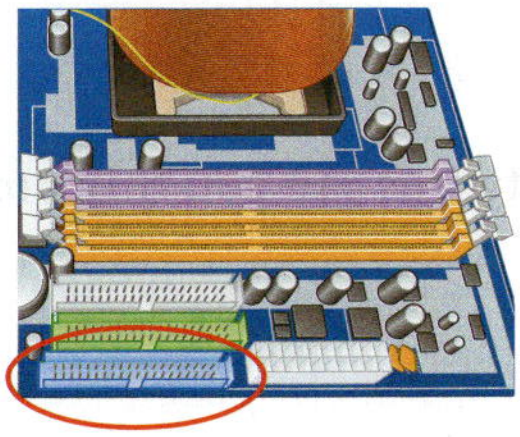
3

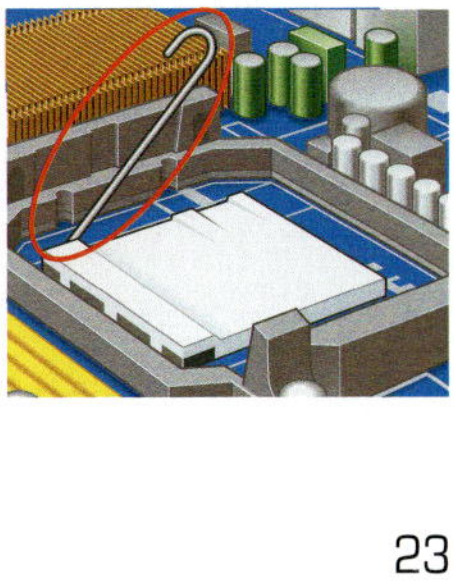
4

1 Installing the central processor

Before lowering the CPU into its socket, lift the retention arm and look at the bottom of the processor. Compare the layout of the pins on the bottom of the CPU to the socket: you'll see that they can only fit one way. Align the processor with the main board and lower it into the socket. Don't insert the CPU at an angle or move it from side to side. This can bend the pins. Finally, lock the lever back in place beside the socket to secure the CPU.

2 Installing the memory

It's quite simple to do but installing memory may need more force than other components. For this reason, the RAM should be installed before the motherboard is in the PC: place the motherboard on a plastic bag on a flat surface to protect it.

Before installing the RAM, make sure that the retention clips are unlocked. Align the notch in the RAM module with the slot. When it's aligned correctly, apply pressure across the top of the module and slide it gently into place. Finally, lock the retention pins firmly in place.

3 Mounting the motherboard

The next step is to mount the main board in the housing. Before you slide it in, check that there are no extra pieces of metal blocking the ports. It's important to do this: if you forget, you may have to disassemble the PC later to fix the problem. If there are any extra pieces of metal, fold them up into the inside of the housing.

Now lower the motherboard into the case. The ports must be aligned with the holes in the ATX backplane. Check that there are motherboard standoffs to line up with all the mounting holes on the mobo. Now screw down the board. Do not over-tighten the screws – too much force will cause damage to the motherboard ...

4 Install the PSU

Now comes the power supply unit. This should be lowered into the housing, fan-side down, and secured from the outside of the case with four screws. Use your fingers to tighten the screws before using a screwdriver – this avoids bending the case. When the PSU is in place, connect the power leads.

c Read the text closely to finish the sentences using your own words.

1 It's important to look at the bottom of the processor because ...
2 To install memory you might have to ...
3 To fit memory to the motherboard, place the mobo ...
4 You should line the RAM module up with the mobo correctly then ...
5 If there are excess pieces of metal on the case, you should ...
6 When installing the PSU, you can avoid bending the case by ...

10 Putting words into action

Webcode: ITMU0201

a Find the expressions (a – f) in the text and match them to their synonyms (1 – 10). There are four synonyms too many!

a align
b lower
c insert
d mount
e disassemble
f secure

1 take apart
2 put into
3 take out
4 fit
5 fix
6 finish assembling
7 line up
8 put onto
9 tighten
10 drop

b Note down which procedures the verbs are used to describe in the text. Then work with a partner and use your notes and the verbs to summarize the text.

Refresh your knowledge

1a Complete the questions a salesperson would use when advising a customer.

1 ... you want to play games on your PC?
2 ... much money ... you want to spend on the PC?
3 ... ... you want to do with your PC?
4 ... sort of software ... you run on the computer?

1b Make four phrases for recommending.

1 should / about / really / you / think / ...
2 advise / I / to / would / you / ...
3 option / be / best / would / your / ...
4 for / you / if / were / I / go / would / I / certainly / ...

1c Using material from exercises 1a and 1b, the unit and your own ideas, collect useful phrases for advising and recommending.

2a Give the English words for these German terms.

1 Werkzeuge
2 Schraubendreher
3 Zange
4 Stromnetz

2b Now make a word field for each of the PC components discussed in the texts in the unit and all the verbs that can be used with them.

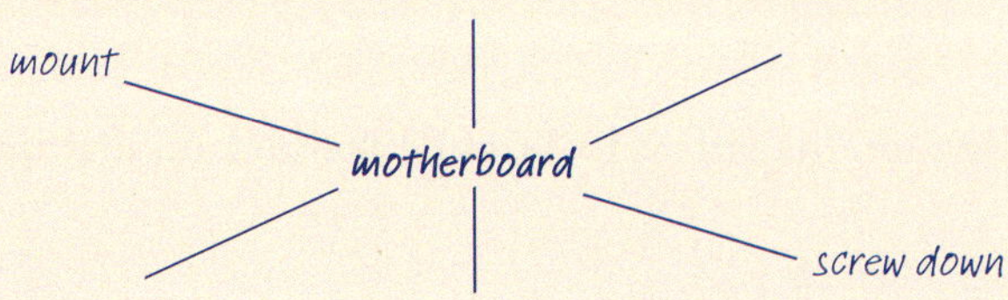

Extra material

Electric shocks are a serious threat for PC technicians. Here's what to do if it happens.

It's crucial that someone who has suffered an electric shock is treated as quickly as possible. Call your local emergency number immediately if any of these signs or symptoms occur:

- Heart failure
- Burns
- Heart rhythm problems
- Respiratory failure
- Muscle pain and cramps
- Unconsciousness

While waiting for medical help, follow these steps:

- **Look first. Don't touch.** Your colleague may still be in contact with the electrical source. Touching them may allow the current to pass through you.
- **If possible, turn off the source of electricity.** If not, move the source away from you and your colleague using a non-conducting object made of cardboard, plastic or wood.
- **Check for signs of circulation (breathing, coughing or movement).** If absent, begin cardiopulmonary resuscitation immediately.
- **Prevent shock.** Lay your colleague down and, if possible, position their head slightly lower than their body with their legs raised. Don't move your colleague unless they are in immediate danger. Keep them warm with a blanket.

1 Symptoms of electric shock

Match the definitions to four of the symptoms of electric shock in the text.

a the person appears to be asleep
b the heartbeat is not regular
c the person has trouble breathing
d the heart stops beating

2 The steps to take

Which picture shows the correct position you should place somebody who has suffered an electric shock in?

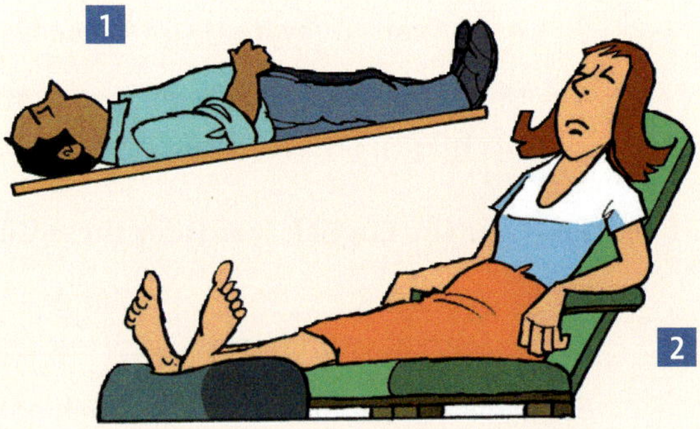

3 Mediation

Work with a partner. Take turns to describe the first aid instructions in German.

4 A poster for the workplace

Work in a group and design a poster. It should include advice about preventing accidents with electricity from the unit as well as the first aid tips from the text.

Looking after customers

3

- telephoning
- arranging meetings
- getting specifications from a customer

1 Start up

a Copy the mind map and then work with a partner to complete it with things an IT company can do to make sure it has good relations with its customers.

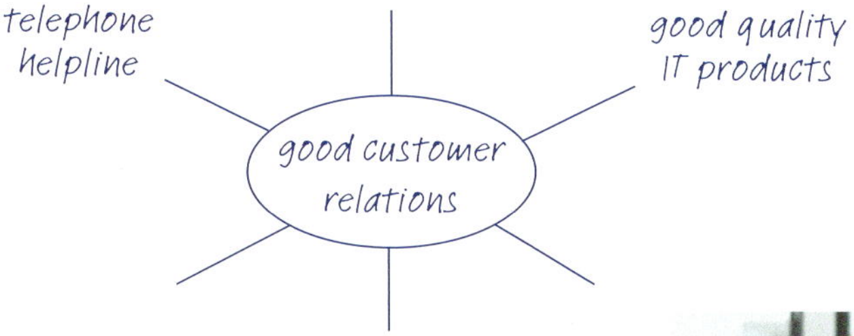

1 *A company should always listen to its customers carefully.*

2 *It should offer special offers to customers who do business with them again.*

b Now discuss the following questions with your partner.

1. Why is it important to have good relations with customers?
2. What could your company do better to help its customers?

2 A customer calls

Track 6

Listen as Sara Knight from AX Design phones Flektek, a company which sets up IT systems. Decide which statement (a–d) best summarizes the reason for her call.

The main reason for Sara Knight's call is ...

a to find out who is responsible for selling IT systems at Flektek.
b to let Flektek know that AX Design now have an office in Berlin.
c to discuss what sort of computer system AX Design will need in its Berlin office.
d to ask if she can have a job in Flektek's Berlin office.

Schröder Flektek, Schröder. Guten Tag.
Knight Oh ... sorry. My German's not very good. Do you speak English?
Schröder Yes, no problem. How can I help you?
Knight My name's Sara Knight from AX Design. We're based in London and we're setting up a new office in Berlin. I've been given the job of organizing everything. I'd like to talk to someone about our IT requirements.
Schröder OK. The best person for you to speak to would be Gunnar Stiller. He's our head of sales. Can you hold, please? I'll put you through to him.
Knight Thank you.
...
Schröder Hello. I'm sorry, Ms Knight. I'm afraid Herr Stiller's extension is busy. Can I take a message for him? Or can I get him to call you back?
Knight Yes, please. Could you ask him to call me back?
Schröder Fine. Could you spell your surname for me, please?
Knight Yes, sure. It's K-N-I-G-H-T.
Schröder Right, thanks. What telephone number can you be reached on?
Knight It's 0044 for the UK, then 20 649 838. My extension is 493.
Schröder OK. Can I just repeat that? So ... country code 0044, then 20 649 838, extension 493.
Knight That's right.
Schröder OK, Ms Knight. I'll let Herr Stiller know that you called. I'm sure he'll return your call soon.
Knight That's great. Thank you very much. Bye now.
Schröder My pleasure. Goodbye.

A few minutes later Gunnar Stiller calls Sara Knight.

Knight AX Design. Sara Knight here.
Stiller Hello, Ms Knight. This is Gunnar Stiller from Flektek.
Knight Hello, Mr Stiller. Thanks for returning my call.
Stiller No problem. I understand you need a new IT system for your Berlin office.
Knight Exactly.
Stiller I think it's best if we meet in person to discuss this. Can we arrange an appointment?
Knight Absolutely. When could you ...

3 Telephone phrases 1

a Find the English equivalents of the following phrases in the dialogue.

1 Können wir einen Termin vereinbaren?
2 Ich denke, es ist das Beste, wenn wir uns treffen und dies besprechen.
3 Können Sie mir bitte Ihren Nachnamen buchstabieren?
4 Ich bin mir sicher, dass er bald zurückrufen wird.
5 Ich gebe Herrn Stiller Bescheid, dass Sie angerufen haben.
6 Könnten Sie ihn bitten, mich zurück zu rufen?

b Now find phrases in the dialogue which have a similar meaning to the following phrases.

1 I'll see if I can connect you.
2 What can I do for you?
3 Thank you for getting back to me.
4 Shall I ask him to return your call?
5 Just a moment, please.
6 He's talking on the phone just now.
7 Would you like to leave a message?
8 Can I speak to someone about …?

4 Telephone phrases 2

Copy the table into your notebook and complete it with phrases from the dialogue and the exercise above.

Making a telephone call

	Phrase 1	Phrase 2
Saying why you're calling		
Asking the caller to wait		
Asking what you can do for the caller		
Offering to take a message		
Offering to take further action for the caller		
Saying somebody is not available		
Thanking the caller for phoning back		

5 Role-play: making a telephone call

page 112

a Work with a partner.

Student A: choose one of the business cards on page 108. You are that person. Call Flektek and ask to speak to Mr Stiller.
Student B: you work for Flektek. Take the call. Mr Stiller is not available. Take a message.
Use as many expressions as you can from the table in Exercise 4.

b Now swap roles and make another call.

Webcode: ITMU0301

6 Making an appointment

Track 7

Copy the diary into your exercise book and then listen to Gunnar Stiller arranging an appointment with Sara Knight. Complete the diary with Sara's appointments.

	a.m.	p.m.
Monday	*Meet with interior decorators*	
Tuesday	*Meeting with advertising agency*	
Wednesday		
Thursday		
Friday		

7 Phrases for arranging appointments

Track 7

a Listen again and put the following phrases into the order they are used in during the conversation.

1 I could come any time in the ... on ...
2 That would be fine.
3 Sorry, I'll be with another client all day ...
4 I'll be free on ... if that's any good for you?
5 Would ... morning be convenient for you?
6 Would ... be possible?
7 I'll be free then.
8 No, I'm afraid my diary is completely full on ...
9 No, sorry. I'll be in London for meetings on ...
10 How about ...?
11 I'm going to be busy all day ..., I'm afraid.

b Now sort the phrases into three categories: a) suggesting a time, b) rejecting a suggestion and c) accepting a suggestion.

8 Role-play: arranging a meeting

page 112

Work with a partner.

Make a diary for next week. Leave one morning and two afternoons free but do not tell your partner which ones.
Phone your partner and try to arrange a meeting. Use your diary and the phrases from exercise 7. Give reasons why you can't meet.

9 At AX Design

Track 8

Gunnar Stiller is now at AX Design for his appointment with Sara Knight. Listen and decide if the statements are true or false. Correct the false statements.

1 Sara is a computer designer.
2 Sara has a clearly defined amount of money to invest in the new system.
3 Five of the staff at the new office are administrators.
4 Three of the designers will be concentrating on print media.
5 Five of the designers will be specializing in animated design.
6 Gunnar suggests keeping the cost of the administrators' PCs down by using standard computer packages.
7 Both the print and animation designers will require customized PCs.
8 Gunnar says that his technical team will work out how much the new system will cost.

10 Dealing with customers

Match the sentence beginnings (1–10) to the sentence endings (a–j) to form useful phrases from the listening.

1 I'm going to ask you a few
2 Could you tell me a bit
3 Could you explain that
4 Would it be possible for you to
5 Now, perhaps you could go into more
6 Could you give me more details
7 I'm going to go back to the office now and draw
8 I'll pass it
9 I'll be able to give you
10 I'll make another

a elaborate upon what the admin staff will use their computers for?
b about what software they'll be using?
c up the specification for you.
d further for me?
e onto our technical team.
f appointment with you and we can look at what I suggest in detail.
g questions about your work here.
h more about your staff and what their jobs are?
i an idea about the price.
j detail about what sort of software the designers will be using?

Track 8 **Now listen again to check your answers.**

Grammar **The future with will & going to**

1 **I'll be** with another client all day Monday.
2 **I'll make** another appointment and then we can look at what I suggest in detail.
3 The other three designers **are going to concentrate** more on animated design.
4 **I'm going to leave** for a three-day business trip on Tuesday.
5 **I'm going to go back** to the office now and draw up the specification.

- Das *will future* wird mit dem Hilfsverb *will* und dem Infinitiv (ohne *to*) gebildet (1–2).
- Das *will future* wird benutzt, wenn man ganz allgemein über die Zukunft spricht (1).
- Es wird manchmal auch verwendet, wenn etwas im Moment des Sprechens entschieden wird (2).
- Das *going to future* wird mit *am/is/are* + *going to* + Infinitiv (ohne *to*) gebildet (3–5).
- Das *going to future* wird für Absichten oder Pläne verwendet (3, 4).

⚠ Man sollte jedoch beachten, dass dies keine starren Regeln sind! Muttersprachler verwenden das *will* und *going to future* gelegentlich in anderen Sprachsituationen. So wird das *going to future* manchmal anstelle des *will future* verwendet, wenn man eine gewisse Entschlossenheit unterstreichen möchte (5). Das *will* und *going to future* können aber auch abwechselnd benutzt werden, um mehrere aufeinanderfolgende Handlungen zu beschreiben.

11 Practice

Read the entries from a diary and make sentences describing your plans for next week. The first example has been done for you.

1	Monday	*9.30: Meeting Martie Crane: discuss cost cutting*

I'm going to meet Martie Crane on Monday at 9.30. We'll discuss cost cutting.

2		*4.30: Presentation from IT contractors*
3	Tuesday	*10.00: Visit new office in Peterborough, check if computer system set up*
4		*2.00: Lunch with Brian Alexander, discuss IT budgets*
5	Wednesday	*9.45: Dentist appointment*
6		*3.00: Interviews for a new system designer*
7	Thursday	*11.00: Team meeting: discuss problems with current projects*
8		*3.30: Leave work early, pick up kids from school*
9	Friday	*10.15: Call Dana Rosford, discuss new software needs*
10		*5.00: Brenda Smith's last day! Leaving party*

12 Role-play: finding out about a customer

page 112

Use the future tenses and the phrases from exercise 10 to carry out the following role-play with a partner.

Customer

Heißen Sie den IT-Spezialisten in Ihrem Konstruktionsbüro willkommen und sagen Sie ihm, dass Sie ein neues Computersystem für Ihr Büro benötigen.

IT specialist

Eklären Sie dem Kunden, dass Sie ihm einige Fragen stellen werden, um mehr über seine Anforderungen/Bedürfnisse heraus zu finden. Sie fragen ihn, wie viele Mitarbeiter in seinem Büro tätig sind.

Sagen Sie, dass Sie zehn Mitarbeiter haben, von denen sieben Designer und drei Administratoren sind.

Fragen Sie, welche Aufgaben die Administratoren an den PCs ausführen werden.

Erläutern Sie, dass die Administratoren die üblichen Bürotätigkeiten mit ihren PCs erledigen: Textverarbeitung, Excel Tabellenkalkulationen und E-Mails.

Darüber hinaus benötigen Sie Informationen, welche Anforderungen die Designer an die PCs stellen.

Erklären Sie, dass die Designer leistungsstarke Computer benötigen, auf denen sie mehrere Design-Programme gleichzeitig verwenden können.

Erläutern Sie dem Kunden, dass die Administratoren nur eine Standardausstattung der PCs benötigen, wohingegen die Designer für sie spezifisch eingerichtete PCs benötigen werden. Sagen Sie dem Kunden, dass Sie nach der Rückkehr in ihr Büro ein Anforderungsprofil erstellen und es an Ihr Technikteam weiterleiten werden.

Skills — Was versteht man unter Mediation?

„Mediation" bedeutet nicht eine wörtliche, sondern eine sinngemäße Übersetzung. Jedes Wort muss nicht genau übersetzt werden, sondern der übersetzte Text muss alle wesentlichen Fakten enthalten, in richtigem Deutsch und für den Fachmann gut verständlich abgefasst sein.

1 Lesen Sie den Text langsam und genau.
2 Konzentrieren Sie sich zu Beginn auf die Übersetzung der Verben, da diese die wichtigsten Informationen im Satz liefern (wie z. B. Wer tut was? Hinweise auf die Zeiten, usw.).
3 Bei langen Sätzen übersetzen Sie zunächst den Hauptsatz, dann die Nebensätze. Beachten Sie: Die englische Wortstellung entspricht häufig nicht der deutschen. Ihre Aufgabe ist es, gutes Deutsch zu schreiben (oder zu sprechen).
4 Da sich auch die Wortarten im Englischen von denen im Deutschen unterscheiden, können Sie z. B. Substantive als Verben übersetzen und umgekehrt.

13 Building skills: mediation

Read the skills box on page 33 and then outline the main points of the advertisement for an IT services company in German for your colleagues.

Choosing a new IT system can be expensive in terms of time and money.

Choose IT Pro Inc. We won't waste your time – or your money.

IT Pro Inc. has years of experience providing businesses with IT solutions which make financial and practical sense. Whether you want to choose a new IT set up for your organization or network and upgrade your existing IT infrastructure, we have the know-how to take the job off your hands at prices you can afford.

Benefit from our experience – talk to our system consultants

Our system consultants are professionals with a lot of experience in working in IT. They will give you an honest opinion about whether you should upgrade your existing IT infrastructure or invest in a new system. If you decide on a new system, they'll look carefully at your requirements and choose a system which will meet your company's needs – and fit your budget.

Installation schedules which work for you

Our installation engineers will work at times which suit you and not us. They'll also ensure that your business can continue to run normally while installation work is in progress and keep down-time to a minimum.

Award winning after-sales service

We'll provide you with an IT solution which works first time and continues to run efficiently. But for the moments when things do go wrong, our after-sales service team and hotline will be ready to sort your problem out as quickly as possible. We've won awards for our after-sales service. Become a customer and find out why.

Refresh your knowledge

1 Find phrases in the unit for saying the following things:

1 asking what the caller would like
2 asking the caller to wait while you check if the person they want is available
3 saying someone can't come to the phone at the moment
4 offering to take a message
5 asking if a certain time would be suitable for an appointment
6 saying that a certain time is (not) suitable for an appointment

2 Now use the phrases and any others that you find useful to make an A4-sized poster to hang by your phone. This will help you when you have to make a phone call in English at work.

Companies present a unified image of themselves to the world. But often their departments don't communicate with each other about what customers want. Now there's a software solution that can change this. Brian Thomas reports.

Acquiring and holding onto customers is a complicated business. It requires key business processes such as product design, marketing, sales and customer service to all work in the same direction. But even in well-organized companies, key departments often live in their own worlds and don't communicate with each other enough.

However, software introduced in the last few years could be changing this. Customer relationship management (CRM) software is designed to maintain a flow of information between customers and the departments in a company. The software helps the company respond intelligently and swiftly to customer needs.

According to Stephanie Brinley from the Watling Business School, CRM is now standard in most large companies. "Companies have realized that they have to fight to keep their customers. To do this they have to listen constantly to what customers want whether that is different product design or better customer service. Using CRM is the best way for them to do this."

Put simply, CRM collects information from customers and feeds it back to departments in the company. This information is in a form which can be analyzed quickly and action can be taken where necessary. Brinley offers an example. "A company which uses CRM will be able to monitor almost in real time what buying decisions customers are taking and what their preferences are. CRM feeds this information back to all the relevant departments so that they can make the appropriate decisions. For instance, product design would have the information it needed to decide whether to build in more of the features which customers like.

Marketing and sales could decide whether to emphasize these features more in existing products."

CRM can help sales and marketing in other ways. "CRM data can help marketing to identify and target its best customers – those that generate the most profit – and give better customer leads to the sales force. In the end, this leads to a company saving money," says Brinley.

In the long run CRM may be about saving money but companies need to invest heavily in selecting, purchasing and implementing the right CRM platform. CRM systems aren't cheap and the companies which produce them, including Oracle, SAP and Microsoft, expect to be paid handsomely for their solutions.

Companies also have to support the staff using the new CRM system. "Identifying what sort of training is called for and implementing it is also expensive. But this is all money well spent. In the end, companies which deploy CRM properly can develop more profitable relationships with their customers."

1 The best headline

Read the article and choose the best headline for it.

1 CRM too expensive for most businesses
2 CRM: How software can help you "listen" to customers
3 Customers like companies that use CRM better

2 Comprehension

Read the article again and answer the questions in your own words.

1 How does the article describe the relationship between departments in some companies?
2 What is CRM software designed to do?
3 Find examples of the type of information from customers that CRM can provide.
4 How can the sales force benefit from CRM?
5 Why is CRM expensive to implement?

3 Vocabulary

Write definitions of the following idioms from the text.

1 to work in the same direction (lines 10–11)
2 to live in their own worlds (lines 12–13)
3 in the long run (line 54)
4 to be paid handsomely (line 60)
5 to be money well spent (line 64)

4 Key information

Summarize the key information from the article in German.

5 Internet research

Work with a partner and complete the following tasks.

1 Look on the internet to identify a CRM product.
2 Do some research into the product to find out what features it offers users as well as what system requirements are needed to run it.
3 Present the information you have researched to the class.

Installing & customizing software 4

- computer usage
- unpacking & installing software
- dealing with problems & errors

1 Start up

a Read what these people say about their computer use. Discuss with a partner which types of software they need.

browser | compression program | database application | encryption program | image editor | spreadsheet | word processor

What I use my PC for? Well, email, of course. I also use it for my hobby which is photography. I like to play around with my photos. You know, change the colours, that kind of thing.

I use my computer for writing reports. These are often confidential so I use a piece of software to make sure that they can only be read by the people who should read them. I also use my PC to do financial calculations. Oh, and I do quite a lot of internet research.

2

3

1

4

The main thing I use my computer for is working with texts. I send these to colleagues using email. Generally my files are pretty big so I use special software to make them smaller for emailing.

Well, I use my PC for lots of things. But mainly I use it to store and manage details about my company's customers. There are thousands of them, so that's a pretty big job.

b Tell your partner what you use your computer for and what software you need.

2 Installing software

Track 9

Listen as a colleague gives Jennifer advice about installing OpenOffice software. Put these stages in the order they are mentioned.

a Unpack and install OpenOffice files.
b Review the system requirements for OpenOffice.org.
c Download OpenOffice.
d Run OpenOffice to ensure that the installation was successful.
e Log onto the PC as the administrator.

3 Installation steps

Decide which of the stages (a–e) above you would put the following instructions and advice about installation under.

1 If your connection is not very fast, you might consider a program that enables you to pause/resume the download.
2 After installation and deletion of temporary installation files, OpenOffice.org will use approximately 440 MB disk space.
3 Windows Explorer users should find the downloaded file and double-click to launch the installation programme.
4 Choose a mirror (download location) closest to you.
5 The Welcome window is displayed to note that you have downloaded OpenOffice.org 3.0. Click Next to continue.

4 Advice about installation

a Match the sentence beginnings (1–8) with the endings (a–h) to make sentences similar to those in the dialogue from exercise 2.

1 If I delete one or two older pieces of software,	a on your hard drive.
2 Just be sure to read the	b sure that it's installed successfully.
3 If it doesn't install for some reason,	c just try downloading it and going through the procedure again.
4 Well, the next step, of course, is to download	d on to your PC as the administrator so that you can run the installation.
5 Then you need to log	e I'll have space for the package.
6 You need at least 650 MB free	f OpenOffice from the internet.
7 The first thing you'll need to do is check	g the system requirements.
8 Don't forget to run the software once you're finished to make	h instructions at each stage before clicking OK.

b Now arrange the sentences in the logical order the tasks would be performed in when installing software.

5 Unpacking and installing the software

Jennifer uses the installation instructions on page 40 to help her install the software. Match the download instructions below to the appropriate stages of the text.

A

OpenOffice.org 3.2 Installation Preparation

Thank you for downloading OpenOffice.org 3.2.

The installation files must be unpacked and copied to your hard disk in preparation for the installation. After that, the OpenOffice.org installation download will start automatically.

B

OpenOffice.org 3.2 Installation Preparation

Select folder

The OpenOffice.org 3.2 installation files will be unpacked and saved in the folder shown below. If you would like to save OpenOffice.org to a different folder, click 'Browse' to select another folder.

C

OpenOffice.org 3.2 Installation Preparation

Set-up Type

Choose the set-up type that best suits your needs. Please select a set-up type.

- ○ Complete — All program features will be installed. (Requires the most disc space.)
- ○ Custom — Choose which program features you want installed and where they will be installed. Recommended for advanced users.

D

OpenOffice.org 3.2 Installation Preparation

Ready to install the program

The wizard is ready to begin the installation.

If you want to review or change any of your installation settings, click Back. Click Cancel to exit the wizard.

6 Understanding the installation instructions

Read the text on page 40 again. Decide which steps you would do the following in.

a Select the elements of the software you want to install.
b Decide where you want to install the software on your computer.
c Confirm that you agree with the terms and conditions of using the software.
d Read general information about the software.
e Find the software files you have downloaded.
f See a progress bar.

File Edit View Go Bookmarks Tools Help

SolveIT Computing Solutions

Carry out the following steps to unpack and install OpenOffice 3.2 on your computer.

1 Either using Windows Explorer or Mozilla's Download Manager, navigate to the OpenOffice file you have downloaded. The Welcome window is displayed to show that you have downloaded OpenOffice 3.2. Click Next to continue.

2 The Select Folder window is displayed. Accept the folder name displayed in the text box or enter the name of the folder in which the unpacked files should be saved and click Unpack.

3 Once the files are unpacked, the OpenOffice 3.2 Installation Wizard is displayed. Click Next to continue installing OpenOffice 3.2. Follow the prompts and OpenOffice will be installed on your system ready for use.

4 The Welcome window contains important information: read this, then click Next. The Licence Agreement window appears. Read the licence, select Accept if you agree with the licence conditions and click Next. The Setup Type window appears.

5 Select a setup type (we recommend Complete) and click Next. The File Type window is displayed.

6 Confirm the file types (for example, spreadsheet, word processing, etc.) that you wish to open with OpenOffice. All the file types are selected in the default configuration. This means that OpenOffice will start when these file types are opened. De-select (click on the ticks) to view, edit and print these file types with your existing word processing, spreadsheet or presentation programme.
Note: If you change your mind after running a complete installation, getting certain file types to open with other software is tedious. You will need to reassociate all word processing, spreadsheet or presentation files with the appropriate file type.

7 Once you have selected the file types, click Next. The Ready to Install the Programme window is displayed. Click the Back button to return to previous windows to change your installation options, otherwise click Install to begin the installation process. The Installation Wizard will keep you informed of the progress of the installation. Click the Finish button when the Installation Wizard Finished window is displayed.

If you logged in as the administrator, logout. Each user can then open OpenOffice from the program menu which will allow them to configure OpenOffice as a workstation copy with no further effort on their part.

7 Useful verbs

a Match the German expressions with English ones from the text.

1 durchführen
2 fortsetzen
3 eingeben
4 beinhalten
5 erscheinen
6 aussuchen
7 empfehlen
8 bestätigen
9 akzeptieren *(two possible English words)*

b Now complete the sentences using eight of the verbs.

1 We ... that you save the programme files in the default folder.
2 Click I agree to ... the terms of the licence agreement.
3 ... your user name and password to log in as the administrator.
4 The Installation Wizard will ... the installation after you click Next.
5 ... that you want the standard installation by clicking OK.
6 This window ... details of the system requirements for the software.
7 If you do not want to ... with the installation, click End now.
8 Click Don't accept if you do not ... with the terms of the licence agreement.

8 Customized installation

Discuss these questions with a partner.

1 What type of options does customizing an installation offer you? Give examples.
2 Describe a customized installation which you have carried out.
3 What sort of problems have you encountered with customized installations?

9 A problem after installation

Track 10

a Listen as Jennifer's colleague gives her advice about a problem with her new software. Choose which statement (1–4) best describes the problem.

1 Jennifer's other software doesn't work with OpenOffice.
2 She has installed OpenOffice incorrectly.
3 She has used the standard installation which means that she can only open spreadsheet files with OpenOffice.
4 She has lost spreadsheet files after installing OpenOffice.

b Jennifer wrote down the advice that Colin gave her. Listen again and complete her notes.

Get an ...1 when you install software that allows you to ...2 certain file types so that they can be opened with other software.

Could put files ...3 by OpenOffice into a format ...4 by Excel using Import / Export or Save As functions in Windows. To ...5 files in this way can take a long time.

Other option: ...6 the main set up and select ...7 to change which file types are opened by which software.

Good idea to ...8 the Custom setup when installing software. Even if you ...9 all the default settings, you know what you're getting.

Grammar **If sentences types 1 & 2**

1 If I **delete** other software I don't use anymore, **I will have** space for the package.
2 I **won't be able to** install the software now if it **takes** so long to download.
3 If the software **worked** better, more people **would use** it.
4 You**'d know** what the default settings were if you **ran** the customized installation.
5 If you **tested** the free version, you **might be able** to decide if it's really useful.

- *If*-Sätze vom Typ 1 drücken eine erfüllbare Bedingung aus. Beachten Sie die Zeitenfolge: Der *if*-Nebensatz steht im *simple present*, im Hauptsatz steht das *will future* (1,2).
- *If*-Sätze vom Typ 2 drücken eine möglicherweise erfüllbare Bedingung aus. Beachten Sie die Zeitenfolge: Der *if*-Nebensatz steht im *simple past*, im Hauptsatz wird *would* + Infinitiv verwendet (3, 4), wobei *would* durch *could*, *might* oder *should* ersetzt werden kann (5).
- Steht der *if*-Nebensatz an erster Stelle, wird er vom Hauptsatz durch ein Komma getrennt (1, 3, 5).

10 Practice

Fill the gaps with the correct form of the verb in brackets.

1 I would have to uninstall the software if it ... other files on my system. (corrupt)
2 If you downloaded a pirate copy of the software, you ... pay for it but it might not work. (not have to)
3 Your system will freeze if you ... it to perform too many tasks at once. (ask)
4 If you have a problem uninstalling the software, you ... to reach me on my office number all afternoon. (be able to)
5 If the software didn't open properly, it could ... a fault with installation. (be due to)
6 I'll call you tomorrow morning if I ... any problems starting my system up again. (have)

11 Practice

Translate the following into English using if sentences.

1 Falls ihr System eine beschädigte Datei entdeckte, müssten sie ihr System neu starten und neu beginnen.
2 Sie werden andere Anwendungen schließen müssen, falls sie eine Fehlermeldung erhalten, die besagt, dass nicht genügend Speicher vorhanden ist.
3 Ich müsste das Softwarepaket deinstallieren, wenn wir für die Lizenz nicht bezahlten.

Webcode: ITMU0401

Skills **Wie kann ich Grammatik lernen?**

1 Suchen Sie sich eine Grammatik, die zu Ihrem Kenntnisstand passt.
2 Schlagen Sie das Problem im Inhaltsverzeichnis (am Buchanfang) und im Stichwortverzeichnis (am Buchende) nach, um die Grammatikregel zu finden.
3 Lesen Sie die Regel genau durch und versuchen Sie zu verstehen, wie die Struktur verwendet wird.
4 Schreiben Sie einige Beispielsätze in Ihr Grammatikheft und heben Sie die wichtigsten Schlüsselwörter durch farbige Markierungen hervor.
5 Formulieren Sie unter den Beispielsätzen kurz, prägnant und in verständlicher Weise selbstständig die Regel. Benutzen Sie zusätzlich Eselsbrücken (z. B. *he, she, it* – das „*s*" muss mit.) oder merken Sie sich Signalwörter (z. B. *ago/last week* = *past simple*).
6 Entwerfen Sie ein Poster mit Beispielen und Regeln, das Sie in Ihrem Zimmer aufhängen und häufig sehen können.

12 Skills: grammar

Read the skills box above and follow the steps to make a poster about if sentences.

13 Dealing with error messages

Work with a partner and carry out the following tasks.

1 Discuss which of the errors below are the most and least serious.
2 Identify any errors you do not know how to solve. Research how to solve them on the internet.
3 Write texts like those that would appear if you clicked *What to do*.

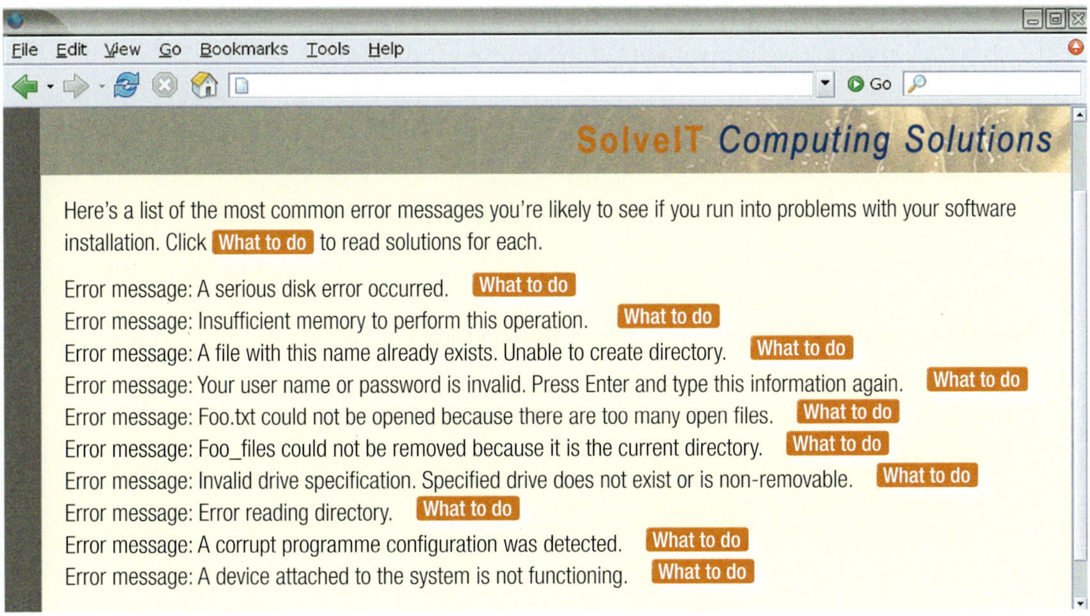

14 Working with words

Complete the sentences with words from the box.

corrupt | detected | insufficient | invalid | occurred | performed | remove | serious

1 A ... system conflict is preventing installation.
2 The system has... a hardware failure.
3 There is ... memory to run this operation.
4 The password or username is ... . Please re-enter.
5 A ... system file is preventing the software from installing.
6 The system failed to find a file: the operation cannot be ... .
7 Click OK to ... malicious files detected on the system.
8 A critical system failure has ... . Please restart the system.

15 Mediation

Translate the error messages and the solutions you wrote in exercise 13 for a colleague who does not understand English.

Refresh your knowledge

1 Which pieces of software can you remember from the unit? Collect them together to make a word spider. Add any other software you can think of.

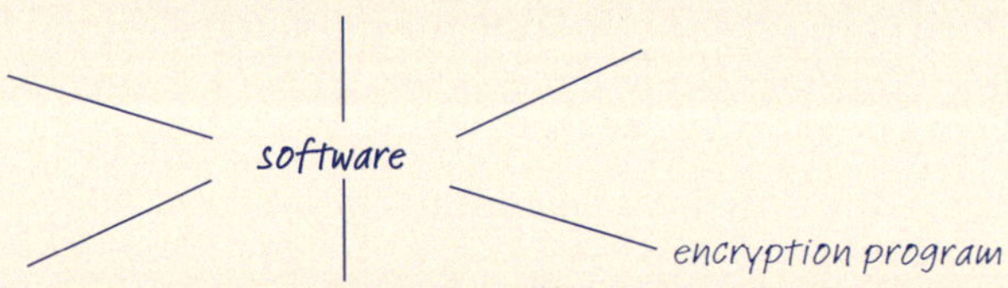

2 Give the German equivalents of these important verbs.

1 enter
2 contain
3 appear
4 agree
5 accept
6 continue
7 select
8 confirm
9 carry out
10 recommend

3a Match the words to their definitions.

1 invalid
2 corrupt
3 error

a damaged
b problem
c not recognizable

3b Now collect more words that you need to understand problems and error messages and make a definition matching quiz for a classmate.

File Edit View Go Bookmarks Tools Help

Go

SolveIT Computing Solutions

Problem-free software installation – top tips

Everyone knows what it's like. You've just bought or downloaded a new piece of software but when you attempt to install it, something goes wrong. You know the kind of thing: your system freezes, the setup program refuses to run or another program on your PC stops working. Often problems like these are caused by a mistake that you've made during installation. So read our list of installation tips and make your next installation a success.

1 ______________________________

First things first! Make a back up of your system files before attempting to install software. If something goes badly wrong, at least you won't lose valuable system information.

2 ______________________________

Close down all programs on your system, including your screensaver, before installing new software: they can interfere with the installation process, lead to incomplete installations and result in software which apparently doesn't work.

3 ______________________________

When you download programs from the internet, leave your virus protection running to detect any malware that comes as a "free extra". If a program will not install with virus protection running in the background, think about whether you trust the software enough to disable virus checking during installation.

4 ______________________________

Software is often accompanied by a text file called Installation Notes or something similar which details known incompatibilities and other issues associated with the software. Even if a software company doesn't refer to this file in the installation instructions, find it and read it over. It could save you time in the end.

5 ______________________________

Some programs, particularly those that work with hardware (such as photo editors that work with scanners), require the installation of additional utilities. Sometimes you have to install programs, utilities and devices in a specific order. Always read the documentation that comes with a program to make sure you do everything in the right order.

6 ______________________________

Finally, once the software is up and running, store the original installation files in a safe place and write the product identification key on the CD. If you need to wipe your hard drive and start again from scratch, you'll have those installation files close at hand.

1 Before reading

Discuss these questions with a partner.

1 What general steps do you take when installing software to ensure that the installation is a success?
2 Which mistakes have you made when installing software which you have learned from?

2 Skim reading

a Read the article quickly and decided which headlines (a–d) match which sections of the text (1–6).

a Read me!
b Do things in the right order
c Close down for clean installation
d Scan the software

b Now write headlines for the two sections which don't match.

3 Close reading

Read the article again and finish the sentences using your own words.

1 The problems you can have if some software doesn't install cleanly can include ...
2 Creating a system backup is important because ...
3 Keep virus protection software running so that ...
4 Find out about potential incompatibilities by ...
5 When installing programmes which work with hardware ...
6 Store installation files safely in order ...

4 A software installation checklist

Work with a small group of students to complete these tasks.

1 Discuss if there are other general tips about installing software which are not mentioned in the article. If necessary, use the internet to help you find these.
2 Write your list of new tips in English in a similar way to the article.
3 Swap lists with another group and mediate the new list into German.

Troubleshooting 5

- typical computer problems
- dealing with flow charts
- telephone hotlines

1 Start up

a Look at the cartoons and decide which IT problems the people are having.

1

2

3

b Make a list of three problems with your computer that you have had to solve.

c Now work with a partner. Tell your partner about the problems: they should explain how you can solve them.

2 Common problems

Track 11

a Listen to the problems a computer hotline operator has to deal with and match them to the advice (a–f) she offers.

Careful: one of the problems and one of the solutions cannot be matched.

A This can be caused by too many unnecessary files, fragmented data, a corrupted registry, spyware or software that you no longer need. Try deleting any unnecessary data and software. You could also try cleaning your registry. That should help boost your computer's performance.

B Check the back of the computer to see if all the connectors are properly in place. The speaker plug should be put into the socket on the soundcard marked "Audio Out". If this doesn't solve the problem, check for loose cables at the back of your speakers.

C You can try to fix this by checking your hardware. You may have a faulty power supply or, more likely, a defective or dirty cooling fan. The dust that accumulates on the fan makes it heat up faster and the computer automatically switches off in order to cool it down. Cleaning the fan is the most likely way of solving this problem.

D This component is sensitive to electromagnetic radiation from TVs, radio, microwaves, dishwashers, mobile phones, etc. Try moving these pieces of equipment away from your PC. That should solve the problem.

E Your problem may be due to spyware or a virus. Update and run your anti-virus software. If it fails to detect malware, the problem may be caused by the fact that you don't have enough RAM. If that is the case, upgrading your RAM should stop your screen turning blue.

F Noises and vibrations are a hardware problem: many of the electronic parts which make up your PC can make high-pitch noises. Try switching off your computer and disconnecting it from the power supply. Then remove the case from the CPU and restart your PC. Try to find where the noise is coming from, then switch off the computer and disconnect the faulty component. You should replace this immediately.

b With a partner look at the two parts that don't match. Write a possible solution and find the missing problem.

3 Working with words

Find words in the texts (a–f) which can be used to complete the sentences.

Note that sometimes more than one word can be used.

1 I have to clean up my laptop. I've got so many ... pieces of software which I just don't need now.
2 It sounds like the file you're having a problem opening has been ... by a virus.
3 Your mouse is .... That's why you can't move the cursor on your screen.
4 It could be that the cartridge in your printer is .... That could be why the pages you are printing have lines across them.
5 Try using the Repair connection wizard. If it can't solve the problem, it should be able to ... what's causing it.
6 OK. First ... the external storage device from your computer. Now plug it back in. It should work now.

4 A problem game

Work with a partner. You will need two cards or pieces of paper.

1 Write a computer problem on a card.
2 Write the solution to the problem on the other card.
3 Put your cards (face down) into two piles, one for problems and one for solutions, together with the cards that the other pairs have written.
4 Mix up the cards in each pile.
5 Each pair takes one card from the 'problems' pile and one from the 'solutions' pile.
6 One pair reads out a problem card.
7 The pair which thinks it has the solution card for the problem reads it out.
8 Continue until all the cards have been read.

5 Getting help

Discuss which of the possibilities below are the most useful when someone has a computer problem. Can you suggest any other common troubleshooting tips?

1 Ring a telephone hotline.
2 Check the cables, wires and power cords.
3 Take notes about error messages.
4 Research the problem on the internet.
5 Use a troubleshooting flow chart.
6 Restart the computer.
7 Check the manual.
8 Press the F1 key on your PC to get the Help window.

6 A troubleshooting flow chart

Use the words in the box to complete the sentences in the flow chart. The flow chart shows what to do if the sound on your PC is not working.

adjust | connector | cord | fix | insert | log | outlet | plugged | sound | speakers | turned | unplugging | volume

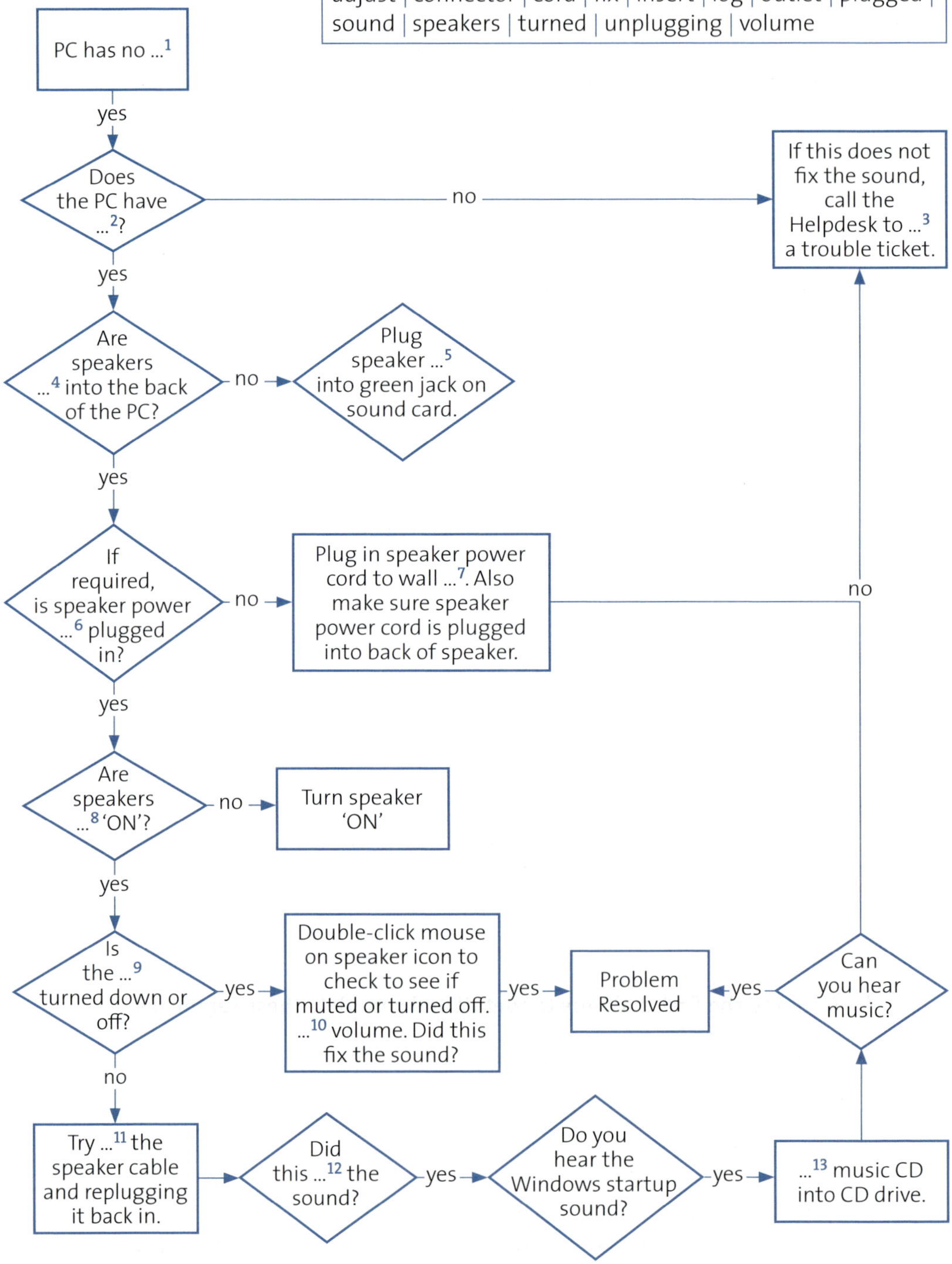

Skills **Wie kann ich einen Hörtext besser verstehen und bearbeiten?**

1 Machen Sie sich vor dem Zuhören klar, um was es beim Hörtext gehen wird. (Welche Thematik? Gibt es Fotos/Diagramme/Illustrationen?)
2 Versuchen Sie beim ersten Zuhören, den Text sinngemäß zu erfassen (*listening for gist*) und verzichten Sie auf das Verstehen von Details.
3 Achten Sie beim zweiten Zuhören auf Einzelheiten und versuchen Sie, Ihr Verständnis des Textes zu verbessern (*listening for detail*).
4 Beachten Sie: Bleiben Sie nicht an Einzelwörtern hängen, sondern versuchen Sie, die Gesamtaussage zu erfassen.

7 Building skills: listening

Track 12

a Read the skills box and then listen to the phone conversations for gist. Match one of the flow charts to each dialogue. There is one flow chart too many.

Flow chart 1

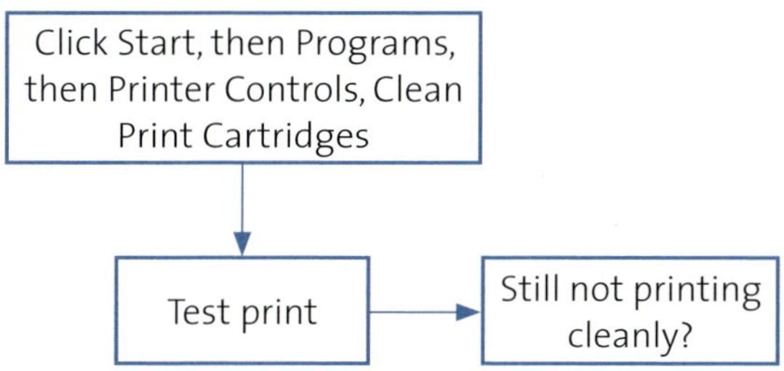

Flow chart 2

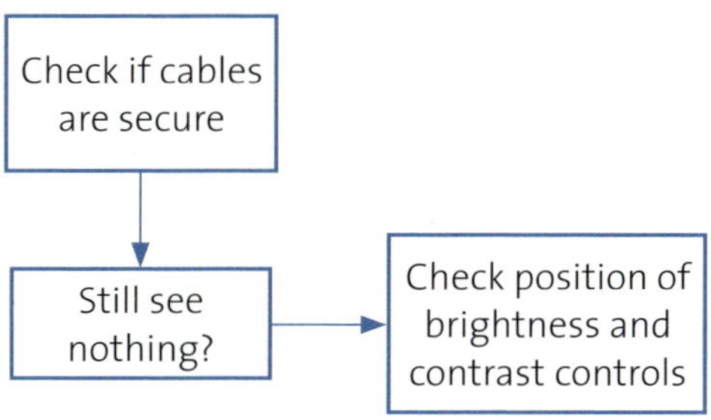

Flow chart 3

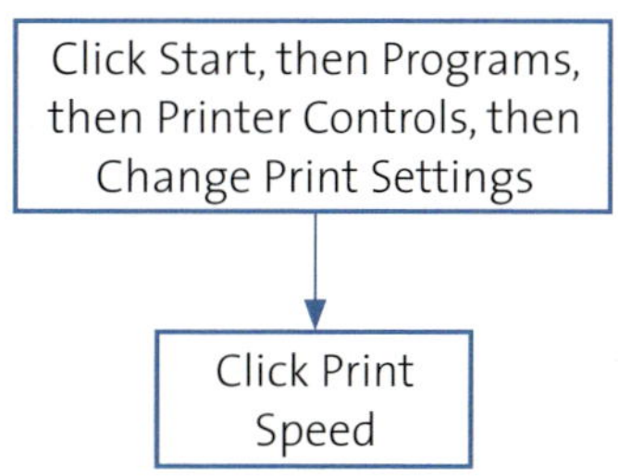

b Listen to the first dialogue for detail and complete these sentences.

1 I'm having some ... with my monitor.
2 I ... if you can help me.
3 I'll ... what I can do. What ... is the problem?
4 Let's ... with the ....
5 Have you ... to make sure that the monitor power cable is in ...?
6 Try ... your mouse or ... a few keys on the keyboard.
7 ... you please ... turning the contrast and brightness controls on your monitor?

8 Asking for and offering help

a Match the sentence beginnings (1–10) to the sentence endings (a–j) to make sentences from the second dialogue.

1 I'm having a problem with my printer	a Start, then Programs.
2 What sort of	b right of the window, beside Change Print Quality.
3 And what seems	c at that then.
4 Let's have a look	d in the list.
5 Tell me when	e telling you that it's finished.
6 Click on	f printing out a single sheet of one of your documents.
7 You should see it	g which I hope you can help me with.
8 That's on the top	h it's open.
9 You'll get a message	i printer do you have?
10 Now, try	j to be the problem?

Track 12 **b Now listen again to check your answers.**

9 Hotline phrases

a Copy the table below. Then read the sentences from exercises 7b and 8 and sort them into three categories.

asking for help	*getting information from a caller*	*directing a caller*
I'm having some difficulties with my monitor.		

b Now sort the phrases below into the three categories as well.

1 Now try clicking on ...
2 I've got a question about ...
3 You'll see that on the top left of your screen.
4 A quick question. How can I ...?
5 I'm having a problem with my ...
6 What should I do?
7 You'll find that in the middle of the screen next to ...
8 Look under ... and click on ...
9 What type of ... do you have?
10 Can you tell me more about ... ?
11 What happens if you ...?
12 You need to make sure that you don't ...

Webcode: ITMU0501

Grammar **The –ing form**

1 Now click 'update'. OK? What**'s happening** now?
2 The contract provides for the **servicing** and **upgrading** of our IT system.
3 There's a meeting on Wednesday to discuss the **existing** service arrangement.
4 The icon on the top right of the screen is **for changing** the user settings.
5 Regular back ups reduce the risk **of losing** valuable data.
6 Right. Let's start **by checking** if the mouse is plugged in properly.

- Die *-ing* Form des Verbs hat viele Funktionen.
- Mit dieser Form drückt man den Verlaufscharakter des Verbs aus, z. B. im *present continuous* (1).
- Sie steht als Gerundium, wenn Verben substantiviert werden (2).
- Sie kann als Adjektiv verwendet werden (3).
- Sie steht nach Präpositionen wie *for*, *of* und *by* (4–6).

10 Practice

Five of these sentences are grammatically correct; the remaining five are not. Correct the mistakes in the incorrect sentences.

1 You can solve that problem by click on Settings, then Alter Page Width.
2 Right. Have you done that? Tell me what's happening now.
3 Clicking on Delete doesn't wipe the file from your hard drive.
4 This icon will give you a menu that displaying your printer options.
5 Try restart your computer, then tell me what happens.
6 My PC is not saving my Word documents.
7 Let's begin by check if the power supply is working.
8 Could you try pushing the cable in further at the back of your laptop?
9 Hold on. I think it's working now.
10 The button at the bottom of the screen is for alter the page width.

11 Practice

Decide if you need the -ing form and write sentences.

1 You can / open / the Help window / by / press / F1
2 What / make / that noise / ?
3 The manual / tell / you how / to open / the correct files
4 Click / on the icon / open / a new window
5 The manual / be / useful for / find out / how to deal with problems
6 Back up / every day / help / to prevent / lose / data
7 Be / there any chance / of / get / a technician / to look at this / ?
8 What / happen / if you / turn off / the speakers / ?

12 Helping a caller

Match each sentence (1–7) with an appropriate response (a–g). Who is speaking in each sentence: the caller or the hotline operator?

1 I'm having a problem with my mouse. 2 What happens if you turn up the volume on your speakers? 3 A quick question. How can I import a photo into Word? 4 What type of internet connection do you have? 5 You'll find that at the bottom left of your screen. 6 What should I do?	a Do you mean what sort of cable? b Let's see what we can do about that. c Well, first you need to close all of your programs. d Hold on. I'll try. Absolutely nothing. e Ah, OK. So I click Start. Then what? f Just right click on the image, select Save, then paste it into the document.

13 Role-play: IT problems

page 113

Work with a partner. Use language from the exercises above.

Student A: Turn to File 1 on page 107. Student B: Turn to File 5 on page 109.

Refresh your knowledge

1 Find words in the unit which have the same meaning as the following German expressions.

1 unnötig
2 beschädigt
3 fehlerhaft
4 schadhaft
5 entdecken/erkennen
6 ab-/ausschalten

2a Form sentences useful for troubleshooting by matching the sentence beginnings (1–7) and sentence endings (a–g).
Be careful: one beginning and one ending cannot be matched.

1 I'm having some
2 I wonder if
3 I'll see what
4 Let's start
5 Have you checked that
6 Click on
7 What sort of

a with the power supply.
b at the top right of your screen.
c operating system do you use?
d you can help me.
e difficulties with my keyboard.
f the keyboard is connected to the PC?
g I can do.

2b Now think of a problem which you have had to deal with regarding a PC and its peripherals such as a printer. Create a flow chart explaining how the problem can be solved.

Computer support services agreement

Following are the terms of a computer support services agreement between Bafford Engineering Inc., hereafter (BE), and IT First Aid Inc., hereafter (ITFA).

1 The period of this contract is defined as ...., 20... through ...., 20....
2 (ITFA) agrees to supply support to (BE); (BE) agrees to the terms as laid out in the Customers' System Manual, the contents of which are outlined below.
3 BE agrees to email a contract service request to (ITFA) as the primary means of requesting support, followed by a phone call for confirmation. Any other means of communicating a service request will not be guaranteed timely response.
4 Call out response time is within 8 (eight) working hours. If equipment is not repaired on the first visit, an equivalent machine will be installed by the end of the next 8 (eight) working hour period.
5 All services shall be provided between the hours 8.30 a.m. to 5.30 p.m., Monday to Friday, excluding Public Holidays. A representative from (BE) is to be present in the case of on-site repair.
6 Only approved products shall be deemed eligible for support under this schedule and shall be inspected prior to commencement of any contract by (ITFA).
7 Only (ITFA) approved personnel shall repair or adjust the products listed under this agreement.
8 All orders of support are subject to acceptance by (ITFA).
9 (ITFA) shall be under no obligation to provide repair services for damage or malfunction resulting from the following: improper use, natural disaster, strikes, riots, war or nuclear disaster, neglect, damage through transit carried out by (BE), failure of (BE) to maintain recommended site specifications.
10 (ITFA) will not be held responsible for any failure or delay beyond their reasonable control.
11 (ITFA) shall not be held responsible under this agreement for service/maintenance of software, stationery media unless specific to the schedule, and duly noted. All software should be copied by (BE) for archival purposes to replace worn copies and for program verification by (BE).
12 Charges shall be those currently in effect.
13 Notice of alterations to the contract must be given to the other in writing at the address shown.
14 (BE) shall be responsible for security of proprietary and classified information.
15 Computer equipment included under this contract includes CPU, RAM memory, hard disk drives, printers, monitors and other peripheral devices. Coverage of consumable items (print heads, toners) is not provided for under the contract.
16 Additional services which can be utilized under this contract include software training, software installation, hardware installation, software programming, general consulting and upgrades.

1 Understanding the text

Read the email excerpts from Bafford Engineering to IT First Aid and decide which requests they are covered for under the terms of their contract.

Say which parts of the contract you used as evidence for your answer.

1 I know its Good Friday, but some of us are working here and we're having problems with the network. Can you come out?

2 We'd like to set up some training on our new ERP package for sales staff. Would you be able to provide this?
3 I think my monitor is faulty. Could you please come out and take a look at it?
4 I seem to have a problem with the cartridge in my printer. Would it be possible for you to take a look at it tomorrow? I know you'll be here then anyway doing some routine network maintenance.
5 I dropped my laptop on the way home last night and now it's not working. I would be grateful for your support.
6 My operating system's playing up. Could you possibly reinstall it?

2 Email questions

Work with a partner.

Student A: you are the customer. Write an 'email' to your partner on a piece of paper asking a question about the contract.
Student B: you work for IT First Aid. When you receive your partner's 'email' write a reply answering their question.
Do not speak to your partner: all communication must be done in writing.

3 Online task

Use a search engine to find other examples of service contracts and answer the following questions.

1 What other elements does this type of contract often contain?
2 Is the contract between IT First Aid and Bafford Engineering typical or is it unusual in any way?

4 Writing a contract

Work with a partner and complete the following tasks.

1 Contracts often use the same standard phrases. Examine the contract on page 55 closely and identify the standard phrases it contains.
2 Make an agreement with your partner. For example, your partner could agree to help you test vocabulary you have learned while you could help to test new phrases which they have learned. Sort out the terms of the contract: when you are both prepared to provide the help, for how long, where, etc.
3 Write a contract based on what you have agreed using the phrases you have collected.
4 Prepare a short presentation which you should give to the class explaining the agreement you have reached with your partner.

6 IT security

- types of security problems
- dealing with viruses
- acceptable use policies

1 Start up

a Read the list of things that people sometimes do on their PCs at work. With a partner decide which are the most risky in terms of security.

a Surfing the internet
b Reading private emails and opening attachments
c Playing online computer games
d Visiting social networking sites like Facebook
e Downloading films or music from peer-to-peer networks
f Uploading photographs to websites like Flickr
g Chatting in chat rooms
h Watching videos or listening to music online

b Aside from any security issues, discuss which of these are acceptable for employees to do briefly at work. Which does your company allow?

I think it is OK to check your emails during your lunch break.

Work computers should only be used for work, not to keep in touch with friends.

We can listen to the radio online in our company but we're not allowed to play games.

2 A virus attack

Track 13 **Listen as Stefan Rehn from Stahlwerk GmbH, an engineering firm in Aachen, calls Henk Baars, a computer specialist based in the Netherlands. Match the German phrases with the English equivalents in the dialogue.**

1 während der Arbeitszeit
2 Ich habe keine Bedenken, dass ...
3 ruhig bleiben
4 Ich erkläre es Ihnen schrittweise.
5 sich verbreiten
6 verhindern

Baars Goedemorgen. Henk Baars.

Rehn Hello, Henk. This is Stefan Rehn from Stahlwerk in Aachen.

Baars Oh, hello, Stefan. How are you?

Rehn Well, not great. I'm afraid we might have a problem with our computer system. I need your help with it.

Baars No problem. That's what I'm here for, Stefan. Tell me more.

Rehn Well, about half an hour ago one of our secretaries' PCs stopped working properly. We think she may have a virus on it.

Baars Oh dear. Did she open an email attachment without checking who it was from?

Rehn I'm not sure, but it seems she wanted to listen to music on some website or other that she'd never used before. She says her machine started acting up after that.

Baars And now she's in trouble for listening to music on-the-job as well as catching a virus.

Rehn I'm not really bothered about her listening to music. Our staff can listen to the radio anyway if they want so I don't really see the difference. But I am concerned about the virus.

Baars Of course. OK ...

Rehn What should I do?

Baars Well, stay calm. That would be my first piece of advice. After that, there are several things you have to do.

Rehn OK.

Baars I'll walk you through the steps.

Rehn Right. Let me just get a pen and paper and I'll note them down ... OK. Go ahead.

Baars So ... the first thing you should do is disconnect from the network. You have to stop this thing spreading to other PCs.

Rehn OK ... got that.

Baars You should also prevent the malware spreading to other machines by turning off the file and printer sharing functions. OK?

Rehn Yes.

Baars Right. The next thing you should do is update the anti-virus software online.

Rehn How can I do that if the PC is disconnected from the network?

Baars Right, sorry. Let me explain more clearly. You shouldn't disconnect from the internet just yet. But you absolutely must close down all networking functions in Windows as quickly as possible.

Rehn Ah, I see.

Baars Right, next. You've updated your anti-virus software. Now quickly run updates on the operating system. Then you should use the firewall to block all internet traffic.

Rehn I'm not sure ...

Baars If you're not sure how to use the firewall, then now's the time to disconnect from the internet. Just pull the cable out of the PC.

Rehn Got you. And then?

Baars Then run the anti-virus software. If that can't remove the virus, it will certainly identify it for you. Then you'll know what you're dealing with. Oh, and until you're absolutely sure you've removed the virus, don't go back on the network and don't send emails with attachments. And the final step you have to take is to make sure that your staff understand and respect the company's AUP.

Rehn Uh? What's that?

Baars I'll explain later, Stefan. Take the steps that I've explained, then call me back when you've got the situation under control. I'll tell you how to avoid problems like this in the future.

Rehn OK, Henk. Thanks. I'll call later.

3 Stefan's notes

Track 13

a Stefan makes several mistakes when noting down Henk's advice. Read the notes and carry out the following tasks.

1 Listen or read again and identify the three pieces of advice Stefan forgot.
2 Find and correct the three mistakes.
3 Put the pieces of advice in the order Henk mentions them in.

– reject updates on operating system
– update anti-virus software online
– if firewall doesn't work, disconnect physically from the internet
– delete anti-virus software to destroy virus
– disconnect from the network
– block all internet traffic with firewall

b Work with a partner and discuss the questions.

1 Are there other steps that should be taken against an attack on a computer? What are they?
2 What was the worst attack you have had to deal with on your PC? How did you deal with it?

4 Different types of attack

a Use the verbs in the box to complete the texts. You will have to change the form of some of the verbs.

distribute | execute | generate | hack | hijack | infect | launch | self-replicate | spread | wipe

Adware
A program that ...[1] pop-ups on your computer or displays advertisements. It is important to note that not all adware programs are necessarily considered malware. There are many legitimate, free programs that display ads to generate revenue. As long as this information is provided up front, they are not considered malware.

Backdoor
A program that allows a remote user to ...[2] commands and tasks on your computer without your permission. These types of programs are typically used to ...[3] attacks on other computers, ...[4] copyrighted software and media or ...[5] other computers.

Hijackers
A program that attempts to ...[6] certain internet functions like redirecting your start page to the hijacker's own start page, redirecting search queries to an undesired search engine or replacing search results from popular search engines with their own information.

Virus
A program that, when run, has the ability to ...[7] by infecting other programs and files on your computer. These programs can have many effects. They may ...[8] your hard drive, display a joke in a small box or do nothing at all except replicate themselves. These types of infections tend to be localized to your computer and don't have the ability to spread to another computer on their own.

Worm
A program that, when run, has the ability to ...[9] to other computers on its own using either mass-mailing techniques to email addresses found on your computer or by using the internet to ...[10] a remote computer using known security holes.

b What other types of security attack do you know about? Research these on the internet and identify the key verbs which are used to describe how they work. Then write your own definitions similar to those above.

5 What's the problem?

Decide which type of attack happened to these people. The texts in exercise 4 may help you.

1 *Help! After I started up my computer this morning, I discovered that I'd lost all my files and that I couldn't control my mouse cursor.*

2 *Last week, my PC started defaulting to a website I had never seen before. The website was ... well, not exactly professional in nature. I find this pretty embarrassing but I don't know how to get rid of it.*

3 *I suddenly started getting pop-ups promoting strange products on my PC. I don't know why. I didn't have the problem before and I didn't clicked on any links to the pop-ups.*

6 Dealing with the problem

Track 14 **Listen as Stefan calls Henk to report his progress. Choose the correct sentence ending (a, b or c).**

1 Stefan tells Henk that he has ...
  a prevented the virus spreading onto some of the computers on the network.
  b failed to prevent the spread of the virus onto the network.
  c prevented the spread of the virus onto other computers on the network.

2 Stefan says that he has ...
  a installed new anti-virus software.
  b updated the operating system and anti-virus software.
  c reinstalled the operating system and anti-virus software.

3 Stefan says that the anti-virus software ...
  a has removed the virus.
  b can't identify the virus.
  c has identified the virus.

4 Henk says that the virus ...
  a cannot be spread by means other than email.
  b is normally spread via email attachments.
  c was spread on this occasion via an email.

5 Henk advises Stefan to ...
  a get some more specialist anti-virus software.
  b buy a new hard drive for the infected PC.
  c reinstall the operating system.

6 Henk tells Stefan that AUP stands for ...
  a Acceptable Use Policy.
  b Accepted User Policy.
  c Accepted Use Policy.

7 Working with words

Track 14 **Listen again and complete the sentences from the dialogue.**

1 The software has identified the virus but it ... seem to remove it.
2 I would say that you ... probably wipe the computer clean.
3 Quite a lot of viruses these days ... evade attempts to remove them with software.
4 I ... be able to drive over in the morning and take care of it for you.
5 I'll ... let you know by the end of the afternoon if I can.
6 Before I come, the best thing ... be to back up all the data on the PC.
7 We ... talk about an AUP for your office.
8 An AUP ... help you avoid problems like this in the future.

Grammar **Modal verbs**

1 We **must** talk about improving data security in our company.
2 You **should** back up your data every day.
3 You **can** block viruses by using the right anti-virus software.
4 I **can't** identify the problem with my PC but I think it's a trojan.
5 I want to **be able to** work online without worrying about attacks on my system.
6 You **don't have to** reinstall the operating system: the anti-virus software will deal with the problem.

- Modale Hilfsverben haben folgende Eigenheiten:
  - Sie haben in allen Personen dieselbe Form (1–4).
  - Bei der Verneinung gibt es zusammengezogene Formen (4, 6).
  - Sie werden mit dem Infinitiv ohne *to* verwendet (1–4).
- Wenn andere Formen nötig sind, benutzt man die Ersatzverben *to be able to (can), to be allowed to (may), to have to (must)* (5, 6).
- Achtung: *must not* bedeutet „nicht dürfen"; *do(es) not have to* bedeutet „muss nicht" (6).

Positive	Negative		German
	Full	**Contracted**	
can	cannot	can't	können
may	may not	–	dürfen
should	should not	shouldn't	sollte
must	must not	mustn't	müssen; nicht dürfen

8 Practice

Choose the best alternative to complete each sentence. Careful: you will have to change the form of some of the verbs.

1 You *can / have to* update anti-virus software daily if you want to avoid viruses.
2 Companies *can / be able to* use an AUP to tell their staff what they can do on their IT systems.
3 He *can / be able to* delete the trojan yesterday by updating his operating system.
4 Staff *shouldn't / don't have to* download music onto the company's IT system.
5 You *can / must* log back onto the network. I've deleted the virus on your computer.
6 I want to *can / be able to* surf the internet without worrying about viruses.
7 You will *have to / must* reinstall the operating system to solve this problem.
8 Staff *mustn't / don't have to* use their internet connections for activities which are not related to their work.

9 Giving your opinion

a Match the sentence beginnings (1–10) with the sentence endings (a–j) to make sentences that can be used in meetings to discuss opinions.

1 I have a few	a true, however ...
2 I'm not so	b the case, but ...
3 I'm sorry but I	c don't think that's true.
4 I agree with	d doubts about that.
5 I'm afraid I can't	e I don't agree.
6 Up to a point that may be	f really the case.
7 You're absolutely	g sure about that.
8 To an extent that's	h you there.
9 I don't think that's	i agree with that.
10 Sorry, but	j right.

b Now work with a partner to decide which phrases are for agreeing, disagreeing or expressing doubt about someone's opinion.

10 A meeting about an AUP

Stefan's colleagues have a meeting about an AUP. Discuss their opinions and use phrases from exercise 9 to say whether you agree, disagree or are doubtful.

11 Role-play: a meeting about an AUP

page 113

Work with a partner to carry out the role-play.

Student A: turn to File 6 on page 109. Student B: turn to File 2 on page 107.

12 Stahlwerk's AUP

a Match the English words with their German translations.

1 inappropriate
2 alter
3 removable
4 permission
5 destroy
6 respected
7 forbidden
8 review
9 access
10 copyright
11 harming
12 behaviour

a entfernbar
b Urheberrecht
c Genehmigung
d zugreifen auf
e unangemessen
f nachprüfen
g zerstören
h ändern
i schaden
j respektiert
k Benehmen
l verboten

b Now complete the English version of Stahlwerk's AUP using the words above.

Stahlwerk GmbH Acceptable Use Policy

Equipment

- Always get ...[1] before installing, attempting to install or storing programs on the company's computers.
- Damaging, disabling or otherwise ...[2] the computers or intentionally wasting resources puts your work at risk and is strictly ...[3].
- Only use the computers for work purposes. Activities such as buying or selling goods, listening to music and visiting social networking sites are ...[4].
- Always check files brought in on ...[5] media (such as CDs, flash drives, etc.) or on mobile equipment which will be connected to the network with anti-virus software and only use them if they are free of viruses.

Security and privacy

- Other computer users should be ...[6] and should not be harassed, harmed, offended or insulted.
- To protect yourself and the systems, you should respect the security on the computers; attempting to bypass or ...[7] the settings may put you or your work at risk.
- Data on your PC belongs to the company. IT staff may ...[8] your files and communications to ensure that you are using the system responsibly.

Internet

- You should ...[9] the internet only for company activities.
- Respect the work and ownership rights of people outside the company. This includes abiding by ...[10] laws.

Email

- Only open attachments if they come from someone you know and trust. Attachments can contain viruses or other programs that could ...[11] all the files and software on your computer.
- Be polite and appreciate that other users might have different views from your own. The use of strong language, swearing or aggressive ...[12] is as anti-social on the internet as it is on the street.

13 More rules

Read these rules from the AUP and decide which section they come from.

1 If you receive material of a violent, dangerous, racist or inappropriate content, always report this to a member of IT staff.
2 Only access suitable material: using the internet to download, send, print, display or otherwise access materials which are unlawful, obscene or abusive is not permitted.
3 Protect the computers from spillages by eating or drinking away from your PC.
4 Always be wary about revealing your home address, telephone number, school name or picture to people you meet on the internet.
5 Protect your work by keeping your password to yourself; never use someone else's logon name or password.

Webcode:
TMU0601

14 Mediation

Summarize the AUP in exercise 12 in German for a colleague who does not understand English.

Refresh your knowledge

1 **Make a word spider of all the verbs from the unit that can be used with virus.**

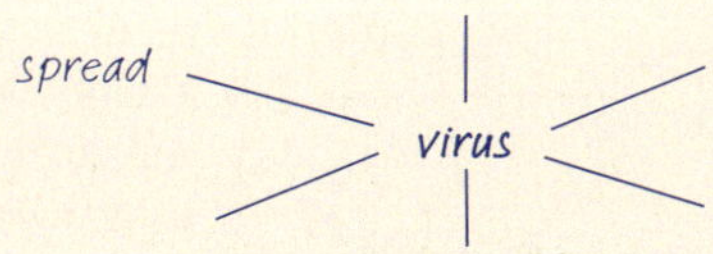

2 **Rearrange the words to make phrases for agreeing, disagreeing and expressing doubt.**

1 few / I / a / that / doubts / about / have
2 agree / I / can't / I'm / with / afraid / that
3 right / absolutely / you're
4 not / that / sure / so / I'm / about
5 you / there / with / agree / I

3a **Find the English equivalents for the German sentences from an AUP.**

1 Schützen Sie die Computer vor Verschmutzung, indem Sie in ausreichendem Abstand zum PC essen oder trinken.
2 Schützen Sie Ihre Arbeit, indem Sie Ihr Passwort für sich behalten; nutzen Sie niemals den Anmeldenamen oder das Passwort eines anderen Nutzers.
3 Fragen Sie immer um Erlaubnis, bevor Sie Programme – egal welchen Typs – auf Firmencomputer installieren oder zu installieren versuchen.

3b **Using ideas and vocabulary from the unit, decide what you think is acceptable when using computers at work and write the beginning of an AUP.**

Extra material

1 Read the questions and then scan the texts to find the answers.

1 What role did Twitter play in the two stories?
2 Which hacker may get into further trouble for their actions?
3 Which hacker has got a job as a result of their actions?
4 What argument is presented by critics of the hackers' activities in the text?

A

The 21-year-old who created the first ever iPhone worm has been given a job developing apps for the phone. Ashley Towns revealed via his Twitter account that he's been hired by apps developer mogeneration. Towns has said he created the "ikee" worm – it changed users' wallpaper into a photo of Rick Astley – to point out flaws in security and has not faced charges. Critics point out that his worm paved the way for a more malicious version that tries to steal financial data.

B

The kids who crashed the social networking site Twitter have not only come clean about their antics but have apparently asked the outfit for a job.

"Mikeyy" and "StalkDaily" crashed the site leaving thousands of unwanted messages in their wake. Messages directed users to StalkDaily.com and said things such as "Mikeyy I am done", "Twitter please fix this" and "Twitter hire Mikeyy".

It looks like, while Twitter will not hire Mikeyy, someone else has thought it would be a good idea to give 17-year-old Michael "Mikeyy" Mooney a job. The teenage programmer told ABCNews.com that, after claiming responsibility for the attacks, two companies contacted him with job offers. Despite this, Mikeyy is being investigated by the police who may take the case to court.

Mooney said that he created the Twitter worm, to show the social networking site that there was a problem.

2 Find words and expressions in the texts which have the same meaning as the following ones.

1 announced
2 given a job
3 defects
4 laid the ground
5 admitted
6 tricks
7 company

3 a Work in groups and discuss when you think it is ethically acceptable that hackers are rewarded for their actions with job offers and when not.

b Now work in groups and draw up a list of guidelines that could be used by technology companies considering offering jobs to ex-hackers.

7 Trade fairs

- participating at a trade fair
- presentations
- small talk

1 Start up

a Match the appropriate trade fair to the companies. Give reasons for your choice.

A
CeBIT
Venue: Hanover, Germany
Category: IT and telecommunications
Visitor's profile: industry, retailers, passionate users

B
GITEX
Venue: Riyadh, Saudi Arabia
Category: Computer networks, multimedia technology, internet products
Visitor's profile: Trade visitors only

C
Web 2.0 Expo
Venue: New York, USA
Category :Computer and IT, web design and web development
Visitor's profile: Business leaders, web designers and developers, advertising agencies

D
Convergence India
Venue: New Delhi, India
Category: ICT industry, focus on green IT
Visitor's profile: Vendors, operators, service providers, IT companies

E
PT/Expo COMM China
Venue: Beijing, China
Category: Internet, multimedia, telecommunications (telecom networking, mobile communications)
Visitor's profile: Professionals: Industry, traders

F
IEEE International Conference on Peer to Peer Computing
Venue: Delft, Netherlands
Category: computer science, web services, peer to peer computing
Visitor's profile: Professionals and passionate users

1 FutureWorld, a company focusing on environmentally-friendly IT products
2 EuroCom, a retailer for telecommunication solutions throughout Europe
3 InterMobil, an international and steadily expanding seller of mobile phones and telecommunication services who want to move into the Asian market
4 WorldTravel, a travel agency with innovative web presentations
5 Future Technologies, a company focusing on innovative technologies and specialized in peer-to-peer networking
6 Telefonikom, a network specialist wanting to explore the Middle Eastern market

b Your head of department asks you to prepare a visit to a trade fair. Carry out the following tasks.

1 What does the ideal trade fair for your company look like? What does your company hope to achieve when taking part at a trade fair?
2 Check the internet and find a suitable trade fair for your company.

2 The PT/Expo COMM China

Read the text and answer the questions.

1 How successful was the P&T/Expo COMM China last year?
2 Who attends the trade fair?
3 Why is the P&T/Expo COMM China especially suitable for foreign exhibitors?
4 Which of the ten reasons to exhibit at the trade fair could be important for your company? Name three.
5 What exhibits are displayed at the fair? Which would be interesting for your company?

http://

P&T/EXPO COMM™ CHINA 2010

Accelerate your business

P&T/Expo COMM China – Accelerate Your Business

For over 20 years the P&T/Expo COMM China exhibition and conference has allowed ICT service providers and equipment manufacturers to promote their products on the Chinese market. It is the largest international fair and conference on telecommunications, internet and wireless technology in Asia. Over 500 exhibitors from 19 countries participated in P&T/Expo COMM China last year, with 50,000 square metres of exhibition space. More than 150,000 attendees visited the fair, most of them professional visitors from the IT and telecom sectors representing a variety of interests and industries. The media provided thorough, complete and comprehensive coverage of this ICT event, giving participating exhibitors a name and face in Asia.

Top 10 reasons to exhibit at P&T/Expo COMM China

- Meet decision makers from telecom, satellite and internet service providers
- Meet thousands of buyers from the government and China's expanding enterprise community
- VIP tours by industry leaders and key government officials
- Conference keynotes and panel speaker opportunities
- Technical seminars and product presentation available on site
- Announce new products and services at China's leading forum for technology development
- Nationwide press and media coverage that will extend your brand name beyond the show floor
- TV and radio coverage throughout Asia and the Pacific Region
- Meet agents and distributors eager to represent your company

Analysis of attendee objectives

Looking for new technology, new products	67.23%
Business negotiation/looking for partnership	19.56%
Face-to-face meetings with exhibitors	6.78%
Purchasing	4.40%
Other objectives	2.04%

Exhibits content

At P&T/ Expo COMM China you will find all the innovations in the market. Visitors can look at networking (mobile communications, wireless LAN/WAN, Gateway), telecom manufacturing (antennas, personal terminals, IC/Smart cards), telecom applications (billing systems, VoIP/IP telephony, e-commerce), and satellite communications.

3 Working with words

a Match the words from the text (1–10) with the explanations (a–j).

1 accelerate	a detailed
2 exhibitor	b a person who displays something at a show
3 thorough	c make something known publicly
4 promote	d discussion aimed at reaching an agreement
5 booth	e increase
6 announce	f the activity of buying things
7 throughout	g give publicity in order to sell sth
8 objectives	h in every part
9 negotiation	i a small, temporary area at a fair
10 purchasing	j purposes

b Work with a partner and decide what the German equivalents are for the English terms.

Grammar **Comparatives & superlatives**

1 Our trade fair stand was **smaller than** the one we had last year.
2 The presentation should have been **simpler** so that everyone could understand it.
3 The location of the stand is **more important than** its size.
4 We shouldn't just take **the cheapest** stand.
5 We should spend **as much** money **as** necessary on advertising.

- Alle einsilbigen Adjektive werden mit *-(e)r* und *-(e)st* gesteigert (1, 4).
- Einzelkonsonanten nach einem kurzen Vokal werden dabei verdoppelt: *big – bigger – the biggest.*
- Zweisilbige Adjektive mit den Endungen *-y*, *-er* und *-le* werden ebenfalls mit *-(e)r* und *-(e)st* gesteigert (2). Dabei wird *-y* in *-i* umgewandelt.
- Alle anderen zwei- und mehrsilbigen Adjektive werden mit *more* und *most* gesteigert (3).
- Einige Adjektive haben unregelmäßige Steigerungsformen: *good – better – best; bad – worse – worst; little* (wenig) *– less – least; much/many – more – most*
- Vergleiche bildet man mit *than* (als) (1,3) oder *as ... as* (so ... wie) (5).

4 Practice

Complete the sentences with the comparative or superlative of the adjectives in brackets.

Webcode: ITMU0701

1 P & T/Expo COMM China is the ... IT trade fair in Asia. (large)
2 ... exhibitors came to the fair than last year. (many)
3 China is the ... growing market in the world at the moment. (fast)
4 The fair was huge – it wasn't the ... fair to find your way around in! (easy)
5 The cost of the stands was ... than at the fair in India. (expensive)
6 The media coverage was ... than any other trade fair I've been to. (good)

5 A trade fair planning meeting

InterMobil Plc wants to exhibit at the next trade fair in China. Read the agenda and then link the sentences below to a) the speaker and b) the correct item on the agenda.

InterMobil Plc

Venue: Conference room, main building, second floor
Date: 21 July 20..
Time: 9.00 a.m. to 12.30 p.m.

Participants

John Strawford (Chairperson)
Davis Brown (Research and Development)
Peter Hunt (International Relations)
Christoph Meisner (IT Technician)
Wesley Miller (Customer Service Manager)
Maggie Wang (Marketing Manager, IT International)
Madeleine Proulx (Finance)
Jane Seymore (Minutes)

Agenda

1 Welcome and introduction of participants
2 Introduction of the agenda
3 Meeting objectives
4 Current situation and experience
5 Future action
6 AOB

1 Welcome to the meeting, everyone. (John Strawford, agenda item 1)
2 As the expert in international affairs in our company, I must say we don't have enough experience in taking part at trade fairs in China. I'd suggest we ask Ms Wang to give us a presentation on trade fair participation at our next meeting.
3 Do you all have a copy of the agenda?
4 The purpose of today's meeting is to discuss which trade fair would be best to represent our company on the Asian market.
5 Ms Wang has some experience in working with Asian companies. She will give us some advice about cross-cultural differences.
6 Peter has asked me to tell you about the arrangements for today. I'll be taking the minutes and John is chairing. We will have a 15-minute break at 11.00, and then ...
7 Any other points? No? Then I'd like to thank you all for coming. See you at the same time next week.
8 Well Peter, you've been to a trade fair in Kuala Lumpur. Could you say a few words about your experience?

6 Working with words

Complete the sentences with words from the box.

advice | agenda | aim | future action | intercultural differences | item | minutes | participants | participate

1 The first ... on the agenda was to welcome and introduce the ... .
2 Jane was there to write the ... .
3 John called the meeting because the company is planning to ... at a trade fair.
4 The ... of the meeting was to discuss how to find the right trade fair in Asia.
5 It is important to get ... on ... .
6 After having discussed most items, we talked about ... .

7 Participating at a trade fair

Track 15

a Maggie Wang gives a presentation on successful trade fair participation. Copy the mind map and then listen and complete it with the points Maggie makes.

b Listen again and complete the questions with words or phrases from the presentation.

1 Why should our company ... at a trade show?
2 How can we find out if our products ... to Asian buyers?
3 Why should we only ... on a few key products?
4 How can we choose the most ... trade fair?
5 How ... will it be to take part in a trade fair?
6 Why is the ... design so important?
7 Why are ... relations so important?
8 What kind of stand ... do we need to be successful?
9 What are the best ways to ... our success at the trade fair?
10 What ... do we need to be successful in China?

8 Language for presentations

Track 15 **a Listen again and decide which of the sentences below Maggie uses.**

1 If there are any questions, I'll be happy to answer them.
2 Good morning, ladies and gentlemen.
3 Thank you very much for listening.
4 Before I finish, let me summarize the key points.
5 Let me point out ...
6 My name is ... and I'm ...
7 The presentation will take around ... minutes.
8 If there are no questions, I'll move on to ...
9 Today, I'd like to ...
10 That brings me to the end of my presentation.

b Decide which of the sentences are used at the beginning of a presentation, which signal the direction of the presentation and which come at the end.

9 A good presentation

a Discuss what you think is important for a successful presentation. Mention at least five different items.

b Summarize the text in English. Do not translate word for word.

12 goldene Regeln für eine gute Präsentation

1 Bereiten Sie sich sorgfältig auf die Präsentation vor. Erscheinen Sie frühzeitig, um bereits Kontakt mit den Zuhörern zu knüpfen.
2 Sagen Sie zu Beginn der Präsentation immer klar, um was es geht, und stellen Sie Lösungen in Aussicht. Versuchen Sie, einen guten Eindruck zu machen.
3 Versuchen Sie, Ihre Präsentation mit einer Anekdote oder einem ‚Wachmacher' zu beginnen. Berücksichtigen Sie aber die interkulturellen Unterschiede.
4 Denken Sie genau darüber nach, was Sie sagen, wann Sie es sagen, und wie Sie es sagen.
5 Stellen Sie ein Handout zur Verfügung oder stellen Sie die Präsentation für die Zuhörer zugänglich ins Netz, denn über geschriebenen Text werden mehr Infos transportiert als über verbale Kommunikation.
6 Verwenden Sie visuelle Hilfsmittel wie Bilder, Grafiken usw., denn ein Bild sagt mehr als tausend Worte.
7 Halten Sie Blickkontakt zum Publikum. Jeder muss subjektiv den Eindruck haben, dass sie/er wichtig ist.
8 Zeigen Sie Begeisterung. Die Zuhörer müssen spüren, dass sie im Mittelpunkt stehen und dass es Ihnen Freude macht, mit ihnen zu sprechen. Verstecken Sie sich nicht hinter dem Rednerpult, sondern verwenden Sie Gesten, laufen Sie herum und beziehen Sie das Publikum mit ein.
9 Versuchen Sie die Aufmerksamkeit der Zuhörer z.B. mit Anekdoten, Karikaturen, Fragerunden oder Diskussionen zu gewinnen.
10 Berücksichtigen Sie interkulturelle Unterschiede, wenn Sie eine Präsentation vor Zuhörern aus anderen Ländern oder Kulturen halten. Manche Präsentationen ‚über Grenzen hinweg' misslingen, weil der Redner diese Unterschiede nicht beachtet.
11 Sprechen Sie lebendig und wirkungsvoll: nicht zu schnell, flüssig und klar, mit Pausen an den richtigen Stellen. Benutzen Sie ihre Stimme wie ein Instrument.
12 Fordern Sie das Publikum auf, Fragen zu stellen und gehen Sie mit den Fragen sorgfältig um: die Meinung der Leute basiert vor allem darauf, wie Sie deren Fragen beantworten.

c Compare your ideas about a good presentation with the 12 golden rules. Which similarities and differences are there?

10 Giving a presentation

page 114

Prepare a presentation of your company's key products (or of another company you know well) for a trade fair.

1 Use Maggie Wang's presentation, the language of presentation and the golden rules from the previous exercises for your preparation.
2 Give the presentation with the class acting as your audience.
3 Ask the audience questions at the end to check if they were listening.
4 Give marks from 1–6 for content and delivery of the presentations.

Skills **Wie kann ich mehr Verständnis für interkulturelle Unterschiede entwickeln?**

Ob man im Ausland geschäftlich unterwegs ist oder in Deutschland internationale Kunden betreut, man benötigt interkulturelle Kompetenz, um Missverständnisse und Konflikte zu vermeiden. Interkulturelle Kompetenz bedeutet, die Sinne für die eigene kulturelle Prägung zu schärfen und für andere Sicht- und Arbeitsweisen bzw. Führungs- und Verhandlungsstile sensibel zu werden. Achten Sie daher beim Umgang mit Geschäftspartnern aus anderen Ländern besonders auf folgende Bereiche, in denen sich im Berufsleben häufig interkulturelle Unterschiede zeigen:

- Einstellung gegenüber Zeit (z. B. Pünktlichkeit, Einhaltung von Zeitplänen, usw.)
- Körpersprache (z. B. Körperkontakt beim Begrüßen, Gestik, usw.)
- Haltung gegenüber Arbeit (z. B. Arbeitszeit, Pausen, Urlaubstage, usw.)
- Firmenkultur (z. B. Führungsstil, Hierarchie, usw.)
- Kommunikationskultur (z. B. Smalltalk, Höflichkeit, Dominanz beim Kommunizieren, usw.)

11 Building skills: cross-cultural awareness

To prepare for the trade fair, InterMobil research the Chinese culture. Read the skills box above and then carry out the tasks.

1 In groups choose a category from above and find out information about China.
2 Present your findings to the class.

12 Small talk at a trade fair

Track 16

a Peter Hunt from InterMobil is taking a coffee break at the trade fair. Listen to his conversation with another participant and complete the sentences.

1 Hi. Is there ... left?
2 It's a ... , isn't it?
3 Have you ... to the UK?
4 I was in Birmingham ... last year.
5 Where is your ...?
6 What was ... of the city?

b Decide which small talk topics are covered in the dialogue. Which of the sentences above match which topic?

c In groups brainstorm what other small talk topics you could talk about at a trade fair.

13 Role-play: small talk at the stand

page 113

a **At the InterMobil trade fair stand in China a visitor is talking to the company's representative. Use the language and ideas from exercise 12 to make small talk.**

Mitarbeiter/in

Begrüßen Sie den Besucher / die Besucherin und stellen Sie sich vor.

Besucher/in

Begrüßen Sie den Mitarbeiter / die Mitarbeiterin am Messestand und fragen Sie, wo die Firma in Deutschland ansässig ist.

Antworten Sie, dass die Zentrale in München ist. Fragen Sie, ob der Besucher / die Besucherin schon einmal in Deutschland war.

Antworten Sie, dass Sie bereits in Deutschland auf einer Geschäftsreise waren.

Fragen Sie, welchen Eindruck der Besucher / die Besucherin von Deutschland bekommen hat.

Antworten Sie, dass Sie viele gute Erfahrungen gemacht haben. Fragen Sie, welche Schlüsselprodukte die Firma anbietet.

Antworten Sie, dass Sie auf Handys und Telekommunikationsdienste spezialisiert sind.

Sagen Sie, dass Sie diese Produkte interessieren. Fragen Sie nach mehr Informationen.

b **Swap partners and make small talk with a new visitor at the stand. Use the topics you collected in exercise 12 to carry out your own role-play.**

Refresh your knowledge

1 **Rearrange the words to make phrases for structuring a presentation.**

1 to / would / to / like / conclude / I / ...
2 point / me / that / on / out / let / moving / ...
3 presentation / minutes / around / take / the / twenty / will
4 at the end / if / any / them / there / are / happy / I'm / to / questions / answer

2 **Using topic ideas and language from the unit, compile a list of useful small talk phrases for when you have to talk to business partners from abroad.**

The power of body language in presentations

What makes body language so important? Well, your appearance subconsciously affects your audience. In other words, they just look at you and go with their gut. However well supported and prepared the content of your speech is, it is your non-verbal delivery that establishes your credibility for an audience. Most importantly, however you hold yourself, however you move through space and however you gesture, your body sends messages back to your brain. So, if you are standing with your shoulders drooping and head bowed, your brain creates, and sends, negative chemicals into your bloodstream in less than a fortieth of a second – to make you feel the way you look.

How does a speaker become positively powerful then? Attributes like the full use and control of space, relaxed body language, an open posture and a strong, authentic presence. To begin feeling that power yourself, imagine a lion in the jungle. She establishes her space and territory; she's queen of the jungle. She's relaxed; she moves gracefully and carries her confidence and stability with her. Hold on to that image of the lion as you begin to become aware of your presentation body language. Walk around the room taking long purposeful strides and allowing your arms to swing freely.

But does body language make a great difference? It does. Research shows that 55% of communication is conveyed by body language, 38% by your voice and only 7% by the words we use. So to be a great presenter you have to start becoming aware of your body language and what it is saying. With the right body language, your presentations will be much more successful. Let's look at some of the most important factors:

Space and territory: Imagine yourself in a conference room or banquet hall. The whole room is yours so you should take control of it. Don't just get stuck standing behind the podium. Talk to the people at the back of the room. You want to connect with even the quiet group sitting on the back row.

Movement: How you move affects your audience. Move quickly and it stirs up the audience, move slowly and you keep them entranced. Use your space to create transitions in your speech: state your first point and pause. Move and then address your second point. Speak formally from far away. Silently come forward to get more intimate when giving your personal opinions. Make positive points from one side of the room and negative ones from the other.

Posture: When we are fearful or stressed, our shoulders tend to draw up towards our ears and our backs arch slightly. Instead of being powerful and open, we may hunch forward so our shoulders curve in, protecting the heart. If we continue to do this, the muscles across the chest will shorten and grow tight and it will become difficult to take full complete breaths. Deep breaths are crucial to relaxation.

Gestures: The answer to the FAQ 'What do I do with my hands?' is simple: 'Just do something!' Animated gestures help audiences understand and retain more information by creating visual images that appeal to the right side of the brain. Keep your hands in view rather than behind your back or in your pockets. When making points, use your fingers to count, hold your hand high so the audience will know that you are counting for them.

Eye contact: As speakers, it is vital to make eye contact with our audience. Maintaining eye contact with an audience is proven to make the speaker appear more skilled, experienced and powerful and the people we look at are more likely to remember what we've said. Since we take in 80% of information via the eyes, monitoring the audience throughout a presentation is critical. It allows us to be authentic. The primary function of eye contact is to establish relationships. Each person in the audience with whom eye contact is established will feel connected to you and that energy will give you even more confidence. Make sure to give the most contact to the people who need it, for example, someone who may be losing concentration or talking with a neighbour.

Extra material

1 Understanding the text

Read the text on page 75 and then answer the questions.

1 How are the body and brain connected?
2 What makes a speaker powerful?
3 Which example does the author give to visualize the impact of body language? Is it a good example? Why (not)?
4 What does research show about the importance of body language?
5 What is the author's opinion on movement in presentations? Do you agree?
6 Why is good posture so important?
7 What key point does the author make about gestures?
8 To whom should you give most eye contact as a presenter?

2 Right or wrong?

Look at the cartoons below and decide what they are doing right or wrong according to the text.

3 Over to you

a Do cross-cultural factors influence how you use body language in daily life / in presentations? Discuss this issue in groups and then report to the class.

b Use the internet and compare presentation etiquettes for different countries. Present your findings.

Handling orders & complaints 8

- placing & taking an order
- complaining
- formal & informal correspondence

1 Start up

a **Work with a partner and describe the ways that customers can order products and services from the company you work for.**

b **Discuss which method can lead to the most mistakes with orders.**

2 Placing an order

Track 17

Listen as Mary Crane calls Hardware Computer Supplies Ltd and write down the English equivalents of the German words and expressions below.

1 Preisnachlass
2 Mehrwertsteuer
3 etwas auf Lager haben
4 die Bestellung bestätigen
5 als Standard
6 Vor-Ort-Garantie / Gewährleistung
7 auf Wunsch
8 Lieferanschrift

3 The details of Mary's order

Track 17

Listen again and choose the correct ending (a–p) for each sentence beginning (1–8).

1 Mary Crane met Niles Simpson at
2 Mary wants to order
3 She's interested in ordering two
4 Niles offered a discount of
5 Without the discount, the EPL N2 55ODTs would cost
6 The C2500Ns will be with Mary
7 The total price of £3,396 for the scanners
8 Mary's email address is

a in three days.
b five scanners from Epson.
c excludes VAT.
d the CeBit fair in Germany.
e EBL N2 55ODEs.
f mary_crane@cranephotography.co.uk.
g eleven per cent.
h £1,990.
i at the MediaTech fair in Cambridge.
j two scanners from Epson.
k includes VAT.
l by next Thursday at the earliest.
m £995.
n Mary.Crane@cranephotography.co.uk.
o EPL N2 55ODTs.
p 12 per cent.

4 Talking about orders

Rearrange the words to make sentences about orders from the dialogue.

1 in / are / models / which / you / interested / ?
2 cost / the / will / £1,990 / for / total / two / be
3 12% / offered / me / a / Niles / ordered / discount / if / two / I
4 the / equal / discount / £3,396 / that / minus / would
5 price / inclusive / is / VAT / the / of
6 the / currently / we / stock / in / have / C2500N / don't
7 next / be / scanners / earliest / the / with / by / you / at / would / the / Thursday
8 email / confirm / I'll / order / by / your

Skills Wie kann ich meine Sprechfertigkeit verbessern?

Wie kann ich mir die notwendigen Sprachmittel und Verhaltensregeln aneignen?

- Suchen Sie Situationen, die Sie zum Sprechen bringen. Fahren Sie ins englischsprachige Ausland (z. B. im Urlaub, durch Austauschprogramme der Schule oder des Betriebes, usw.). Versuchen Sie, Kontakte zu Muttersprachlern in Ihrem Land zu bekommen (z. B. durch internationale Freundschaftsklubs).
- Hören Sie sich einen Text auf DVD oder CD an und sprechen Sie ihn mit.
- Eignen Sie sich eine Sammlung von Redewendungen an, die bei Gesprächen und Diskussionen häufig verwendet werden.

Welche Kommunikationsstrategien helfen mir, wenn mir Wörter fehlen?

- Benutzen Sie Umschreibungstechniken wie z. B. das Paraphrasieren eines unbekannten Wortes mit eigenen Worten, damit Sie Ihre Gedanken auch dann noch ausdrücken können, wenn Ihnen einzelne Wörter fehlen. Wenn Ihnen z. B. das Adverb *currently* nicht einfällt, können Sie stattdessen *at the moment* oder *now* sagen: *We don't have the parts here now / at the moment.*
- Formulieren Sie einen Satz völlig um, wenn Ihnen mehrere Wörter fehlen oder Sie große Schwierigkeiten haben, einen bestimmten Gedanken auszudrücken. Anstatt *Accompanying software is always included in the sale price* könnten Sie *You don't have to pay extra for the software* sagen.

5 Building skills: speaking

You are on the phone but can't remember all the English words you need. Form these sentences without using the direct translation of the words in bold.

1 Der Preis enthält die **Mehrwertsteuer**. *(VAT)*
2 Leider sind die Mäuse gerade **nicht auf Lager**. *(not in stock)*
3 Wir können Ihnen heute einen **Rabatt** von 10% anbieten. *(discount)*
4 Können Sie mir bitte die **Lieferanschrift** geben? *(delivery address)*
5 Das kostet €2.000 **insgesamt**. *(in total)*

6 Role-play: ordering

page 114

Work with a partner to carry out the role-play using phrases from exercise 4.

Don't forget to use the communication strategies from the skills box.

Student A

Nehmen Sie den Telefonanruf für Hardware Computer Supplies entgegen und nennen Sie Ihren Namen.

Student B

Stellen Sie sich mit Ihrem Namen vor und nennen Sie den Namen Ihrer Firma. Sagen Sie, dass Sie daran interessiert sind, Druckerkartuschen zu bestellen.

A: Fragen Sie, welche Art von Druckerkartusche der Kunde / die Kundin bestellen möchte.

B: Sagen Sie, dass Sie 25 Kartuschen für den Epson C 4000 Drucker bestellen möchten. Fragen Sie, wieviel diese insgesamt kosten werden.

A: Bieten Sie dem Kunden / der Kundin einen Preisnachlass von 3% an, weil er/sie eine große Anzahl Farbkartuschen bestellt. Sagen Sie, dass der Gesamtpreis £151.25 beträgt.

B: Fragen Sie, ob die Mehrwertsteuer im Preis enthalten ist.

A: Bestätigen Sie, dass der Preis die Mehrwertsteuer beinhaltet.

B: Fragen Sie, wann die Kartuschen geliefert werden.

A: Sagen Sie, dass Sie in der Datenbank überprüfen, ob die Kartuschen zurzeit auf Lager sind. Sagen Sie, dass die Kartuschen momentan nicht auf Lager sind, dass Sie diese aber umgehend bestellen werden. Sie werden am nächsten Freitag beim Kunden / bei der Kundin sein.

B: Sagen Sie, dass es so in Ordnung ist.

A: Bitten Sie den Kunden / die Kundin um seine/ihre E-Mail Adresse, damit Sie die Bestellung per E-Mail bestätigen können.

B: Nennen Sie Ihre E-Mail Adresse.

A: Bedanken Sie sich beim Kunden / bei der Kundin für die Bestellung.

7 Confirming the order

a Complete Lynton North's email confirming the order using the words in the box.

additional | address | deliver | discount | hesitate | order | product | total | within

Order for Epson scanners

From: Lynton North
To: Mary Crane
Cc:
Subject: Order for Epson scanners

Dear Ms Crane

Thank you for your telephone call today. I am writing to confirm your ...1. You ordered the following products:

...2 code	Description	No. items	Price per item minus 12% ...3	Price for items ordered
EPL N2 550DT	Epson scanner	2	£995.00	£1751.20
C2500N	Star desktop scanner	3	£623.00	£1644.72
	...4 charges		Installation charge	£106.00
			Delivery charge	£78.00
			Subtotal	£3579.92
			VAT	£626.49
			...5 price	£4206.41

Delivery ...6: 34 Sheldon Avenue, Croydon, CR9 1SD

We will ...7 your order ...8 the next six working days. Thank you again for your order. Please don't ...9 to call us if you have any questions.

Best wishes

Lynton North

b Read the email again and answer the questions.

1 What costs does it include which were not mentioned during the telephone conversation between Mary Crane and Lynton North?
2 In what other way do the prices in the email vary from those mentioned on the telephone?

8 Writing an email

Write an email from Hardware Computer Supplies to the customer confirming the order from the role play in exercise 6. Use the email in exercise 7 as a model.

Grammar | **Relative pronouns**

1 Thank you for your order **which** we received today.
2 Only users **who** register with the provider can access the central server.
3 You did not mention delivery during the phone call **(that)** I made to order the printers.
4 Select the payment option **(which)** you want to use then click 'buy now'.

- *which* bezieht sich auf Sachen (1).
- *who* bezieht sich auf Personen (2).
- *that* bezieht sich sowohl auf Personen als auch auf Sachen und kann *who* und *which* ersetzen (3).
- In notwendigen Relativsätzen können Relativpronomen wegfallen, wenn sie Objekt sind (3, 4).

9 Practice

a Decide which relative pronoun is not possible in these sentences.

1 This is the scanner *who/which/that* I was telling you about earlier.
2 Can I speak to the technician *who/which/that* set up our new laser printer?
3 This is the invoice *who/which/that* is causing all the problems.
4 I'd like to talk to the person *who/which/that* is responsible for after sales service, please.
5 The cable *who/which/that* connects the scanner to the PC is faulty.
6 What's the product code of the part *who/which/that* you need?
7 Here's the customer's email address *who/which/that* you were looking for.
8 Can you tell me the name of the person *who/which/that* I spoke to last week?

b Now decide in which sentences the relative pronoun can be left out.

10 Practice

Write sentences with relative clauses. Only use a relative pronoun where necessary.

1 Where / be / the sales person / I / speak to / at the trade fair last week / ?
2 Do / you / sell / any other software / be / compatible with / this program / ?
3 We / receive / an order / be / incomplete
4 She / be / the person / deal with our order / last Friday
5 I cannot / find / the order / I / be looking for

11 An email from Mary

Mary has received her order. Read her email and then match the phrases (1–6) to the highlighted phrases in the email which have the same meaning.

1 bill
2 to bring up some issues
3 to forgo
4 further cost
5 I'd appreciate it if
6 had the distinct feeling

Order for Epson scanners

From: Mary Crane
To: Lynton North
Cc:
Subject: Order for Epson scanners

Dear Lynton

I received my order for five Epson scanners today along with your invoice. This is just a quick email to raise a few points with you about this.

I was surprised to read that there is an additional charge of £78.00 for the delivery of the scanners in your invoice. You didn't mention this on the phone and, if you had, I would have asked you to waive the charge because of the size of my order. The more important point about the invoice is, however, that VAT has been put on top of the price you quoted me. I was under the strong impression that the prices you quoted included VAT. I'd appreciate it if you could look into this for me soon as I won't be in a position to settle the bill until this has been clarified.

Unfortunately, there was also a problem with the order itself. On the phone you told me that the software came as standard with the scanners. However, the scanners arrived minus the software. When I asked the technician who helped us get the EPL N2 550DTs up and running about this, he told me that I would have to order – and pay for – the software separately. I'd be grateful if you could supply the software at no additional cost as we agreed on the phone.

Thanks in advance for your help with this.

I look forward to hearing from you soon.

Best

Mary

12 Mediation

Work with a partner and take turns to summarize Mary's email in German for a colleague who doesn't understand English.

13 Discussion

Work in a group and discuss the following questions.

1 How serious do you think the mistakes Mary mentions in her email are?
2 Which steps should Lynton North take in response to the email?

14 An email from Lynton

a Lynton replies to Mary. Complete the email with the phrases (a–f).

a ... at no extra cost to you
b ... let me say that I am sorry about ...
c ... inclusive of VAT
d I have amended ...
e Apologies ...
f To make up for any inconvenience ...

Re: Order for Epson scanners

From: Lynton North
To: Mary Crane
Cc:
Subject: Re: Order for Epson scanners

Dear Mary

First off, ...[1] the mistakes which were made in your invoice as well as in your order. ...[2] the invoice to include the original prices we discussed on the phone ...[3]. I have also sent the software you require: it should be with you tomorrow. ...[4] as a result of our oversights, I have included five packs of photo paper ...[5].

...[6] once again for our mistakes. Please get in touch if you have any questions.

Regards

Lynton

b Complete the discussion tasks with a partner.

1 Say whether you think Lynton has responded to Mary's email appropriately.
2 Identify the issue in Mary's email which Lynton does not include in his.

Info **Formal and informal emails**

Emails are often less formal than business letters but, depending on the subject or who is sending and receiving an email, they can be just as formal as a letter. Here are some ways you can begin and end emails with the right tone of formality.

Beginning an email	**Ending an email**
Dear Mary Crane *(formal)*	Best wishes/regards *(formal)*
Dear Ms Crane *(formal)*	Regards *(informal)*
Dear Mary *(informal)*	Best / All the best *(informal)*

15 Formal or informal?

a Decide whether the phrases below are from formal or informal emails.

1 Apologies for ...
2 First off, ...
3 To begin with ...
4 I am writing to ...
5 Please do not hesitate to contact us if you have further questions.
6 This is just a quick email to ...
7 Please accept my apologies for ...
8 Please get in touch if you have any questions.

b Read the three emails in this unit again. Which are more formal in tone?

16 A formal letter of complaint

a Read the parts of Mary's letter (a–f) to Lynton and match them to the right sections (1–6).

a ... sincerely
b ... doing business with you in the future but only on the condition that the delivery charge is, on this occasion, removed from my invoice.
c ... I am writing to complain in the strongest possible terms about your having disregarded my complaint about the addition of a delivery charge of £78.00.
d ... you did not mention this charge during the telephone call that I made to order the scanners, and that there were several mistakes with my invoice and order, I feel that it is only fair that you waive the delivery charge.
e ... to hearing from you soon.
f ... received your revised invoice for my order of five Epson scanners yesterday and note your inclusion of five packs of photo paper with my order which I will not be charged for. I am grateful for this gesture on your part.

Crane Photography
34 Sheldon Avenue, Croydon, CR9 1SD

Mr Lynton North
Hardware Computer Supplies Ltd
96 Warwick Road West
Coventry
CV3 9TD

24 April 20XX

Dear Mr North

Delivery charge for Epson scanners

I ...[1]

However, ...[2]

Given that ...[3]

I anticipate ...[4]

I look forward ...[5]

Yours ...[6]

Mary Crane

Mary Crane

b Now answer the questions about the letter.

Webcode: ITMU0801

1 Does Lynton appear to have taken any steps regarding the delivery charge since his last email to Mary?
2 What words does Mary use to express the strength of her complaint?
3 What action does she want Lynton to take?
4 What argument does she use to encourage Lynton to take the action she wants?
5 Which features of the letter indicate that it is formal in tone?

17 Lynton writes to Mary

Lynton decides to waive the delivery charge and to write formally to Mary to apologize for not having told her about it.

Use formal phrases from exercise 15 and the letter in exercise 16 as a model to write Lynton's letter to Mary.

Refresh your knowledge

1 Match the words on the left (1–6) with words on the right (a–f) to make expressions from the unit.

1 on-site	a address
2 optional	b charges
3 delivery	c warranty
4 total	d code
5 additional	e extra
6 product	f price

2a Complete the mind maps with formal and informal ways of beginning and ending an email.

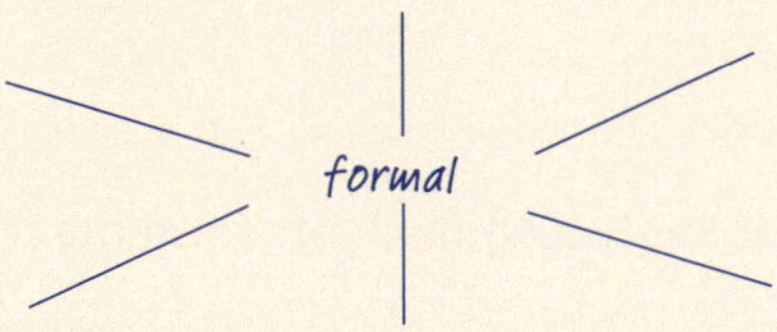

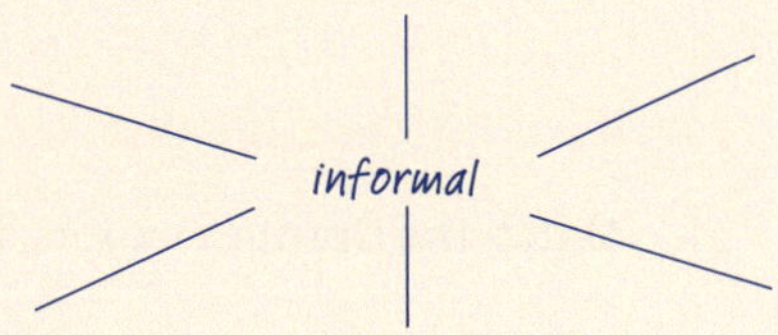

2b Make these informal sentences more formal.

1 Hi there!
2 This is just a quick email to ask about the price of your modems.
3 Apologies for not replying sooner.
4 Get in touch if you have any questions.
5 All the best

5 rules for dealing with angry customers

Even if your company's products and service are excellent, things can go wrong – and customers can get angry. Here's what to do when this happens.

Don't get into an argument

If a customer is angry, one of your first aims is to calm them down. Stay calm yourself and use positive and professional behaviour to take the heat out of their anger. Never argue back: this will just make the customer angrier.

Listen more, talk less

You can only understand what a customer's angry about if you listen carefully. So, it pays to do less talking and more listening. That way you will understand the problem faster and be able to offer the customer a satisfactory solution.

Show that the customer is important to you

At the first opportunity let the customer know that you are sorry about their problem and that you will do everything possible to solve it. This will help calm the customer down and make it easier to reach a solution.

Be patient

It's important that you show an angry customer that you have time for them. Maintain eye contact with the customer and do not give them the impression that you are impatient for the discussion to end, for example, by glancing at your watch. Stay with the discussion until you've solved the problem and never walk away.

Be positive

Try to adopt a positive attitude towards the customer's problem. Remember that your aim is to solve the problem as quickly and effectively as possible. You can only do this if you have a positive frame of mind. Avoid being sucked in by the customer's negative feelings and watch how the customer grows more positive as a result.

1 True or false

Decide whether the statements are true or false. Correct the false statements.

1 Let the customer express their anger: don't speak until they have expressed themselves fully.
2 You should try to calm the customer down by talking as much as possible.
3 The customer will calm down if you apologize for any mistakes.
4 You should let the customer know that you have time for their problem.
5 It's a good idea to tell the customer that their negative feelings do not affect you.

2 Working with words

Match the German expressions to their English equivalents from the text.

1 ruhig bleiben
2 argumentieren
3 zu zahlen an
4 bei der ersten Gelegenheit
5 Augenkontakt halten
6 positiv bleiben

3 Discussion

Work in a group and discuss the following questions.

1 Have you ever had to deal with an angry customer? Why was the customer upset? How did you resolve the problem?
2 Have you ever been angry in your role as a customer? Why? Did the person dealing with your complaint handle the situation properly?

Managing a networking project 9

- different types of topology
- organizing a networking project
- dealing with problems in a project

1 Start up

With a partner think of possible advantages a computer network has for a business. Copy and complete the mind map with your ideas.

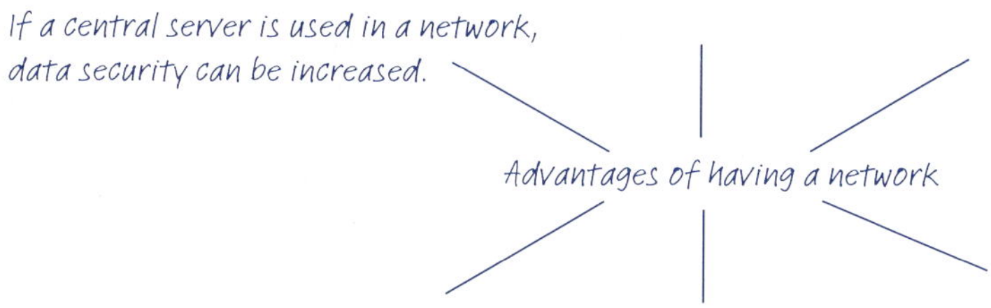

2 Network topologies

a Edward Cybulski, the owner of UK Travel Ltd, wants to network his new office in Oxford. He does some research online about network topologies and finds the text on page 88. Use the words in the box to complete the text.

destination | distributed | hub | interconnection | logical | physical | signal | transmission

b Now read the advantages and disadvantages of the various approaches to networking below and match them to the appropriate topologies.

1 Does not require a central server
2 Due to limited cable length, the number of stations that can be connected is limited
3 Due to its centralized nature, the topology is simple to operate
4 Only performs well with a limited number of nodes
5 Easy to handle and implement
6 Network requires a central hub: if this fails, the entire network goes down
7 Changes made to one or more network nodes affects the performance of the whole network
8 Failure of a single network node can cause the entire network to fail
9 Best suited to small networks
10 Achieves an isolation of each device in the network

Choosing the right network topology for your business

Want to network your business but confused about network topologies? Then read on. Our quick guide will help you to make the best choice quickly.

Let's start with the basics. Network topologies are classified as physical, logical and signal topologies. A ...[1] topology describes the mapping of the network nodes and the connections between them. ...[2] topology describes the paths which signals take as they pass over the network. The mapping of the paths taken by data as they travel over the network is known as a ...[3] topology. Let's look at the different types of network topologies in detail.

Types of Network Topologies

Bus Topology: In this type of topology, all network nodes are connected to a common ...[4] medium known as the bus or backbone of the network. If this medium has two endpoints, the network topology is a linear bus topology. If it has more than two endpoints, the network is called a ...[5] bus topology.

Advantages:
Disadvantages:

Ring Topology: In a ring topology, every node in the network is connected to two other nodes: the first and the last nodes are connected to each other. Transmitted data travels in a single direction and passes through each of the nodes in the ring until it reaches the ...[6] node. A dual ring topology, however, has two connections between each of the network nodes and allows data to flow in two directions.

Advantages:
Disadvantages:

Star Topology: In this type of topology, each node is connected to a central node, which is known as a ...[7]. Data transmitted between the network nodes passes through the central hub. A distributed star network is formed by the ...[8] of two or more individual star networks.

Advantages:
Disadvantages:

c **In groups discuss which of these topologies are no longer up-to-date, which topologies are currently state of the art and what their advantages are over these older types. Use language from the text to describe these.**

3 A network for UK Travel Ltd

a Edward has a meeting with Jim Struthers from Network Pros to decide what sort of network he wants. Read Jim's email to a colleague and match the German words and expressions to their English equivalents in the email.

1 informieren über
2 Auftrag erteilen
3 Übergabetermin
4 überzeugen
5 Lieferanten
6 Subunternehmer
7 Angebot

UK Travel Ltd - network

From: Jim.Struthers@networkpros.co.uk
To: Brian.Clegg@networkpros.co.uk
Cc:
Subject: UK Travel Ltd - network

Hi Brian

I wanted to fill you in on my meeting this morning with Edward Cybulski from UK Travel Ltd.

Edward has decided to contract us to install his network. He needs it to be up and running by next Friday. I assured him we can manage this: I think he decided to give us the business because I promised we could meet his deadline so we need to get going immediately.

Edward and I spent a good deal of time talking about the various technical options. I tried to convince him that he should go for a wireless network but he was concerned about security and has decided to use Ethernet. In the end we agreed that a client-server architecture using a star topology would best meet his security needs.

Here are the details of the job. Edward wants to network seven PCs and three printers. He also wants a high-speed internet connection (he has already arranged for DSL with his telecoms provider which will be operational at the beginning of next week).

I want to put you in charge of this, Brian: can you please get onto it? You'll need to order the network components from our suppliers, make an appointment with Edward for next week, make sure our cabling subcontractor can come in to lay the cables next week, etc. Could you also please send a quotation to Edward by tomorrow (Thursday)? I've promised him he won't have to pay more than £1,500 so please bear this in mind: it's the other main reason we're getting the contract. You may have to look online to see if you can get better prices than our usual suppliers can offer.

OK. I'm going to be out of the office until next week so let's catch up on Monday. I'd like to see an action plan for the project by this Friday: please email it to me.

Kind regards

Jim

b Read the email again and complete the tasks.

1 Summarize in your own words why Jim is writing to Brian.
2 Security is one factor identified in the email which is important to Edward: what are the other two factors?
3 Which components will Brian need to order for the job? Make a list.

c Now draw the network that Network Pros will build for UK Travel Ltd.

4 A quotation for the network installation

a Read the quotation which Brian sends Edward and answer the questions.

1 How does Brian indicate that he is not sure if the work will take five hours?
2 Do the prices he quotes include VAT?
3 What action does Brian indicate that he will take in the quotation?
4 What action should Edward take and when?

b Compare the quotation with a quotation sent by your company. How does it vary in terms of layout and style?

Network Pros
6 Parkway West
Oxford
OX1 3DW

Mr Edward Cybulski
UK Travel Ltd
38 Straightmile Walk
Oxford
OX2 5DW

21 September 20..

Dear Mr Cybulski

Quotation

Following your meeting with Jim Struthers on Wednesday, I am sending you a quotation for networking your office.

Cisco Small Business NSS2050 NAS Server	£ 601.45
8-port hub D-Link DUB-H7 USB 8-port hub	£ 27.45
Netgear DM111 PB DSL modem	£ 42.79
1 ARX uninterrupted power supply	£ 97.40
25 m Belkin CAT5e network cable	£ 11.56
Labour costs: 5 hours (estimated) @ £135/hour (including work by cabling sub-contractor)	£ 675
Total	£1455.65

Please note that all prices are inclusive of VAT.

I will be in contact with you tomorrow to make appointments for our installation team and cabling subcontractor to carry out their work. In the meantime, if you have any questions, please do not hesitate to get in touch with me.

Your sincerely

Brian Clegg
Brian Clegg

5 An action plan for the project

a Brian has prepared an action plan which will help him with the installation of Travel UK Ltd's network. Use the words in the box to complete the plan.

call
compare
confirm
install
make
order
provide
research
test

1 ... network equipment
2 ... network together with cabling
3 ... online for cheaper sources of network equipment
4 ... network performance and troubleshoot
5 ... Travel UK with complete documentation for the network
6 ... installation date with Edward Cybulski
7 ... internet prices with those of usual suppliers
8 ... provisional appointment with Travel UK for installation
9 ... cabling subcontractors to see if appointment is suitable for them

b Now work with a partner and put the action plan points in the order that you think Brian should do them in. Tell the class why you put them in this order.

6 A problem with the network installation project

Track 18

Listen as Jim and Brian meet to discuss the installation of Travel UK Ltd's network. Choose either a, b or c to complete the statements correctly.

1 Brian did some research on the internet ...
a to find out if his usual suppliers supply the parts more cheaply online.
b to find out if the parts are available more cheaply from other suppliers.
c to order the parts directly from the manufacturers.

2 The quotation sent by Brian was ...
a within the budget set by Travel UK.
b much lower than the budget set by Travel UK.
c for the exact price set by Travel UK.

3 After receiving the quotation, Edward Cybulski said ...
a he'd have to think again about whether Network Pros should do the job.
b he would rather not have the job done at that price.
c that Network Pros could do the work.

4 The parts will arrive later than planned because ...
a Brian did not check the delivery times carefully enough.
b Brian did not understand the delivery times.
c the online suppliers do not have them in stock and will have to order them.

5 Jim says that Brian should have ...
a called Edward Cybulski to tell him about the later delivery of the components.
b gone back to Network Pros' usual suppliers.
c called him to let him know about the problem.

7 Phrases for project meetings

a Match the sentence beginnings (1–7) to the sentence endings (a–g) to make sentences from the dialogue.

1 Fill me in
2 Where are we up
3 He's given the official
4 Bring me up
5 That's a bit
6 Well, if we have to deal with unforeseen
7 At least I could have talked to Edward and smoothed things

a difficulties, we could have real problems.
b to with the project?
c over a bit.
d on how the Travel UK installation is going.
e tight, don't you think?
f to speed with the appointment for installation.
g go-ahead for the project.

Track 18 **b Now listen again to check your answers.**

8 Softening criticism

During their conversation Jim strongly criticizes Brian. Work with a partner and read the different version of the conversation below. Which words, phrases and reformulations does Jim use here to soften his criticism?

Jim Well, if we have to deal with unforeseen difficulties, we could have real problems.

Brian Yes, but ...

Jim Look, Brian. I don't want to be too critical here. However, I'm afraid this is not up to your usual standards. Perhaps you could have checked these delivery times more carefully. The market we work in is pretty competitive. If we don't deliver when we say we're going to deliver, our reputation will suffer and we'll lose business.

Brian I know but I was pretty excited about finding the parts at cheaper prices and I just forgot ...

Jim How long have you known about this anyway?

Brian Since the day before yesterday.

Jim Well, perhaps you waited a little too long to say something about this. Maybe you could have called me earlier to tell me about the problem, Brian. At least I could have talked to Edward and smoothed things over a bit. It might have been better if you had been a little more communicative.

Brian I'm sorry, Jim.

Webcode: ITMU0901

9 Mediation

Imagine you were at the meeting. Summarize the last part of the conversation from exercise 8 in German for a colleague who does not speak English.

Grammar | Simple past

1 We **developed** a customer database to keep a record of our sales.
2 I **designed** the online shop for the company's website.
3 I **worried** all of last week about missing the deadline.
4 Ben **misunderstood** the project plan and **didn't finish** on time.
5 They **gave** us a deadline of 28 June to finish the project.

- Das *simple past* benutzt man, um zu sagen, was zu einem bestimmten Zeitpunkt oder in einem bestimmten Zeitraum der Vergangenheit (z. B. *last week, two years ago, yesterday*) abgeschlossen wurde (1–5).
- Das *simple past* bildet man mit der zweiten Form des Verbs (1–5).
- Regelmäßige Verben werden durch das Anhängen von *–ed* gebildet (1, 2).
- Ein *y* am Ende des Infinitivs wird zu *i* (3).
- Verneinungen werden mit *didn't* gebildet. Nach *didn't* steht die Grund-, nicht die Vergangenheitsform des Verbs (4).
- Einige unregelmäßige Verben haben besondere Formen (4, 5).

10 Practice

Use the verbs in the box to complete the sentences in the simple past.

Be careful: some of the verbs are irregular.

bring | build | draw | forecast | input | lay | lead | preset | report | write

Tip If you come across an English verb you do not know, quickly check in your dictionary if the verb is irregular and note its irregular simple past form if it is.

1 They ... our network last year and since then we've had nothing but problems.
2 I ... a diagram to help the customer understand what I was suggesting.
3 Claire ... the project to upgrade our network last year: she's in a strong position to be network manager.
4 I ... that we would finish the project by the end of next month but we'll finish three weeks early.
5 Neil ... the action plan for the project yesterday.
6 I ... the system up to date by installing the latest plugs-ins: you'll be able to view the website properly now.
7 Bill ... the system so that it always defaults to 'safe mode' when you start it up.
8 We ... the cabling incorrectly and now we have to do it again.
9 Gordon ... the wrong code: that's why it doesn't work when you click 'send'
10 We ... the fault in the network yesterday but they haven't repaired it yet.

11 Role-play: a progress report

page 115

Carry out the role-play with a partner. Student A should use expressions from the dialogue in exercise 8 to soften the criticisms they make.

Student A

Bitten Sie Ihren Kollegen um einen Tätigkeits-/Zwischenbericht zu einem Projekt, bei dem ein Netzwerk für einen Kunden installiert wird.

Student B

Sagen Sie, dass Sie einen Termin mit dem Kunden für nächste Woche Donnerstag und Freitag während der Arbeit arrangiert haben.

Fragen Sie Ihren Kollegen, ob er günstige Netzwerkkomponenten gefunden hat, die im Rahmen des Budgets bleiben.

Sagen Sie, dass Sie Netzwerkteile zu einem guten Preis bei einem Internetzulieferer gefunden haben. Sie haben dem Kunden ein entsprechendes Angebot geschickt.

Sagen Sie Ihrem Kollegen, dass er einen guten Job gemacht hat.

Sagen Sie Ihrem Kollegen, dass es ein oder zwei kleinere Probleme mit dem Projekt gibt. Das erste Problem ist, dass der Router nicht vor Freitagmorgen als frühestem Termin geliefert wird: Sie haben vergessen, die Lieferzeiten sorgfältiger zu überprüfen, als Sie die Komponente bestellten.

Sagen Sie Ihrem Kollegen, dass dies nicht gut ist und dass sie sorgfältiger hätten überprüfen sollen, wie lange die Lieferung brauchen würde, als sie den Router bestellt haben.

Sagen Sie Ihrem Kollegen auch, dass der Kabel-Subunternehmer nur am Freitag kommen kann und nicht am Donnerstag. Sie haben den Subunternehmer nicht rechtzeitig angerufen.

Sagen Sie Ihrem Kollegen, dass er den Subunternehmer früher hätte anrufen sollen. Fragen Sie, wie lange der Kollege schon davon wusste.

Sagen Sie Ihrem Kollegen, dass Sie von diesen Problemen seit Anfang der Woche wussten.

Sagen Sie Ihrem Kollegen, dass er Sie früher hätte informieren sollen, damit Sie hätten helfen können.

Entschuldigen Sie sich für den Fehler.

Sagen Sie, dass Sie den Kunden anrufen werden, um zu fragen, ob ein weiterer Termin Anfang nächste Woche möglich sei.

12 An end of project report

a The networking project is now complete and Brian has written a short report. Complete it with words from the box.

budget | client | Ethernet | hit | miss | on time | smoothly | suppliers | time plan | troubleshooting

End of project report – network installation at UK Travel Ltd

The customer requested a network connecting seven PCs and three printers using ...[1] due to security concerns with a wireless network. For this we decided upon a ...[2]-server architecture with a star topology. The customer had a strict ...[3] of £1,500 so we could not use our usual ...[4]. New suppliers from the internet provided us with a small business NAS server, an 8-port hub, DSL modem and 25m of network cable. Unfortunately we ...[5] a snag with the ...[6] as the delivery times were longer than expected. It was essential that we did not ...[7] the deadline so we had to carefully plan the installation for the final day of the project. All cables were laid and everything installed by Friday afternoon for testing. The tests went ...[8] and no ...[9] was required. The project was completed ...[10] and on budget.

b Discuss whether the project was ultimately successful and what could have been done better. Compile a list of tips to help prevent a project going wrong.

Refresh your knowledge

1 Rearrange the words to make sentences for giving criticism.

1 this / not / I'm / up / is / your / standards / usual / afraid / to
2 could / have / times / carefully / checked / these / you / delivery / perhaps / more
3 this / something / waited / a / about / you / little / too / perhaps / to / long / say
4 could / you / have / me / called / problem / earlier / to / tell / me / maybe / about / the
5 communicative / have / had / been / better / if / more / you / it / been / a / little / might

2 Think of as many topology types as you can. Write a mini-profile explaining the advantages and disadvantages of each type and include a diagram showing how the system works.

Software	Collaborative software	Issue tracking system	Scheduling	Project portfolio management	Resource management	Document management
Basecamp	Yes	No	No	No	Yes	Yes
Central Desktop	Yes	Yes	No	No	No	Yes
Dolibarr ERP/CRM	Yes	No	No	Yes	Yes	Yes
dotProject	No	Yes	No	No	No	Yes
FastTrack Schedule	No	No	Yes	Yes	No	Yes
Feng Office Community Edition	Yes	No	Yes	Yes	No	Yes
GanttProject	No	No	Yes	No	Yes	No

1 Functionality of project management software

Look at the table detailing the functionality of different pieces of project management software and match the descriptions to the right software.

Which software:

1 features a system for monitoring the development of various elements of a project so that users can see what progress has been made?
2 allows two or more users to input their own information thus helping them to complement each others' work on a project?
3 allows a timeline for the project to be created in which the various parts of the project can be given their own schedules?
4 allows project managers to plan the most effective use of the things they need to complete a project such as financing, staff and logistics?
5 includes a feature for keeping track of all the paper work relevant to a project?
6 enables project managers to view one project in combination with other current projects in order to maximize efficiency?

2 A group discussion

Work in a group and complete the tasks below.

1 Discuss the advantages of the different functions of project management software.
2 Discuss what the most and least important functions for effective project management are and rank the various functions.
3 Discuss which piece of software from the table would be most effective for the projects you work on. Present your choice to the class saying why it would suit your company's purposes.

Applying for a job 10

- job adverts & qualifications
- CVs & covering letters
- interviews

1 Start up

a What makes a job ideal? Read the speech bubbles and add your own ideas. Then put the statements in order of importance. Discuss in class.

1 I need the freedom to use my own initiative.

2 I like taking responsibility.

3 I'm a team player.

4 The pay must be good.

5 I like to organize other people's work.

6 My job has to give me social status.

7 My job has to offer me the chance to learn something new.

8 The working conditions have to be pleasant.

9 I have to receive praise from colleagues or customers.

10 There has to be the opportunity of promotion.

b Are there any elements which you definitely don't want in your job? Make a list and then discuss in a group.

2 A job advertisement

Daniela Kropp, a newly qualified software developer, is looking for a job on the internet. She is interested in the advertisement on page 98.

Read the advert and complete the sentences in your own words.

1 The company will pay ...
2 The type of contract of employment on offer is ...
3 Candidates should have their applications in by ...
4 The company's employment policy says ...

http://www.jobs-in-it.com/juniordeveloper/Medteccov

www.jobs-in-it.com

Junior Developer

Salary: £20,000 – £25,000 per annum (depending on experience and age)

MEDTEC Ltd is a fast-growing manufacturing company based in Coventry and specializing in the production of medical scanning equipment. We are seeking a full-time, permanent Junior Developer to support the team at our high-tech production facility.

As the successful candidate, you will be highly-motivated and possess the ability to work on your own initiative to plan and develop solutions using Perl, Ruby, Javascript and Python, as well as other appropriate application tools.

You will need experience of developing applications within a SQL Server 2005 database environment. Additionally, you will need to be a good team player who can think on his/her feet and work under pressure while still having an eye for detail. Good communication skills are also a must as you will be required to liaise effectively with all levels of the business.

Requirements:

- Accredited qualification in programming / solution development
- 2 – 3 years of work experience in production
- Ability to demonstrate practical understanding of development in a high-pressure, commercial environment
- Experience of assessing the performance and functionality of solutions with a view to improving them
- A full, current and clean driving licence
- Good knowledge of English with strong communication skills in oral and written English

Closing date for applications: 20 April 20..

To apply send your CV together with a covering letter and the names of two referees to Mark Thwaite.
Post:
45 Blair Avenue
Coventry
CV3 4WM

Email: mark_thwaite@medtec.co.uk

MEDTEC Ltd is an equal opportunities employer. We select candidates according to their skills and experience regardless of gender, ethnicity, sexual orientation, religion or age.

3 Working with the text

Read the advert again and make two lists of what the company is looking for.

Skills and experience	Personal qualities
Experience of developing business applications	highly-motivated

4 Working with words

Match the German expressions (1–10) with English ones from the advert.

1 abhängig von
2 ansässig in
3 unterstützen
4 Bewerber/in
5 Fähigkeit
6 eigenständig arbeiten
7 Erfahrung
8 Lebenslauf
9 Anschreiben, Begleitbrief
10 Referenzen

5 Key vocabulary: education and vocational training

a Match the English terms in the box (1–8) with their definitions (a–h).

1 vocational school/college | 2 primary school (GB) / elementary school (US) | 3 General Certificate of Secondary Education (GCSE) (GB) | 4 A level (GB) / High School Diploma (US) | 5 apprenticeship | 6 comprehensive school (GB) | 7 vocational training | 8 grammar school (GB) / high school (US)

a The first school you attend at the age of five or six.
b You attend this school at eleven or twelve. Only students who performed well at their first school go here.
c A two to three-year, on-the-job programme in which you learn how to do a certain type of work.
d An educational institution you can go to when you leave school to complete a course about a certain type of work.
e The second set of school qualifications: the entrance qualifications for university.
f The first formal set of qualifications you receive at school.
g You attend this school at around eleven or twelve. Students of all educational ability go here.
h A programme of learning, usually relatively short in length, which trains you for a specific type of work.

b With a partner decide what the German equivalents for the English terms are.

6 Writing a CV in English

a Read the text and make a list of the things which are different from Germany.

Applying for jobs in other countries

In most countries, you should not include copies of your school certificates or references with your application. You may be asked to produce these at a later time, for instance, after you have been offered the job. But in the UK, for example, you should include the names and contact details of two referees at the end of your CV, one of whom should be your current employer.

Unless asked, don't sign and date your CV and don't include a photograph of yourself. This is particularly the case in the US where employment laws against discrimination insist that photographs are not used. For this reason, it is also not necessary to give your date of birth, although you may if you wish. You should, however, provide your full name and contact details.

Provide details about your education, training and work experience in reverse order: you should start with the present and work your way back through your personal history.

Don't forget to include a section called 'Skills and experience' in which you can list other interesting things about yourself, for example, your language skills or whether you can drive. You should also include details of hobbies on your CV. Employers in the US and Britain are especially interested in this.

Your CV may be up to two pages in length but should not exceed this. If your CV is longer than one page but there is not enough material for two pages, space out the sections so that your details fill the two pages: this will make it easier to read.

Potential employers often provide an application form for candidates instead of asking for a CV. If this is the case, don't enclose a CV but include all the details you want to mention on the form.

b With a partner make a list of dos and don'ts about writing a CV in English.

7 Daniela's CV

Daniela decides to apply for the job with MECTEC Ltd. Copy the outline of her CV then write the information under the appropriate headings.

Mr Jörg Stefan, Training Manager
Pharmafix AG
Baumweg 57, 04107 Leipzig

Unix

Apprenticeship as software developer with Pharmafix AG – September 20.. – May 20..:

Linux

Schilling Allee 93,
04246 Leipzig, Germany

Personal details

Name: Daniela Kropp

Address:

Telephone number:

Nationality:

Work experience

Education and qualifications

Skills and experience

Operating environments:

Programming languages:

Interests

Referees

Ms Sandra Kossak
Berufliches Schulzentrum Connewitz
Leipziger Straße 103
04592 Leipzig

PHP

German

September – December 20..
Volkshochschule (Adult Education College) Leipzig: course in internet development with XSL and XML

Windows (XP, Vista, Windows 7)

Python

Javascript

+49 (0) 341 4873 987

Ruby

Football, cinema

Perl

20 .. Abitur (equivalent to A levels), Max Roth Gymnasium, Leipzig

Office assistant with Leipziger Urbrau GmbH –
July 20.. – January 20..

8 Your CV

a Complete your own CV in English using the one above as a guide for layout and content.

b Swap CVs with a partner. Read his/her CV and suggest improvements.

9 A covering letter

Daniela writes a covering letter to accompany her CV. In which line(s) does Daniela do these things?

1 say where she learned about the job
2 explain why she is qualified to do the job
3 ask for the chance to meet
4 indicate that she is sending her CV with the letter
5 list her skills
6 list her personal qualities

Mark Thwaite
HR Assistant
MEDTEC Ltd
45 Blair Avenue
Coventry
CV3 4WM

Schilling Allee 93
04246 Leipzig
Germany

12 April 20..

Dear Mr Thwaite

Application for the position of Junior Developer

I am writing to apply for the position of Junior Developer with MEDTEC Ltd which I saw advertised on jobs-in-it.com. Please find enclosed a copy of my curriculum vitae.

I have just successfully completed my apprenticeship as a software developer with Pharmafix AG, a manufacturer of pharmaceutical products in Leipzig. During the three years of my apprenticeship I gained experience of developing software solutions in a manufacturing context. In particular, I developed expertise in programming using Perl and Python, as well as experience of programming in Javascript and Ruby. I believe that the experience and skills I gained during my apprenticeship equip me well for the position at MEDTEC Ltd.

I consider myself to be hard-working and reliable. In addition, though I am able to take responsibility for my own workload and work on my own initiative, I enjoy the collaborative experience of working as part of a team. Moreover, I am a fast learner and am very keen to develop myself further in an interesting commercial context, something which I am sure MEDTEC Ltd would provide me with.

I would greatly welcome the opportunity to talk to you about the position and how I can fulfil its requirements. I have attempted to include all relevant information in my curriculum vitae. However, should you require additional information, please do not hesitate to contact me.

Thank you for taking the time to read this letter and my CV. I look forward to hearing from you soon.

Yours sincerely

Daniela Kropp

Enc

10 Writing a covering letter

page 115

Write a covering letter for a job which you might be interested in.

1 Visit an English-language jobs website and find a job which you would be interested in applying for.
2 Write a covering letter for the job as if you were applying for it.
3 Now swap your letter and job advertisement with a partner. Read your partners' covering letter and say why it is good and where it could be improved.

11 Daniela's interview

Track 19

Craig Simon from MEDTEC Ltd interviews Daniela for the job. Listen and say whether the statements are true or false. Correct the false statements.

1 Craig doesn't understand Daniela's CV.
2 Daniela wants to work at MEDTEC to develop her experience of programming in a manufacturing company.
3 Daniela thinks that her English is not very good.
4 She became interested in programming during her apprenticeship.
5 The interface Daniela describes was designed to provide sales managers with information about production.
6 Daniela says that, although she enjoys team work, she would rather work on her own.

12 Interview language

Track 19

Listen again and complete the sentences Daniela uses during her interview.

1 I'm glad to be here. Thank you for ... me.
2 The job here would let me ... my experience of developing solutions in a production environment.
3 I really want to work in Britain and continue to ... my English.
4 I ... interested in programming while I was at school.
5 In the last three years, I ... really learned a lot about programming.
6 I was ... of a team which developed an interface for production managers.
7 The ... of our solution was to present managers with relevant information.
8 In the end, our solution ... in clear management information for production.
9 I ... from having a really good team to work with.
10 During the last three years, I've ... so much from colleagues in my team.

13 Further questions

With a partner brainstorm the questions that Daniela could ask at the interview.

Grammar **Simple past & present perfect**

1 I **became** interested in programming while I **was** at school.
2 Our solution **resulted** in clear management information for production.
3 Since starting my current job, I'**ve learned** a lot about programming.
4 I'**ve learned** so much from colleagues in my team.

- Das *simple past* bildet man mit der zweiten Form des Verbs. Man verwendet es, um zu sagen, was zu einem bestimmten Zeitpunkt in der Vergangenheit abgeschlossen wurde (1, 2).
- Das *present perfect* wird mit dem Hilfsverb *have* und dem Partizip Perfekt (3. Form) des Verbs gebildet. Man verwendet es, um zu sagen, dass etwas irgendwann in der Zeit bis jetzt geschehen ist (z. B. *today, this week, since January*). Es wird oft mit Signalwörtern wie *since, for* und *ever* gebraucht (3, 4).

14 Practice

Daniela is blogging about her apprenticeship and experience. Complete each gap with the simple past or the present perfect.

Technology-blog.com
http://www.technology-blog.com/
Google

Technology blog

My interest in programming ... [1] (start) when I was at school. I ... [2] (do) some basic programming at school before I started my apprenticeship three years ago. Since then, I ... [3] (grow) even more interested in programming and ... [4] (become) a competent software developer. My apprenticeship ... [5] (come) to an end a few weeks ago. During my training I ... [6] (develop) and ... [7] (design) solutions for my company. Most of the systems ... [8] (is) aimed at improving data-flows within the company. Since the end of my apprenticeship, I ... [9] (apply) for a job with a company in England. In fact I ... [10] (go) to Coventry for an interview yesterday. It ... [11] (seem) to go well – I hope I get the job!

15 Practice

Write sentences using the simple past or present perfect.

1 I / learn / a lot about customising software in the last three years
I have learnt a lot about customising software in the last three years.
2 We / start / making websites / when we / be / at school
3 He / be interested in online gaming / for years
4 I / attend / a vocational college / between the ages of 16 and 18
5 We / finish / our training / three months ago
6 You / ever / be involved in programming a new system / ?

Webcode: ITMU1001

16 Interview questions

Discuss how you would answer these questions in a job interview with a partner.

1. Why would you like to have this job?
2. What experience did you gain during your apprenticeship which is relevant to the job?
3. Do you have any other work experience aside from your apprenticeship?
4. Do you like working as part of a team?
5. Can you give me examples of how you have taken responsibility for your work?
6. What is your greatest weakness?
7. What is your greatest strength?

17 Role-play: a job interview

a Work with a partner.

Student A: Turn to File 3 on page 108.
Student B: Turn to File 7 on page 110.

b Now find a new partner and swap roles.

Refresh your knowledge

1 Look over the unit and make a mindmap of all the examples of skills and experience you can find.

skills
applying for jobs
experience

2 Use the English equivalents of the German words in the box to complete the sentences.

Begleitbrief | Bewerber/in | Lebenslauf | Referenzen

1. Do you think I can use my lecturer from college as a ... on my CV?
2. Oh, no. I've included my photo on my ... . The job's in the US – I'll never get it.
3. Did you send a ... with your CV?
4. She's clever, well-organized and has excellent IT skills: the perfect ... for the job!

3 Write a list of tips for someone looking for a job abroad.

Use information from the unit. Think about the CV and covering letter as well as tips for an interview.

Europass

http://www.europass.ie/europass/

★ Home ★ Contact Us ★ Site Map ★ Search

You are here: Home

What is Europass?

Europass is a new initiative which aims to help you make your skills and qualifications clearly and easily understood in Europe by providing an EU-wide standard CV format. Whether you are enrolling in an education or training programme, looking for a job or getting experience abroad, Europass will make the process easier and more straightforward.

What is Europass?
What is Europass for?
Benefits of Europass
Frequently Asked Questions

1 Europass will be used by people who wish to communicate their qualifications and competences in an effective way. People will be able to use Europass when they are seeking jobs and when they wish to enter education and training programmes. Europass will be especially helpful when people move between countries to study or work because:

- Europass will make it easier for employers to understand the qualifications and competences of job seekers from other EU member states.
- Europass will help education, training and guidance practitioners to advise people about the most suitable learning paths and opportunities.

2 Europass is a new initiative which aims to help people make their skills and qualifications clearly and easily understood in Europe, therefore aiding the mobility of both learners and workers. The Europass documents have been designed to help people outline their skills and competences in a coherent manner.

Europass consists of a portfolio of five documents as follows:

Two documents which individuals can complete independently:

- Europass Curriculum Vitae (CV)
- Europass Language Passport

Three documents which are completed by the organisation on behalf of the individual:

- Europass Mobility
- Europass Certificate Supplement
- Europass Diploma Supplement

3 Europass has a number of advantages associated with it, the principal ones being:

- It will help citizens to convey their qualifications and competences in an effective way.
- It provides a comprehensive tool for users based on an accessible electronic format.
- It enables people with diverse backgrounds and experiences to gain access to opportunities for learning and employment throughout Europe, particularly by helping people to move between countries or across employment sectors.
- It will promote strong links between education and training, business and industry, ensuring the continuing relevance and adequate appreciation of competences and qualifications.
- Europass is an open system that supports European policy developments related to the transparency of competences and qualifications.

Extra material

1 Understanding the texts

a Read the information from the Europass website quickly and match the texts (1–3) to three of the links in the information box.

b Give information from the texts in your own words.

1 Describe how Europass is designed to help citizens of the EU.
2 List which groups of people Europass is aimed at.
3 Which elements of Europass are not completed by job candidates?
4 How will Europass make life easier for employers?
5 In what way does Europass complement the policies of the EU?

2 Discussion: the advantages of Europass

Work in a group to complete the following tasks.

1 Discuss and list as many additional advantages of Europass as possible.
2 Does Europass have disadvantages? Discuss and list these.
3 Has a member of your group completed a Europass? Find out what his/her experience of this was.
4 Present the results of your discussion to the class.

3 Creating your own Europass

Go to the Europass website (http://www.europass.ie/europass) and carry out the following tasks.

1 Complete your Europass CV online in English.
2 Complete your Europass Language Passport. Use the self-assessment grid to help you judge your language level.
3 Share your experience of completing your Europass with your classmates and discuss any difficulties which you or other students encountered.

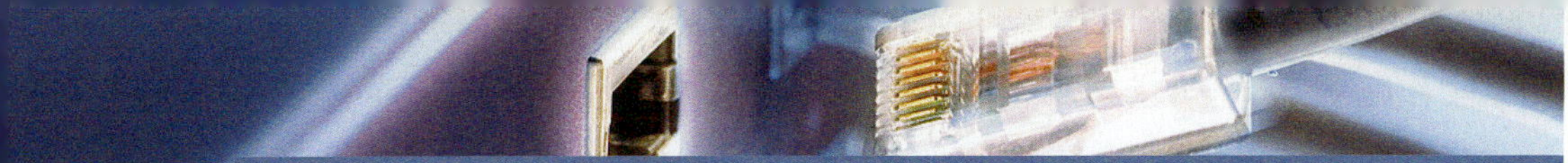

Partner files

File 1 Unit 5, Exercise 13

Student A

Conversation 1
You have a problem with your printer. When you print, your pages come out dirty. Telephone your partner for advice.

Conversation 2
Here is an extract from a mouse troubleshooting guide. Use it when your partner asks you for help.

Problem	Possible cause	Solution
Cursor isn't moving	Mouse cable is not inserted properly	Check that mouse cable is secure
	Mouse is defective	Replace mouse
Cursor moves erratically	Mouse is old and dirty	Remove bottom of mouse and clean wheel
Cursor moves without mouse being moved	Computer infected with malware	Scan system with anti-virus software

File 2 Unit 6, Exercise 11

Student B

Your company needs to develop an AUP. You are at a meeting with colleagues to discuss what should be included in the policy.

Your position
You feel that the role of an AUP should be to ban activities on the internet which have risk attached to them such as downloading music or visiting websites which you can't be certain you trust.

However, you feel that as staff in your company often work long hours without paid overtime, the company has to show a little flexibility and allow staff to listen to online radio or spend time on social networking sites like Facebook during their breaks from work.

Argue your case using as many of the phrases from exercise 9 as possible.

File 3 Unit 10, Exercise 17

Student A

Find an advertisement for a job in an English-speaking country which you would find interesting and that is relevant to your experience. Imagine that you have been invited to an interview for the job. Prepare yourself for the interview by thinking about the following questions:

- How is your experience relevant to the job?
- Why do you want the job?
- What are your strengths and weaknesses?

Before the role-play, give the job advertisement to your partner who will play the role of the interviewer.

At the interview go into as much detail as possible about your skills and experience. Keep your answers to questions about your strengths and weaknesses short.

After the role-play, check that the notes your partner has taken about your skills and experience are accurate.

File 4 Unit 3, Exercise 5

File 5 Unit 5, Exercise 13

Student B

Conversation 1

Here is an extract from a mouse troubleshooting guide. Use it when your partner asks you for help.

Problem	Possible cause	Solution
Horizontal lines	Toner cartridge defective or not installed correctly	Replace toner cartridge
Thin, vertical white lines/stripes.	Toner cartridge is nearly empty or defective	Replace toner cartridge
Dirty paper	Toner has leaked from cartridge	Replace toner cartridge
	Inside of printer is dirty	Send printer to service department to be cleaned

Conversation 2

You have a problem with your mouse. Even when you don't move it, your cursor moves around your screen. Telephone your partner for advice.

File 6 Unit 6, Exercise 11

Student A

Your company needs to develop an AUP. You are at a meeting with colleagues to discuss what should be included in the policy.

Your position

You feel that an AUP should make it clear to staff that they may only use the company's IT system for the purposes of their work. You think that the policy should explicitly forbid:

- surfing the internet
- using sites like eBay
- listening to music or watching videos online
- downloading music or videos
- visiting sites like Facebook

Argue your case using as many of the phrases from exercise 9 as possible.

File 7 Unit 10, Exercise 17

Student B

Your partner has found an advertisement for a job which he/she finds interesting and has the experience to apply for. He/she has been invited for interview. You are the interviewer.

After your partner has given you the job advert, read it and prepare the questions you are going to ask during the interview. Be sure to get as much information from your partner about their relevant skills and experience. Make notes of these to show to your partner when the role-play is over.

Additionally, you should ask questions about your partner's strengths and weaknesses. Don't be satisfied with short answers from your partner to these questions.

Useful language

Unit 1

Describing a company

The company designs/assembles/repairs/sells ...
The headquarters are in ...
The company is located in ...
They specialize in ...
... are employed there.

Welcoming a visitor

How can I help you?
I'm ... . I have an appointment with ...
I'm afraid I'm a few minutes / half an hour / a little bit late/early.
I'll let ... know that you're here.
If you could just wait a moment, I'm sure he/she'll be here soon.
That's fine. I don't mind waiting.
Hello. May I introduce you to ...? / This is ...
Pleased to meet you.
I hope you enjoy your stay here.

Describing a department & its staff

This department is responsible for ...
They specialize in ...
This is where the company ...
... is in charge of the department.
... works for ...
... reports to the head of department / the CEO / ...

Describing jobs

I work in an office / a factory / on site / ...
My main duties include...
I mostly work with ...
I work fixed hours / flexitime / shifts.
I am sometimes on call.
I do a lot of overtime.

Unit 2

Asking a customer for information

What software do you use on your PC?
What do you want/need your PC to be able to do?
Do you need to be able to run the software at the same time?
How much money do you want to spend?
Do you want to play games / use design software / ... on the PC?
What operating system / software / ... would you like to have?

Advising a customer

You should really/certainly think about ...
I'd advise you to ...
My advice would be to ...
You're going to need a ...
In my opinion ...
The better / Your best option would be ...
If I were you, I would ...
I'd suggest/recommend ...
Have you thought about ...?

Unit 3

Making a telephone call

Answering the phone
Good morning. ... speaking.
Hello. ... here.
What can I do for you?
How can I help you?

Saying why you're calling
I'd like to talk to someone about ...
Can I speak to someone about ...?
Could someone help me with ...?

Putting a caller through
Can you hold, please? I'll put you through to him/her.
Just a moment, please. I'll try and connect you.
Please stay on the line and I'll see if his/her line is free.

Saying somebody is not available
I'm afraid his/her extension is busy.
Sorry, but the line's not free at the moment.
... is away from the office this morning. He/she will be back this afternoon.
I'm afraid there's no answer at the moment.

Offering help
Shall I ask him/her to return your call?
Can I get him/her to call you back?
Can I take a message for him/her?
Would you like to leave a message?

Thanking the caller for phoning back
Thanks for returning my call.
Thank you for getting back to me.
I appreciate you calling back so quickly. Thank you.

Making an appointment

Suggesting a time
Can we meet on ...?
What are you doing on ...?
I could come any time on ...
I'll be free on ... if that's any good for you.
Would ... morning/afternoon be convenient for you?
Would ... be possible?
How about ...?

Accepting a suggestion
That would be fine.
I'll be free then.
Good. I'll see you then.

Rejecting a suggestion
Unfortunately I have a meeting / business trip / presentation on ...
Sorry, I'll be with another client all day ...
No, I'm afraid my diary is completely full on ...
Sorry, I'll be ... on ...
I'm going to be busy all day, I'm afraid.

Getting information from a customer

I'm going to ask you a few questions about ...
I'd like to know more about ...
Could you tell me a bit about ...?
Could you explain that to me in more detail, please?
Could you give me some more details, please?

Unit 4

Explaining a process

The first thing you'll need to do is ...
The next step is ...
Then you need to ... so that you can ...
After that you ...
Be sure to ...
And don't forget to ...
Finally, you should ...

Unit 5

Troubleshooting

Asking for help with a problem
I'm having some problems with ...
I've got a question about ...
My ... doesn't work. Do you know what the problem might be?
How can I ...?
Can you tell me how to / more about ...?

Solving the problem
Let's see what we can do.
What type of ... do you have?
What happens if you click on ... / turn the speakers up / ...?
First of all, you need to...
Try clicking on ...
You'll find that at the top of the screen / under ...
You can solve that problem by ...

Unit 6

Giving your opinion

Agreeing
I agree with you there.
You're absolutely right.
I couldn't agree more.
I think so too.
Without a doubt.
I think you're right about ...

Disagreeing
I have a few doubts about that.
I'm not so sure about that.
I'm sorry but I don't think that's true.
I'm afraid I can't agree with that.
Up to a point that may be true, however ...
To an extent that's the case, but ...
I don't think that's really the case.
Sorry, but I don't agree.

Unit 7

Making small talk

Asking about personal things
Is this your first trip to ...?
Do you like ...?
Where do you live ...?
Have you ever been to ...?
What is your impression of ...?
What are you interested in?
What do you do in your free time?
What do you do for a living?
What is your favourite food/hobby/film/sport/...?

Asking about the company
Where is your company located?
Does it operate worldwide?
How many people does your company employ?
What are your key products?
Where are your headquarters?
What do you specialize in?

Giving a presentation

Introduction

Greetings	Good morning, ladies and gentlemen ...
Personal details	My name is ... and I'm ... (company/position/responsibilities)
Objective	Today, I'd like to ...
Main points	First, I'll ..., secondly, I'll ... , finally, ...
Timing	The presentation will take around ... minutes.
Additional information	I have some handouts / internet sites for you at the end.

Signalling what you are doing

Starting a section	I'd like to look at ... / I'd like to comment on ...
Ending a section	That's all I wanted to say about ... Now that brings me to the end of ...
Moving on	If there are no questions, I'll move on to ... I'm now going to turn to ...
Coming back	Well, let me come back to the main issue ...
Drawing attention	As you can see ... (Just) let me point out ... Let's look closely at ...

Conclusion

Signalling the end	That brings me to the end of my presentation.
Summarizing	Before I finish, let me summarize the key points / let me review what I have said.
Final statement	In conclusion, I'd like to say that ...
Closing	Thank you (very much) for listening.
Inviting questions	If there are any questions, I'll be happy to answer them.

Unit 8

Ordering

I would like to order a ..., please.
Which models are you interested in?
How much would that cost?
I can offer you a discount of ... % if you order ...
The price includes VAT/delivery/...
I'm afraid we don't have those in stock at the moment.
I'll order them in for you.
The ... will be with you by/on ...
I'll confirm the order by writing / in an email.

Complaining

I have just received our order and unfortunately there was a problem.
There should have been 5 items but we only received 4.
Unfortunately the invoice was wrong / didn't state the prices we agreed on the phone.
I apologize for the errors in dealing with your order.
I will send the missing items immediately / by post tomorrow.
To make up for any inconvenience, I have sent ... free of charge / at no extra cost.

Formal & informal correspondence

Formal	Informal
Dear Mr/Ms Andrews	Dear Jane/Ian
Best wishes	Best / All the best
Best regards	Regards
I am writing to ...	This is just a quick email to ...
Please accept my apologies.	I'm sorry about ... / Apologies for ...
Please do not hesitate to contact us.	Get in touch.

Unit 9

Discussing a project

How is ... going?
Bring me up to speed with ...
Fill me in on the details.
We've been given the go-ahead to ...
Everything is going according to plan.
Unfortunately we had a few problems with ...
I'm afraid I don't think we're going to make the deadline because...
That's a bit tight, don't you think?

Softening criticism

I'm afraid this isn't up to your usual standard.
It might have been a better idea to ...
Perhaps you could have ... instead.
You should have really ...
I'm not sure it was a good idea to ...

Unit 10

Writing a covering letter

I am writing to apply for ...
I saw your job advertisement on your website / in the local paper / ...
Please find enclosed a copy of my curriculum vitae.
As you can see from my enclosed CV, ...
I consider myself to be ...
During my apprenticeship / work experience / ... I gained experience of ...
In my current job I am responsible for ...
I believe that the experience and skills I gained there equip me well for the position.
I would welcome the opportunity to talk to you about the position.
Should you require additional information, please do not hesitate to contact me.

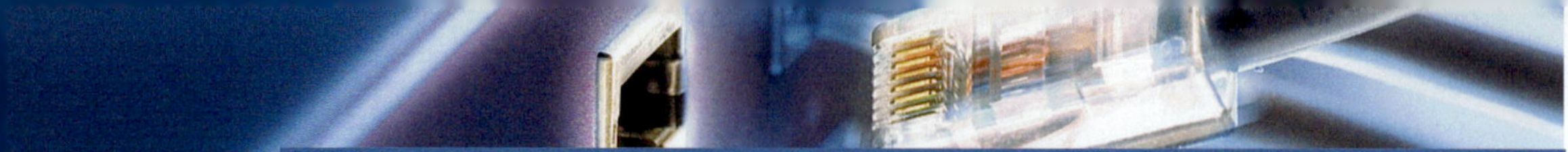

Transcripts

Track 2 Unit 1, Exercise 6

Receptionist Guten Morgen. Wie kann ich Ihnen helfen?

Matthews Oh, guten Morgen. I'm afraid I don't speak much German. Do you speak English?

Receptionist Of course. How can I help you?

Matthews Well, I have an appointment with Ms Wang but I'm afraid I'm a few minutes early. It's my first day here on placement, you see, and I didn't know how long it would take to get here.

Receptionist Well, it's always best to be early – especially on your first day! Could you give me your name, please?

Matthews Of course. It's Matthews, Tobi Matthews. I'm from the subsidiary in Manchester.

Receptionist Well, welcome to Munich, Mr Matthews. I'll let Maggie know that you're here. If you could just wait a moment, I'm sure she'll be here soon.

Matthews That's great, thank you. I don't mind waiting.

Receptionist So what do you do in Manchester?

Matthews I'm an IT specialist there. I haven't been working at IT International long so they thought it would be a good idea to get to know a bit more about the company by coming here.

Receptionist Sounds like a good idea. Ah, here's Maggie now. Maggie, this is Tobi Matthews from Manchester.

Maggie Hi Tobi. Pleased to meet you.

Matthews Pleased to meet you too.

Receptionist Well, I'll leave you with Maggie then. I hope you enjoy your stay in Munich.

Matthews I'm sure I will. And thank you for your help.

Receptionist You're welcome.

Track 4 Unit 1, Exercise 13

Good morning, my name's Klaus Ziegler and I'd like to give you a brief insight into the organization of IT International.
Though job titles and responsibilities vary, you will find common IT management roles in most companies. The highest position in IT International is the Chief Executive Officer, or CEO as he is mostly called. He is responsible for overseeing the different branches of the company and takes an active role in managing the company and in setting goals.

The CIO (Chief Information Officer) and CTO (Chief Technology Officer) are our company's top technological gurus. The CIO reports directly to the CEO and is responsible for the strategic direction of technology in our company. CIOs do not only have to be good at IT management, they also have to be great leaders and I am glad to say that Mrs Khor of IT International is doing a really good job. The CTO is more concerned with the company's technology, e.g. with R & D. Our CTO, Mr Meissner, deals with system architecture, platforms, data processing, system analysis, computer programming, etc. In smaller companies, in our subsidiaries for example, CTOs don't have that title, but they are in charge of the company's future technology as well. In broad terms you can say that the CIO is more business-oriented, while the CTO is more technical, with an in-depth understanding of computer and information systems.
But the CIO and CTO cannot do the job alone. The front line managers such as the Project Manager, Development Manager, QA (which is quality assurance) Manager and IT Operations Manager report to the executive level of IT International. They are responsible for the different departments in our company, such as Marketing, Finance, Human Resources, Research and Development, Communication Technology and Customer Service, just to name the most important ones.
Well, that's the end of my talk on the organization of IT International. I understand that you will now have a closer look at some of our departments so you will get a better understanding of what each department does ...

Track 5

Unit 2, Exercise 2

Salesperson	Hello. Can I help you?
Karen	Yes, thanks. I've decided to build a PC, you know, rather than buy a pre-built model. I was wondering if you could tell me what I'll need.
Salesperson	Of course. What do you want your PC to be able to do?
Karen	Well, all the usual stuff, of course. Word processing and the internet. I definitely won't want to store lots of music or films on it. It's mostly for working on. I use some pretty big pieces of graphic design software for my work so my PC needs to be able to handle that. Oh ... and there are also one or two games I occasionally like to play.
Salesperson	Do you need to be able to run these pieces of design software at the same time?
Karen	Yes. That's the point. My existing computer just isn't powerful enough for that. It crashes all the time.
Salesperson	Right. I know the problem. You should really think about getting an Apple. Lots of people think they're better for graphics work.
Karen	Well, I've thought about it but ... No, I'm used to Windows. I want to stick with that.
Salesperson	OK. Well ... how much money do you want to spend on the PC?
Karen	I think £1,500 is about my limit. Though I'd rather spend a little less.

Salesperson Hmm. I'd advise you to invest the full £1,500. You should be able to put a really good PC together for that. Anything less and you're going to have to compromise on some key components which will cut down on performance.

Karen OK. So ... what do you recommend?

Salesperson Well. Let's start with the video card. You're going to need a video card capable of handling your games. These components are quite expensive and will eat into your budget. I'd recommend the Cyclon 4839 HD. It can handle most games and costs just under £400. It'll also handle your graphics programs with no problem.

Karen OK.

Salesperson Then you're going to need a pretty powerful CPU to run these graphics packages and games. Your best option would be the Textos RD 200. It's a quatro core processor which can handle multi-tasking. It's really stable and won't let you down. It's also energy saving.

Karen That sounds good. What about memory? How much will I need?

Salesperson Right. If I were you, I would certainly go for a minimum of 8GB RAM. You're going to need that to optimize the performance of the processor and get the most out of the PC's multi-tasking capabilities.

Karen OK.

Salesperson Now, my advice would be to get about 500 GB for the hard drive. You're not going to need more than that if you're not saving music and films on the computer.

Karen Right.

Salesperson Now, if you'd just come over here, I'll show you the ...

Track 7

Unit 3, Exercise 6

Knight When could you come in to see me? Would next week be possible? I'm afraid I'm going to be rather busy but I still have a couple of spaces in my diary. How about Monday afternoon?

Stiller Hmmm. Sorry, I'll be with another client all day Monday. Would Tuesday morning be convenient for you?

Knight No, I'm afraid my diary is completely full on Tuesday. I'm going to a meeting with our advertising agency in the morning and in the afternoon I'm going to interview new staff.

Stiller I'll be free on Wednesday morning if that's any good for you?

Knight Wednesday ... let me see. No, sorry. I'll be in London for meetings on Wednesday.

Stiller How about Thursday afternoon, then?

Knight I'm going to be busy meeting new customers all day Thursday, I'm afraid.

Stiller OK. I could come any time in the morning on Friday ... let's say up until 11.30?

Knight That would be fine. I'll be free then. There's a telephone conference with my head office ... but I'll be free by ten.

Stiller Great. Ten a.m. on Friday it is, then. I look forward to meeting you, Ms Knight. See you then.

Knight Goodbye, Mr Stiller. See you on Friday.

Track 8

Unit 3, Exercise 9

Knight Hello, Mr Stiller. Good to meet you in person. Welcome to AX Design.

Stiller Nice to meet you too, Ms Knight.

Knight Let's use first names. I'm Sara.

Stiller Fine by me. I'm Gunnar. So ... Sara ... you need a computer system for your new offices here.

Knight Exactly. I'm a designer by trade and not a computer expert so I'm hoping that you can advise me what we need. I'd like to keep the cost of it all as low as possible. I have a tight budget.

Stiller That should be no problem. I need to find out a little more about your requirements. So, I'm going to ask you a few questions about your work here.

Knight Good.

Stiller OK. Could you tell me a bit more about your staff and what their jobs are?

Knight Well, to begin with we're going to have eleven people in the team. Three of them will be administrative staff. Then there are the designers. Five of them will be doing design work mostly for print – you know, adverts in magazines, that kind of thing. The other three designers are going to concentrate more on animated design.

Stiller That sounds interesting. Could you explain that further for me?

Knight Sure. They'll be doing a lot of work for the internet with animated features ... for banner advertisements and so on. And they're also going to do some animation for TV adverts.

Stiller OK. Would it be possible for you to elaborate upon what the admin staff will use their computers for?

Knight Yes. All the usual stuff, you know, writing letters, using Excel, etc.

Stiller Fine. Well, we can certainly offer a standard PC package for them which won't cost too much. Now, perhaps you could go into more detail about what sort of software the designers will be using?

Knight The five designers concentrating on magazine and newspaper work will be using packages such as Quark and InDesign.

Stiller OK. They're going to need quite a lot of processor speed. I'd suggest that we upgrade our standard PCs for them. That should give them enough power for their work and keep your costs down. Now, what about the three designers who'll be doing the animated work? Could you give me more details about what software they'll be using?

Knight Well, lots of different animation packages. And sometimes they need to run several at once. It's really important that their PCs can handle this without crashing.

Stiller Of course. That's why I'd recommend fully-customized machines for them. I'm afraid you can't cut costs here. They'll need top-of-the-range PCs to keep them working effectively.

Knight OK. That's what I thought. Well ... that all sounds fine.

Stiller Good. I'm going to go back to the office now and draw up the specification for you. I'll pass it onto our technical team and, after they've had a look at it, I'll be able to give you an idea about the price.

Knight OK.

Stiller Then, I'll make another appointment with you and we can look at what I suggest in detail.

Track 9

Unit 4, Exercise 2

Jennifer Hi Colin. How are you?

Colin Great thanks, Jennifer. And you? How are your computer problems?

Jennifer I'm fine thanks. As for the computer, I've decided to try the OpenOffice package. I was wondering if you could tell me how to install it?

Colin Hm, that's a very good idea. It's a good package. Easy to use and easy to install as well.

Jennifer Great. So, how do I go about installing it?

Colin Well, the first thing you'll need to do is check the system requirements. You need at least 650 MB free on your hard drive.

Jennifer Ah ... that might be a problem. My computer's pretty full. But if I delete one or two older pieces of software I don't use anymore, I'll have space for the package.

Colin Good. OK. Well, the next step, of course, is to download OpenOffice from the internet.

Jennifer Right.

Colin Then you need to log on to your PC as the administrator so that you can run the installation. After that you can unpack and install the software. It's really straightforward. Just be sure to read the instructions at each stage before clicking OK.

Jennifer Oh, that sounds straightforward. Great. Thanks, Colin.

Colin And don't forget to run OpenOffice once you're finished to make sure that it's installed successfully.

Jennifer Ah ... OK.

Colin It usually installs first time no problem. But if it doesn't install for some reason, just try downloading it and going through the procedure again.

Track 10

Unit 4, Exercise 9

Colin Colin here.

Jennifer Hey Colin. Listen. I managed to download and install OpenOffice ...

Colin Good.

Jennifer ... but I'm having a few difficulties with it.
Colin Ah, OK. What's the problem?
Jennifer Well, I've tried to use the spreadsheet software but I just don't like it as much as Excel. I'd rather stick to that because I'm used to it. But when I try to open spreadsheet files, they only open with OpenOffice. What do I need to do to open them with Excel?
Colin OK, yeah. Did you run the standard installation?
Jennifer Yes. Was that wrong?
Colin No, no. But you're given an option when you install the software that allows you to deselect certain file types so that they can be opened with other software.
Jennifer Oh dear. Well I didn't do that.
Colin It's not a major problem. Basically, you have to put files recognized by OpenOffice into a format preferred by Excel. You do this using Import/ Export or Save As functions in Windows. To reassociate files in this way can take a bit of time though. Your other option – and this is what I'd recommend – is to re-run the main set up. You can then select Modify to alter which file types are opened by which software.
Jennifer Ah. That sounds like repeating the installation.
Colin Well, it's similar. But doing it that way takes you back to the set up controls and allows you to choose specifically what you want OpenOffice to do ... and not to do. I think it's always a good idea to choose the Custom setup when you're installing software. You just click the appropriate button and follow the prompts to make the right installation choices. Even if you accepted all the default settings, at least you'd know what these are and what you can expect. Anyway ... like I said, just try re-running the main set up. OK?
Jennifer Great, Colin. Thanks. I'll give it a go.
Colin Just call if you have any other problems ...

Track 11

Unit 5, Exercise 2

1 My PC's gone mad. It keeps shutting down and starting up all on its own.
2 My computer is so slow. I have to wait ages for it to do the simplest things.
3 My monitor sometimes gets so fuzzy and unclear I can't even read large text on it.
4 I just tried listening to music on my PC but the sound's not working.
5 Windows seems to be having difficulties shutting down my PC.
6 My computer is so loud I can't turn it on when my girlfriend's watching TV because she can't hear anything.

Track 12 Unit 5, Exercise 7

Dialogue 1

Brian Eptix customer helpline. Brian speaking.

Caller Oh, hello. I'm having some difficulties with my monitor. I wonder if you can help me.

Brian Yes, of course. I'll see what I can do. What exactly is the problem?

Caller I turned my PC on this morning as usual but my monitor screen is black. I hope it's not broken.

Brian Right. Let's start with the basics. Are you sure that your PC is turned on?

Caller Oh, yes. The light at the front's on and I can hear the fan so it must be.

Brian Good. Now, have you checked to make sure that the monitor power cable is in properly?

Caller Yes, of course. I'm sure that power is getting through to it because the light is on at the front of my monitor. But nothing's happening.

Brian OK. Have you checked to see if the cable between the monitor and your PC is plugged in?

Caller Yes. I've done that as well.

Brian OK. Try moving your mouse or hitting a few keys on the keyboard.

Caller Well, of course I've tried that already. But I'll give it another go. ... No, still nothing.

Brian OK. Could you please try turning the contrast and brightness controls on your monitor?

Caller Ah, OK. Well I haven't done that yet, but I'm sure ... No, wait. I don't believe it. My screen is on now. Oh, how embarrassing. I should have thought of that myself. My young son has probably been playing with the computer again. It wouldn't be the first time.

Brian Never mind. At least we've solved the problem.

Caller Well, thank you. Sorry for taking up your time with something so silly.

Brian No problem at all. That's what we're here for.

Dialogue 2

Claire Hi. Central Computing Services. Claire here.

Simon Hey Claire. It's Simon Britten from Marketing here. Listen, I'm having a problem with my printer which I hope you can help me with.

Claire Hi, Simon. Sure. What sort of printer do you have?

Simon It's a JX Officejet.

Claire OK. And what seems to be the problem?

Simon I've tried printing a few documents this morning but all of them have black lines across the page. I haven't got a clue what to do and I have a meeting in twenty minutes which I need to do some printing for straight away.

Claire Right. Let's have a look at that then. Have you tried cleaning the printer cartridge?

Simon Eh, no. How do I do that?

Claire Open the JX Printer Management Suite. Tell me when it's open.

Simon Wait, wait. Where do I find that?
Claire Click on Start, then Programs. You should see it in the list.
Simon Right. Got that.
Claire So, click on it to open up the printer controls.
Simon OK.
Claire Now click on Clean Print Cartridges.
Simon Where is that?
Claire Sorry. I'll go more slowly. That's on the top right of the window, beside Change Print Quality.
Simon OK. Got that.
Claire So, click on it ... and then we have to wait a few seconds while the cleaning takes place. You'll get a message telling you that it's finished. So ...
Simon Right. Finished cleaning print cartridge. It seems to be finished.
Claire Now, try printing out a single sheet of one of your documents.
Simon OK ... Great. No black lines, Claire, thanks. You've saved my life.
Claire I wouldn't go that far but at least you can get your printing done for the meeting.

Track 14

Unit 6, Exercise 6

Baars Henk Baars.
Rehn Henk. It's Stefan again. Listen, I've done everything you suggested half an hour ago and I think I've stopped the virus in its tracks.
Baars You mean it hasn't spread onto any other computers on the network.
Rehn Exactly. None of the other machines seem to be affected.
Baars That is good news.
Rehn Yes, but the thing is, I can't get rid of it from the secretary's PC.
Baars Did you run updates on the operating system?
Rehn Yes, but ...
Baars And have you updated the anti-virus software and scanned the PC with it?
Rehn Yes. That's just it. The software has identified the virus but it can't seem to remove it.
Baars What is the virus called?
Rehn The anti-virus software says it's something called Nitpikker.
Baars Oh.
Rehn Is that bad?
Baars It's not good. Nitpikker is quite new and quite difficult to get rid of. I believe that it's normally distributed via email attachments but this time it seems to have got into your system by another route.
Rehn Yes, well that's interesting but what should I do?
Baars I would say that you should probably wipe the computer clean and reinstall the operating system.
Rehn Really! Why? What do I have anti-virus software for then?
Baars The problem is that quite a lot of viruses these days can evade attempts to remove them with software. Your best bet is a reinstall.

Rehn This is embarrassing, Henk. I've no idea how to do that.

Baars Don't worry, Stefan. I may be able to drive over in the morning and take care of it for you. I'll be able to let you know by the end of the afternoon if I can. Before I come, the best thing might be to back up all the data on the PC. I'll bring some specialist software with me, which will mean we will be able to see if the virus has infected any of this data. Then we can reload the data once the operating system has been reinstalled.

Rehn Thanks, Henk.

Baars No problem. And Stefan, after that we must talk about an AUP for your office.

Rehn Right, you mentioned that earlier. What is it anyway?

Baars AUP stands for Acceptable Use ... or User ... Policy. It's a code of conduct for anyone who uses your system and internet connections.

Rehn Ah. OK.

Baars An AUP may help you avoid problems like this in the future. I'll help you draw it up. Look, I've got to go now, Stefan. Hopefully, I'll be with you at about 10 o'clock tomorrow. As I say, I'll be able to confirm that later ...

Track 15

Unit 7, Exercise 7

Maggie Good morning, ladies and gentlemen. My name is Maggie Wang, and I'm the marketing manager at IT International. This means I'm responsible for organizing our presence at trade fairs, especially in Asia.

This morning I'd like to tell you about reasons for exhibiting at a trade fair and give you some guidelines showing how to be successful there.

First, I'd like to mention some reasons for an exhibitor to attend a trade fair. Trade shows are a very powerful marketing medium because they bring together thousands of exhibitors and potential customers. Most companies use trade shows as a primary marketing vehicle for introducing new products and services. For your company it provides a chance to enhance your image and visibility and establish presence in the Asian marketplace – something which is important for conquering the new Asian market. You can observe your competitors on the market and see if your products appeal to Asian buyers, therefore giving you the possibility of adapting to the market.

Now let me talk about the main issue, how to take part in such a trade fair. First and foremost, set measurable objectives. Focus on only a few key products so that the visitors are not confused. Equally important is choosing the most appropriate trade fair. Pick the fair that offers maximum exposure to your target market. You will recognize the appropriate show because your prime competition will already be signed up and has probably been attending the show for many years.

Let me also point out that participating at a trade fair is not cheap. The stand, travel and accommodation costs, stand personnel, display and presentation expenses – as well as providing hospitality to visitors – are expensive, but with careful preparation this is money well spent.

Now let me move on to your trade fair stand, which should make a strong statement about your company. Your stand design should match your corporate identity. Location is everything, so try to get the best space possible for your trade show exhibit. Your stand should be in a prominent position, next to other companies offering similar products or services. Effective public relations before and at the trade fair are also very important. Each exhibitor should inform potential and existing customers about its participation. Advertising should mention the stand number and the products that will be exhibited.
Next let's talk about when you're at the fair. You need well-informed and highly motivated stand personnel. These should be the people who can best answer the questions you think your customers will ask. Remember, these may not necessarily be the best sales people in your company.
Finally, decide how you will review your success at the trade fair. Collect as many business cards and as much information from your potential clients as you can. Follow these contacts up right after your return to your office either by phone or by email.
Before I close, I'd like to say something about your intention to establish your company in Asia, in particular in China. Here you have to watch out for some cross-cultural differences. The Chinese market is very competitive. To be successful in China, you need three qualities: specialist expertise, the ability to realize goals quickly and a high degree of social competence with a strong interest in people. The Chinese do not make such a clear distinction between work and private life as we do here.
Now that brings me to the end of my presentation. To conclude, I'd like to say that it is essential to learn from your experience at the trade fair and make any necessary changes in products or marketing strategy afterwards. Thank you very much for listening. If there are any questions, I'll be happy to answer them.

Track 16

Unit 7, Exercise 12

Peter Hi. Is there any coffee left?
Visitor Yes, there's a little bit. I'll pour some for you. Here you are.
Peter Thanks. It's a lovely day, isn't it? Much better than the weather at home!
Visitor Oh, it's always like this here. Where do you live then?
Peter I'm from the UK. And unfortunately the stereotype is true – it's often rainy there! Have you ever been to the UK?
Visitor Yes, I have. I was in Birmingham on business last year. And you're right, it was rainy… Where is your company located?
Peter Funnily enough, InterMobil has its headquarters in Birmingham.
Visitor What a coincidence!
Peter What was your impression of the city?
Visitor Well, the people were very friendly and the food was much better than I'd expected. Everyone says how bad the English food is but I quite enjoyed it.

Peter Yes, it's not that bad really!

Visitor So what does your company specialize in?

Peter Well at the moment we're developing some innovative new smartphones actually. That's what we're here to promote.

Visitor Well, that sounds interesting. I'll have to come to your stand at some point.

Peter Great. Here's my card. My name's Peter Hunt and our stand is in Hall A ...

Track 17

Unit 8, Exercise 2

North This is Hardware Computer Supplies. Lynton North speaking. How can I help you?

Crane Hello. Mary Crane from Crane Photography here. I'd like to speak to Niles Simpson, please.

North I'm sorry but Mr Simpson won't be in the office all week. He's at the CeBIT trade fair in Germany. Perhaps I can help you further.

Crane Well, perhaps you can. I met Niles at the MediaTech fair in Cambridge last week. I expressed interest in buying some scanners.

North Which models are you interested in, Ms Crane?

Crane Two models from Epson. Niles showed me several of them in action. The scanner which I was particularly interested in was the EPL N2 55ODT. I'd like to order two of these.

North OK. The EPL N2 55ODT costs £995. So, the total cost for two will be ... let me see ... £1,990.

Crane Well, that's the thing. Niles offered me a 12% discount if I ordered two plus a further three scanners. The model which I'm interested in ordering three of is the Star C2500N.

North OK. Well three C2500Ns would cost ... hold on a moment ... £1,869. So that would make £3,859 in total. Minus the discount, that would equal £3,396.

Crane Does that include VAT?

North Yes, the price is inclusive of VAT. But there's just one thing. We don't currently have the C2500N in stock. I'd have to order the scanners for you. It'll take them three days to arrive here, so the scanners would be with you by next Thursday at the earliest.

Crane That would be no problem.

North Fine. Then I'll order those for you. And I'll confirm your order by email. Could I have your email address, please?

Crane Yes, of course. It's mary underscore crane ... all in lower case ... at crane photography dot co dot uk.

North OK ... got that.

Crane Good. I have another quick question. Do the scanners come with accompanying software?

North Yes, the software comes as standard with the scanners. So does the on-site warranty.

Crane Ah, fine. And will we be able to install and set up the scanners ourselves?

North You should be able to set up the C2500Ns with no problems but the EPL N2 55ODT is another story. As an optional extra we can send out a technician who will take care of the set up for you.

Crane How much does that cost?

North Let me see ... two scanners ... that would be £106 plus VAT.

Crane OK. I think we'll go for that. We're not exactly computer experts here.

North Fine. Now if I can just confirm the delivery address ...

Track 18

Unit 9, Exercise 6

Jim So, Brian. Fill me in on how the Travel UK installation is going. Where are we up to with the project?

Brian Well, I did some research online to see if I could find network components at better prices than our usual suppliers could offer ...

Jim And ...

Brian I found a Cisco server, a network hub and the power supply at different online suppliers at really quite low prices.

Jim Excellent, Brian. Well done.

Brian So, I was able to keep well within the budget set by Edward Cybulski.

Jim Great.

Brian He's given the official go-ahead for the project based on the quotation I sent him.

Jim So, bring me up to speed with the appointment for installation. Ideally, we should carry out the work on Wednesday and take care of the testing and troubleshooting on Thursday so that the network is up and running by our deadline on Friday.

Brian Well, unfortunately, there's a small problem with that.

Jim Oh.

Brian You see, I ordered the network server and the hub from online suppliers based in Germany and the Czech Republic. Unfortunately, I didn't check their delivery times properly. It's going to take a bit longer for these components to arrive than I had hoped.

Jim Go on.

Brian Well ... the server will get here on Thursday afternoon. But we'll have to wait until Friday morning for the hub to arrive. So ...

Jim But that would mean that we could carry out the installation on Friday at the earliest. That's a bit tight, don't you think? Friday is our deadline.

Brian I know, Jim. But we could still do the work, including testing and trouble-shooting, on Friday and have the job completed by the early evening.

Jim Well, if we have to deal with unforeseen difficulties, we could have real problems.

Brian Yes, but ...

Jim Look, Brian. I really have to criticize you here. This is just not good enough. You should have checked these delivery times carefully. The market we work in is pretty competitive. If we don't deliver when we say we're going to deliver, our reputation will suffer and we'll lose business.

Brian I know but I was pretty excited about finding the parts at cheaper prices and I just forgot ...

Jim How long have you known about this anyway?

Brian Since the day before yesterday.

Jim Well, you waited far too long to say something about it. You should have called to tell me, Brian. At least I could have talked to Edward and smoothed things over a bit. You need to be a bit more communicative, you know.

Brian I'm sorry, Jim.

Track 19

Unit 10, Exercise 11

Simon Well, Daniela. Welcome to MEDTEC Ltd. I'm glad you could attend the interview.

Daniela I'm glad to be here. Thank you for inviting me.

Simon So, if I understand your CV correctly, you've just finished your apprenticeship, haven't you?

Daniela That's right. A few weeks ago.

Simon And now you'd like to come and work for MEDTEC. Why is that?

Daniela Well, for two reasons really. The job here would let me broaden my experience of developing solutions in a production environment. That's important to me.

Simon OK ...

Daniela And I really want to work in Britain and continue to improve my English.

Simon Your English is pretty good at the moment.

Daniela Thank you.

Simon Can you tell me a bit about your interest in programming? When did it all start?

Daniela I became interested in programming while I was at school. That's why I chose to do my apprenticeship in solutions development. In the last three years – I mean during my training – I've really learned a lot about programming. I find it fascinating. And I like that the results of the work make things easier and more efficient for other people.

Simon Could you give me an example of some programming that you've carried out?

Daniela Sure ... Well, for example, I was part of a team that developed an interface for production managers with the company's sales database. Basically, the production managers needed information about sales performance so that they could modify production schedules. But the sales database was full of information that they didn't actually need. The aim of our solution was to present managers with relevant information in a form that they could easily understand.

Simon Sounds interesting.

Daniela It was. In the end, our solution resulted in clear management information for production with no additional data input.

Simon Great. I must say that your programming qualifications are splendid. Really in line with what we're looking for. Now ... you mentioned team work. That's important to us here. Do you enjoy working in a team environment?

Daniela Oh, yes. I benefited from having a really good team to work with at the company where I did my apprenticeship. During the last three years, I've learned so much from colleagues in my team, not just about programming, but also about work in general.

Simon But you can do your own thing, right? I mean work on your own initiative, take responsibility for your own work, that kind of thing.

Daniela Yes, I can. I need a job where I have my own areas of responsibility but where my work feeds back into the team's.

Simon Fantastic. Well, your application is impressive. I'm very pleased. But before we move onto the specifics of working at MEDTEC, are there any questions you want to ask me?

Daniela Well, yes. I wanted to ask ...

Basic word list

Diese Liste enthält ca. 900 Grundwörter, die in *IT Matters* als bekannt vorausgesetzt werden. Nicht aufgeführt, jedoch vorausgesetzt, sind einige elementare Wörter, wie Pronomen, Zahlen, Wochentage sowie Wörter, die im Englischen und Deutschen die gleiche Bedeutung haben, wie z. B. *monitor*, *restaurant* und *hotel*.

A

able, to be ~ können, in der Lage sein
about über, etwa
above über, oben(stehend)
absolutely absolut, völlig
accept annehmen, akzeptieren
access Zugang, Zugriff
accident Zufall, Unfall
accompany begleiten
according to zufolge, laut, nach
account Bericht, Konto
across (quer) über
active aktiv(iert)
activity Tätigkeit, Aktivität
add zusammenzählen, hinzufügen
addition, in ~ to zusätzlich zu
address Adresse; adressieren
advantage Vorteil
advice Ratschlag, (guter) Rat
affect betreffen, beeinflussen
afraid, I'm ~ leider
after (all) schließlich (doch)
afternoon Nachmittag
again wieder
age Alter
agree zustimmen, vereinbaren
aim Ziel, Absicht
air Luft
airport Flughafen
all alle(s)
allow erlauben, gestatten, (zu)lassen
almost fast, beinahe
alone allein(e)
along entlang
already schon, bereits
also auch, außerdem
alternatively alternativ
although obwohl
altogether insgesamt
always immer
a.m. vormittags
among zwischen, unter
amount Menge, Betrag
angry wütend, verärgert
another noch eine/r/s
answer Antwort, Lösung; (be)antworten
any irgendetwas, -welche, jede
anybody jemand, jede/r
anyone jemand, jede/r
anything etwas, alles
anyway jedenfalls, sowieso
anywhere irgendwo(hin)
apart from abgesehen von, außer
appear erscheinen, auftauchen
appointment Termin, Verabredung
approximately ungefähr, etwa
area Gebiet, Bereich
arrange arrangieren, vereinbaren
arrival Ankunft
arrive ankommen
ask fragen, bitten
assistant Assistent/in
away weg, entfernt

B

back zurück; Rückseite, Rücken
bad schlecht, schlimm
badly sehr
bag Tasche, Tüte, Beutel
basic grundsätzlich, einfach
because weil
become werden
before vor(her)
begin anfangen, beginnen
beginning Anfang
behind hinter, hinten
believe glauben
belong gehören
below unter, unten(stehend)
best beste, am besten
best wishes Viele Grüße
better besser
between zwischen
big groß
birth Geburt
blue blau
board Brett, Tafel, Platine
body Körper
book Buch; buchen, bestellen
boss Chef/in
both beide
bottom Unterseite, Unterteil, Boden
box Kasten, Kästchen
bracket Klammer
break Pause
brilliant großartig, glänzend
bring bringen, holen
broken kaputt
build bauen, aufbauen
building Gebäude
business Geschäft, Firma, Sache, Anglegenheit
business card (Visiten-)Karte
busy beschäftigt, besetzt
button Taste, Knopf
buy kaufen
buyer Käufer/in
bye tschüs

C

call Anruf; (an)rufen
caller Anrufer/in
can dürfen, können
cannot nicht können
canteen Kantine
car Auto
case Fall, Kiste
cash Bargeld
cause Ursache, Grund; verursachen
certain sicher, gewiss, bestimmt
challenge Herausforderung
change (Ver-)Änderung; (aus) wechseln, (sich) ändern
cheap billig, günstig
check überprüfen, kontrollieren
choice Wahl, Auswahl
choose (aus)wählen
cinema Kino

city (Groß-)Stadt
class Klasse
classmate Klassenkamerad/in
clean sauber; reinigen, säubern
clear klar, deutlich
clever klug, intelligent
close schließen, zumachen
close (to) nahe
clothes Kleidung, Kleider
clue Hinweis, Tip
coffee Kaffee
collection Sammlung
college Fachhochschule
color (AE)/**colour** (BE) Farbe
combine verbinden, kombinieren
come kommen, geliefert werden
command Befehl
common üblich, gemeinsam
commonly häufig, gewöhnlich, üblicherweise
complain sich beklagen, sich beschweren, reklamieren
complete vollständig; vervollständigen
completely völlig
computing Computerwissenschaft
conflict Konflikt
connect (miteinander) verbinden, anschließen
construct bauen, konstruieren
contact Kontakt, Verbindung
contain enthalten
content zufrieden; Inhalt
control Kontrolle; kontrollieren, regeln, steuern, überwachen
copy Exemplar, Kopie; abschreiben, kopieren
corner Ecke
correct richtig, genau; korrigieren
corridor Gang, Flur
cost Kosten; kosten
could konnte/n, könnte/n
count zählen
country Land, Staat
couple Paar
course Kurs, Lehrgang, Gang
create (er)schaffen, erstellen
creative kreativ, schöpferisch
cross (an)kreuzen
culture Kultur
cup Tasse
current gegenwärtig, aktuell

D

danger Gefahr
dangerous gefährlich
dark Dunkelheit, dunkel
date Datum, Termin
date of birth Geburtsdatum
day Tag
dear liebe/r
decide entscheiden, beschließen
decision Entscheidung
definite(ly) (ganz) sicher, bestimmt
delay Verzögerung; verzögern
delete löschen
deliver (aus)liefern
delivery Zustellung, Lieferung
demand Forderung; (an) fordern
depend abhängen (von)
describe beschreiben
description Beschreibung, Schilderung
desk (Schreib-)Tisch, Arbeitsplatz
dialogue Gespräch, Dialog
diary (Termin-)Kalender
dictionary Wörterbuch
differ sich unterscheiden
difference Unterschied
different unterschiedlich, verschieden
difficult schwer, schwierig
difficulty Schwierigkeit
dinner (Abend-)Essen
direct direkt, gerade
direction Richtung
dirty schmutzig
disadvantage Nachteil, Schaden
disappear verschwinden
disaster Katastrophe
discover entdecken, feststellen
dislike nicht mögen
divorced geschieden
do tun, machen
door Tür
doubt Zweifel; (be)zweifeln
drink Getränk; trinken
driver Fahrer/in
during während

E

each jede/r/s
early früh
east Osten
easy, easily leicht, einfach
education Erziehung, (Aus-, Schul-)Bildung
educational Bildungs-
effective effektiv, wirksam
either entweder
electrical elektrisch, Strom-
electricity Elektrizität, Strom
electronic elektronisch
else andere/r/s
employ beschäftigen, einstellen
empty leer
end Ende, Schluss; (be)enden
ending Ende
energy Energie
engineer Ingenieur/in, Techniker/in
enjoy genießen, gefallen, gern tun
enough ausreichend, genug
enquiry (An-)Frage, Untersuchung
enter eintreten, betreten, eingeben
entrance Eingang, Einfahrt
environment Umwelt, Umfeld
environmental Umwelt-
equal gleich
era Ära, Zeitalter
especially besonders
essential (absolut) notwendig
even sogar (noch)
evening Abend
ever je(mals)
every jede/r/s
everybody jede/r
everyone jede/r/s, alle
everything alles
exactly exakt, genau
example Beispiel
excellent hervorragend, ausgezeichnet
excited aufgeregt, begeistert
exciting aufregend, spannend
exclude ausschließen
exercise Übung
exercise book (Schul-)Heft
expect erwarten, annehmen
expensive teuer
experience Erfahrung

expert Fachmann/frau
express ausdrücken
extra zusätzlich
extreme äußerst
eye Auge

F

fact Tatsache
factory Fabrik
fairly ziemlich
false falsch
familiar vertraut, bekannt
family Familie
far weit (entfernt)
fast schnell
feel (sich) fühlen, meinen, glauben
feeling Gefühl
female weiblich, Frauen-
(a) few ein paar, wenig/e
file Ordner, Datei
final letzte/r/s
finally schließlich, endlich
financial finanziell
find finden, suchen
find out herausfinden
fine gut, schön
finish (be)enden, abschließen, fertig werden
firm Firma
first(ly) erst; zuerst
fix festlegen, reparieren
flat Wohnung; flach
flight Flug
floor Etage, (Fuß-)Boden
fly fliegen
follow (be)folgen
(the) following der/die/das Folgende
food Essen, Nahrung
football Fußball
foreign ausländisch, Auslands-, fremd
forget vergessen
form Form, Formular
formal(ly) förmlich, formell
forward nach vorne
free frei; gratis, kostenlos
frequently oft, häufig
friend Freund/in
friendly freund(schaft)lich
friendship Freundschaft
front Vorderseite
full voll
fully völlig
funny komisch, merkwürdig
further weitere
future Zukunft; (zu)künftig

G

gap Lücke
general allgemein, generell, normal
generally im Allgemeinen, normalerweise
get holen, bekommen, werden
give geben
glad froh
go gehen, fahren
go ahead anfangen, weitermachen
go for sth sich bemühen um, gefallen
go on weitermachen, fortfahren
go out ausgehen
good gut
good luck viel Glück
goodbye auf Wiedersehen
goods Ware(n), Güter
government Regierung
great groß(artig)
greatly in großem Maße
green grün
greet (be)grüßen
greeting Gruß(formel), Begrüßung
ground Boden, Grund
group Gruppe; gruppieren
grow wachsen, werden
guess Annahme; raten, schätzen
guest Gast

H

half Hälfte; halb
hall Diele, Saal, Halle
handle umgehen mit, bearbeiten, fertigwerden mit
happen passieren, geschehen
happy glücklich, zufrieden
health Gesundheit
hear hören
heart Herz
heavy schwer
height Höhe, Größe
help Hilfe; helfen
helpful hilfreich, nützlich
her ihr
here hier
herself sie selbst, sich (selbst)
high; highly hoch; äußerst
him ihn, ihm
himself er selbst, sich (selbst)
history Geschichte
holiday Ferien, Urlaub, Feiertag
home Zuhause, Heim; nach Hause
honest ehrlich, anständig
hope Hoffnung; hoffen
hopefully hoffentlich
hot heiß
hour Stunde
house Haus
how wie
however doch, jedoch
huge riesig
human menschlich
husband (Ehe-)Mann

I

idea Vorstellung, Idee
ideally ideal, im Idealfall
identity Identität
if wenn, falls, ob
illness Krankheit
image Bild
immediately sofort, unverzüglich
importance Wichtigkeit, Bedeutung
important wichtig
impossible unmöglich
impressive beeindruckend
improve verbessern, sich bessern
include enthalten, umfassen
individual einzeln, individuell
informal ungezwungen, inoffiziell, informell
information Auskunft, Information(en), Angaben
inside innerhalb, drinnen
instant sofortig, augenblicklich
instead stattdessen
interest Interesse, Zins(en); interessieren
interested interessiert
interesting interessant
introduce (sich) vorstellen, (miteinander) bekannt machen, einführen
introduction Einleitung, Einführung, Vorstellung
invitation Einladung
invite einladen
ironic ironisch
itself sich (selbst)

J

job Arbeit(sstelle), Aufgabe
join beitreten, verbinden
just einfach, nur, genau

K

keep (be)halten
key Schlüssel, Taste, Haupt-
kind freundlich; Art, Sorte
knife Messer
know kennen, wissen
knowledge Wissen, Kenntnis(se)

L

language Sprache
large groß
last dauern; letzte/r/s
late spät
later später
latest neueste/r/s
law Gesetz
lead führen
learn lernen, erfahren
least, at ~ wenigstens
leave lassen, verlassen, ab-/wegfahren
left links; übrig
length Länge
less weniger, abzüglich
let erlauben, (zu)lassen
letter Buchstabe, Brief
level Ebene, Niveau
lie Lüge; (be)lügen
life Leben
lift Fahrstuhl, Aufzug
light Licht, Leuchte; hell, leicht
like mögen; (ähnlich) wie
likely wahrscheinlich
line Linie, Leitung, Zeile
list Liste; auflisten, notieren
listen zuhören
little klein, wenig
live wohnen, leben
load laden
local örtlich, lokal
located gelegen, mit Sitz in
location (Stand-)Ort, Lage
log in/on einloggen
log off/out ausloggen
long lang
look Blick, Aussehen; (aus)sehen, blicken
look after sich kümmern um
look for suchen nach
look forward to sth sich auf etw freuen
lose verlieren
lots of / a lot of viel, viele
love Liebe; lieben, sehr gern mögen
lovely schön, hübsch, reizend
low niedrig
lunch Mittagessen

M

machine Gerät, Maschine
magazine Zeitschrift
main Haupt-, wichtigste/r/s
make machen
male männlich
manage leiten, verwalten, regeln, (es) schaffen
many viele
married verheiratet
match zuordnen, (zusammen) passen
maximum Maximum; maximal
may dürfen, können, mögen
maybe vielleicht
mean bedeuten, meinen, heißen
media Medien
medium mittlere; Medium, Mittel
meet (zusammen)treffen, begegnen
meeting Sitzung, Besprechung, Treffen
memory Gedächtnis, Speicher
message Meldung, Nachricht, Mitteilung, Botschaft
metal Metall
method Methode, Verfahren
middle Mitte
might könnte(n) (vielleicht)
minimum Minimum; minimal
miss verpassen, vermissen
missing fehlende/r/s
misspell falsch schreiben
mistake Fehler, Irrtum
mobile mobil
mobile (phone) Mobiltelefon, Handy
money Geld
month Monat
monthly monatlich
more mehr
morning Morgen
most der/die/das meiste, die meisten
mountain Berg
mouse Maus
move (sich) bewegen, umziehen
movement Bewegung
much viel
must müssen
myself selbst

N

name Name; nennen, benennen
national national, staatlich
nationality Staatsangehörigkeit
near in der Nähe von
nearly beinahe, fast
neatly ordentlich
necessary nötig, notwendig, erforderlich
need Bedarf, Bedürfnis; brauchen, benötigen
neither ... nor weder ... noch
never nie(mals)
new neu
news Neuigkeit(en), Nachricht(en)
next nächste/r/s; danach
night Nacht
normal(ly) normal(erweise)
north Norden
note Notiz; beachten, notieren
nothing nichts
now nun, jetzt
nowadays heutzutage
number Nummer, Zahl

O

object Gegenstand
obviously offensichtlich, selbstverständlich
of course natürlich, selbstverständlich
offer Angebot; anbieten, bieten
office Büro
often oft, häufig
old alt
once einmal, einst; sobald
only nur, einzig
open öffnen; offen, geöffnet
opinion Meinung, Ansicht
opposite Gegenteil; gegensätzlich, gegenüber
option Möglichkeit, Option
or oder
order bestellen
ordinary gewöhnlich, normal
organization Organisation

organize organisieren
original original, ursprünglich, Original(-)
other andere/r/s
otherwise sonst
our unser/e
outside außerhalb (von)
over über
own eigene/r/s; besitzen

P

page Seite
pain Schmerz
pair Paar
paper Papier, Zeitung
part Teil, Bauteil
particular besondere/r/s, spezielle/r/s
particularly insbesondere
passport Pass
password Passwort
path Weg, Pfad
pay Lohn, Bezahlung; zahlen, bezahlen
per cent Prozent
perfect vollkommen, perfekt
perfectly völlig
perhaps vielleicht, eventuell
period Zeit(raum)
personal persönlich
philosophy Philosophie
phone Telefon; anrufen
photo Foto
phrase Redewendung, Satz(teil)
picture Bild
piece Stück, Teil
place Stelle, Platz; setzen, stellen
plain einfach
plan Plan; planen
plastic Plastik, Kunststoff
pleasant angenehm, nett
plenty viel, reichlich
p.m. nachmittags
point Punkt; Komma
poor arm, schlecht, mangelhaft
popular beliebt, populär
position Stellung, Lage, Position
positive positiv, bejahend
possibility Möglichkeit
possible möglich
possibly möglicherweise
power Kraft, Strom; antreiben
powerful mächtig, stark
practical praktisch
practice Praxis, Training
practise (ein)üben
prefer vorziehen, bevorzugen, lieber mögen
preference Vorliebe
preparation Vorbereitung
prepare (sich) vorbereiten, zubereiten, erstellen
present Gegenwart; gegenwärtig; vorstellen, präsentieren
press drücken
previous vorherige/r/s, frühere/r/s
price Preis
primary school Grundschule
print Druck; drucken, ausdrucken
printer Drucker/in
printout (Computer-) Ausdruck
priority Vorrang
private privat, persönlich
probably wahrscheinlich
produce Produkt(e); produzieren, herstellen
product Produkt, Erzeugnis
production Produktion, Herstellung
promise versprechen
properly richtig
protect (be)schützen
protection Schutz
proud stolz
provide liefern, bieten
public öffentlich; Öffentlichkeit
publish veröffentlichen
push schieben, drücken
put setzen, stellen, legen

Q

quality Eigenschaft, Qualität
quarter past/to Viertel nach/vor
queen Königin
question Frage
quick(ly) schnell
quite ziemlich, ganz

R

rapid schnell, rasch
rarely selten
rather ziemlich, lieber
reach erreichen, greifen
read lesen
reader Leser/in, Lektüre
ready bereit, fertig
real echt, wirklich
really wirklich, eigentlich, tatsächlich
reason Vernunft, Grund
receive erhalten, empfangen, bekommen
recent aktuell, neu
recently neulich, kürzlich
recommend empfehlen
record Aufzeichnung, Beleg
regular(ly) regelmäßig
relation Verwandte/r, Verhältnis
relationship Beziehung, Verhältnis
relative Verwandte/r; relativ
relatively relativ, verhältnismäßig
remain (ver)bleiben
remember sich erinnern, daran denken
remove entfernen
repair reparieren
repeat wiederholen
replace ersetzen, austauschen
require benötigen, erfordern
reservation Reservierung, Buchung
reserve reservieren
respect Respekt, Achtung; (be)achten, respektieren
response Reaktion, Antwort
responsible verantwortlich, zuständig
restart neu starten
result Resultat, Ergebnis; folgen, resultieren
return zurückkehren, zurückgeben
rich reich
right rechts, richtig
risk Risiko; riskieren
road (Land-)Straße
role-play Rollenspiel
room Zimmer, Raum
round Runde; rund
rude unhöflich
rule Regel, Vorschrift
run betreiben, laufen (lassen)

S

sad traurig
safe(ly) sicher
sales Verkauf, Vertrieb, Umsatz
same gleiche/r/s, der-, die-, dasselbe

satisfied zufrieden
save retten, sichern
say sagen
school Schule
science Naturwissenschaft
score Ergebnis, Punkt(estand)
screen Bildschirm
search Suche; (durch)suchen
second zweite(r,s); Sekunde
secondary school weiterführende Schule
secondly zweitens
secretary Sekretär/in
see sehen, besuchen, verstehen
seem (er)scheinen
sell (sich) verkaufen
send senden, schicken
sentence Satz
serious ernst, ernsthaft
service Dienst, Dienstleistung, Service
set setzen, stellen
several etliche, einige, mehrere
shall sollen, werden
share teilen, gemeinsam (be)nutzen
shelf Regal
shop Laden, Geschäft; einkaufen
short kurz, klein, knapp
shorten kürzen
should solle/n, sollte/n
shoulder Schulter
show zeigen
shut schließen
side Seite
sign Zeichen, Anzeichen, Schild
similar ähnlich
simple einfach
since da, weil, seit
single einzig, einzeln
sit sitzen, sich hinsetzen
site Website
size Größe
skill Fähigkeit, Fertigkeit
slow langsam
small klein
so also, damit, deshalb, so
solution Lösung
some einige, etwas
someone jemand
something etwas
sometimes manchmal
somewhere irgendwo(hin)
soon bald
sorry traurig; Verzeihung
sound Klang, Geräusch; klingen, sich anhören
south Süden
space Raum, Platz, Abstand
speak sprechen, reden
special besondere/r/s
specially speziell, extra, besonders
speed Geschwindigkeit
spell buchstabieren, schreiben
spelling Rechtschreibung, Schreibweise
spend (Geld) ausgeben, (Zeit) verbringen
stand stehen, aushalten
standard Standard; normal, üblich
start Beginn; anfangen, starten
statement Aussage, Feststellung, Erklärung
stay Aufenthalt; bleiben
step Schritt, Stufe
still still, trotzdem, (immer) noch
stop (an)halten, aufhören (mit)
street Straße
strength Kraft, Stärke
strong stark, heftig
student Student/in, Lernende/r
study lernen, studieren, untersuchen, betrachten
stuff Material, Stoff
subject (Schul-)Fach, Thema
success Erfolg
successful erfolgreich
such as wie zum Beispiel
suggest vorschlagen, andeuten
suggestion Vorschlag
sure sicher
surname Nachname, Familienname
surprise Überraschung; überraschen

T

table Tisch, Tabelle
take nehmen, bringen, dauern
take off ausziehen, abnehmen, abheben
take part teilnehmen, mitmachen
talk Gespräch, Vortrag; sprechen, reden
task Aufgabe
tax Steuer
teach unterrichten, lehren
teacher Lehrer/in
team Mannschaft
technology Technik, Technologie
telephone (call) Telefon(anruf)
television Fernsehen, Fernseher
tell sagen, erzählen
test untersuchen, prüfen
than als
thank danken
thank you danke
thanks Dank; danke
their ihr/e
them ihnen, sie
themselves sich selbst
then dann
there da, dort(hin)
these diese
they sie
thin dünn
thing Sache, Ding, Gegenstand
think denken, meinen, finden, glauben
thorough(ly) gründlich
those jene
though obwohl
through durch
throughout überall (in), die ganze Zeit hindurch
throw werfen
ticket Karte, Fahrschein
tidy aufgeräumt, ordentlich; aufräumen
time Zeit, Mal
timetable Fahr-, Stundenplan
tiny winzig, klein
tip Hinweis, Tipp
today heute
together zusammen
tomorrow morgen
tonight heute Abend/Nacht
too zu, auch
tool Werkzeug
top Spitze, Gipfel; Spitzen-
topic Thema
total (Gesamt-)Summe; gesamte/r/s, Gesamt-
touch anfassen, berühren
town Stadt
traffic Verkehr

trainee Auszubildende/r, Praktikant/in
translate übersetzen
translation Übersetzung
travel Reisen; reisen, fahren
trip Ausflug, Reise, Besuch
trouble Mühe, Umstände, Problem(e)
true wahr, richtig
try versuchen, probieren
turn (sich) drehen, wenden, werden
twice zweimal
type Art, Sorte, Typ; tippen
typical typisch

U

unable unfähig
under unter
understand verstehen, begreifen
understanding Verständnis
unfortunately leider
unfriendly unfreundlich
university Universität
unless es sei denn, außer wenn
unlike anders als, im Gegensatz zu
until bis
urgent dringend, eilig
use Gebrauch; gebrauchen, benutzen, verwenden
useful nützlich
useless nutzlos, unbrauchbar
user Anwender/in, Benutzer/in
usual gewöhnlich, normal, üblich
usually gewöhnlich, normalerweise, meistens

V

vary variieren, schwanken
visit Besuch; besuchen, besichtigen
visitor Besucher/in, Gast
voice Stimme

W

wait warten
wall Wand, Mauer
want wollen
watch Armbanduhr
water Wasser
way Weg, Methode, Art (und Weise)
weather Wetter
week Woche
weekend Wochenende
weekly wöchentlich
welcome Willkommen; willkommen heißen
well gesund, gut; also
whatever was auch immer
when wenn, als, wann
whenever immer wenn
where wo(hin)
whether ob
which welche
while während
white weiß
who(m) wen, wem
whole ganz
why warum
wide breit, weit
wife (Ehe-)Frau
will Wille; werde(n), wollen
window Fenster
wish Wunsch; wünschen
with mit, bei
within innerhalb (von), in
without ohne
woman Frau
wonderful wunderbar
wood Holz
word Wort
work Arbeit; funktionieren, arbeiten
worker Arbeiter/in
workplace Arbeitsplatz
world Welt
worldwide weltweit
worried besorgt, beunruhigt
worse schlechter, schlimmer
worst schlechteste/r/s, schlimmste/r/s
would würde/n
write schreiben
wrong falsch

Y

year Jahr
yesterday gestern
young jung
your dein, Ihr, euer
Yours sincerely Mit freundlichen Grüßen
yourself du/Sie selbst, sich

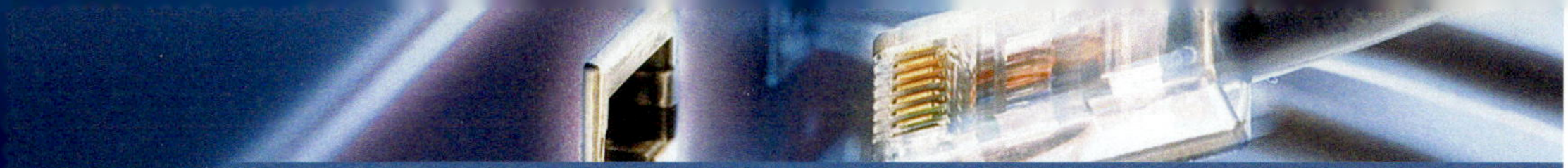

Chronological word list

Die neuen Wörter sind in der Reihenfolge ihres Vorkommens im Text verzeichnet. Hier sind jedoch die Wörter, die zum Grundwortschatz gehören, sowie internationale Wörter wie *software*, *hacker* und *virus* nicht aufgeführt.

P = das Wort befindet sich in den *Partner files*
T = das Wort befindet sich im *Transcript*

Unit 1

page 7

to **explore** [ɪk'splɔː]	erkunden, erforschen
company ['kʌmpəni]	Unternehmen
profile ['prəʊfaɪl]	Porträt, Profil
to **welcome sb** ['welkəm]	jdn begrüßen, jdn willkommen heißen
department [dɪ'pɑːtmənt]	Abteilung
to **discuss sth** [dɪ'skʌs]	über etw sprechen, etw erörtern
to **include** [ɪn'kluːd]	einschließen, einbeziehen, umfassen
to **design** [dɪ'zaɪn]	entwerfen, konstruieren, *(Software:)* entwickeln
to **assemble** [ə'sembl]	montieren, zusammenbauen
customer ['kʌstəmə]	Kunde/-in
mainly ['meɪnli]	hauptsächlich
commercial [kə'mɜːʃl]	geschäftlich, Geschäfts-
industrial [ɪn'dʌstriəl]	industriell, Industrie-
main [meɪn]	Haupt-
to **specialize in sth** ['speʃəlaɪz ɪn]	sich auf etw spezialisieren
specialist ['speʃəlɪst]	Spezialist/-in, Fachmann/-frau
designer [dɪ'zaɪnə]	*(Software:)* Entwickler/in
located [ləʊ'keɪtɪd]	gelegen

page 8

headquarters [ˌhed'kwɔːtəz]	Zentrale
revenue ['revənjuː]	Einkünfte, Einnahmen, Umsatz
to **generate** ['dʒenəreɪt]	*(Umsätze usw.)* erzielen
subsidiary [səb'sɪdiəri]	Niederlassung
including [ɪn'kluːdɪŋ]	einschließlich, inklusive
several ['sevrəl]	einige, mehrere
market ['mɑːkɪt]	Markt
employee [ɪm'plɔɪiː]	Beschäftigte/r, Angestellte/r
abroad [ə'brɔːd]	im Ausland
to **supply** [sə'plaɪ]	liefern, anbieten
network ['netwɜːk]	Netzwerk
access ['ækses]	Zugang
fixed [fɪkst]	Festnetz-
to **focus on sth** [ˌfəʊkəs 'ɒn]	sich auf etw konzentrieren
health care ['helθ keə]	Gesundheitswesen
automotive [ˌɔːtə'məʊtɪv]	Automobil-
to **determine**	bestimmen
principle ['prɪnsəpl]	Prinzip
to **provide sb with sth** [prə'vaɪd wɪð]	jdn mit etw versorgen, jdm etw bieten
grid [grɪd]	Gitter
explanation [ˌeksplə'neɪʃn]	Erklärung, Erläuterung
to **concentrate on sth** ['kɒnsntreɪt ɒn]	sich auf etw konzentrieren
annual ['ænjuəl]	jährlich, Jahres-
income ['ɪnkʌm]	Einkommen, Einkünfte
vehicle ['viːəkl]	Fahrzeug
motor vehicle [ˌməʊtə 'viːəkl]	Kraftfahrzeug
to **be concerned with sth** [bi kən'sɜːnd wɪð]	mit etw beschäftigt sein, mit etw zu tun haben
firmly ['fɜːmli]	fest, bestimmt

page 9

remaining [rɪ'meɪnɪŋ]	übrige/r/s
to **recruit** [rɪ'kruːt]	(Personal) einstellen
to **expand** [ɪk'spænd]	expandieren, sich vergrößern
rapidly ['ræpɪdli]	rasch, schnell
staff [stɑːf]	Personal
support [sə'pɔːt]	Unterstützung, Hilfe
to **develop** [dɪ'veləp]	entwickeln
value ['væljuː]	Wert
good value for money [gʊd ˌvæljuː fə 'mʌni]	günstige/preiswerte Produkte/Dienstleistungen
discount ['dɪskaʊnt]	Rabatt, Preisnachlass

page 10

reception [rɪ'sepʃn]	Empfang

receptionist [rɪ'sepʃənɪst]	Empfangsmitarbeiter/in
stay [steɪ]	Aufenthalt
placement ['pleɪsmənt]	Praktikum *T*
especially [ɪ'speʃəli]	besonders *T*
to **mind** [maɪnd]	etw dagegenhaben *T*
Pleased to meet you. [ˌpli:zd tə 'mi:t ju]	Nett, Sie kennen zu lernen. *T*
to **leave sb with sb** ['li:v wɪð]	jdn mit jdm allein lassen *T*

page 11

order ['ɔ:də]	Reihenfolge
to **identify** [aɪ'dentɪfaɪ]	herausfinden, feststellen, nennen
radio station ['reɪdiəʊ steɪʃn]	Radiosender
findings ['faɪndɪŋz]	Ergebnisse
tour [tʊə]	Rundgang
intern ['ɪntɜ:n]	Praktikant/in
timetable ['taɪmteɪbl]	Zeitplan, Stundenplan

page 12

guide [gaɪd]	(Reise-)Führer/in
to **show sb around** [ˌʃəʊ ə'raʊnd]	jdn herumführen
to divide [dɪ'vaɪd]	teilen, aufteilen
order ['ɔ:də]	Auftrag, Bestellung
order processing [ˌɔ:də 'prəʊsesɪŋ]	Auftragsbearbeitung
customer service [ˌkʌstəmə 'sɜ:vɪs]	Kundendienst
responsible [rɪ'spɒnsəbl]	verantwortlich, zuständig
to arrange [ə'reɪndʒ]	arrangieren, *(Termin)* ausmachen
promotional [prə'məʊʃənl]	Werbe-
tour [tʊə]	Reise, Tour
presence ['prezns]	Präsenz, Anwesenheit
trade fair ['treɪd feə]	(Handels-)Messe
to **place (an order)** [ˌpleɪs ən 'ɔ:də]	(einen Auftrag) erteilen
to **label** ['leɪbl]	etikettieren
to **pack** [pæk]	packen, verpacken
to **ship** [ʃɪp]	versenden
to **deal with sth** ['di:l wɪð]	etw bearbeiten, sich mit etw befassen, mit etw zu tun haben
complaint [kəm'pleɪnt]	Reklamation, Beschwerde
request [rɪ'kwest]	Bitte, Wunsch, Anfrage
canteen [kæn'ti:n]	Kantine
research [rɪ'sɜ:tʃ]	Forschung
development [dɪ'veləpmənt]	Entwicklung
to **demonstrate** ['demənstreɪt]	vorführen
latest ['leɪtɪst]	neueste/r/s
innovative ['ɪnəveɪtɪv]	innovativ
application	Anwendung
day-to-day [ˌdeɪ tə 'deɪ]	Alltags-
currently ['kʌrəntli]	gegenwärtig, im Moment
household ['haʊshəʊld]	Haushalt
result [rɪ'zʌlt]	Ergebnis, Resultat
to **benefit sb** ['benɪfɪt]	jdm zugute kommen, jdm nützen
session ['seʃn]	Runde, Sitzung
I'm afraid [aɪm ə'freɪd]	leider
full-colour [ˌfʊl 'kʌlə]	Farb-
brochure ['brəʊʃə]	Prospekt, Broschüre
to **mention** ['menʃn]	erwähnen
human resources (HR) [ˌhju:mən rɪ'sɔ:sɪz]	Personal(abteilung)
finance ['faɪnæns]	Finanzabteilung

page 13

creative [kri'eɪtɪv]	kreativ
to **promote sth** [prə'məʊt]	für etw Werbung machen
contest ['kɒntest]	Wettbewerb
experiment [ɪk'sperɪmənt]	Versuch, Experiment
details ['di:teɪlz]	Angaben, Einzelheiten
to **make sure** [ˌmeɪk 'ʃʊə]	sicherstellen, gewährleisten, sich vergewissern
on time [ɒn 'taɪm]	pünktlich
responsibility [rɪˌspɒnsə'bɪləti]	Zuständigkeit, Aufgabenbereich
duties ['dju:tiz]	Aufgaben
work pattern ['wɜ:k pætn]	Arbeitsablauf
workshop ['wɜ:kʃɒp]	Werkstatt
on site [ɒn 'saɪt]	vor Ort
supplier [sə'plaɪə]	Lieferant/in
device [dɪ'vaɪs]	Gerät
to **be on call** [bi ˌɒn 'kɔ:l]	Bereitschaftsdienst haben
administration [ədˌmɪnɪ'streɪʃn]	Verwaltung
to **advise sb** [əd'vaɪz]	jdn beraten
fixed hours [ˌfɪkst 'aʊəz]	feste Arbeitszeiten
shift [ʃɪft]	Schicht
flexitime ['fleksitaɪm]	Gleitzeit
to **be in charge of sth** [bi ɪn 'tʃɑ:dʒ əv]	etw leiten, für etw verantwortlich sein
overtime ['əʊvətaɪm]	Überstunden
training ['treɪnɪŋ]	Schulung, Ausbildung
to **take care of sb** [ˌteɪk 'keər əv]	sich um jdn kümmern

page 14

role [rəʊl]	Rolle
to **vary** ['veəri]	unterschiedlich sein

depending on [dɪ'pendɪŋ ɒn]	je nach, abhängig von
specific [spə'sɪfɪk]	konkret, speziell, bestimmt
environment [ɪn'vaɪrənmənt]	Umfeld
to **maintain** [meɪn'teɪn]	betreuen, instandhalten, warten
to **troubleshoot** ['trʌblʃu:t]	Fehler suchen/beheben
related [rɪ'leɪtɪd]	bezogen (auf)
issue ['ɪʃu:]	Frage, Problem
in recent years [ɪn 'ri:snt jɪəz]	in den letzten Jahren
to **broaden** ['brɔ:dn]	sich erweitern
security [sɪ'kjʊərəti]	Sicherheit
to **monitor** ['mɒnɪtə]	überwachen
peripheral [pə'rɪfərəl]	Peripheriegerät
removable [rɪ'mu:vəbl]	austauschbar, Wechsel-
storage ['stɔ:rɪdʒ]	*(Daten:)* Speicherung
to **diagnose** ['daɪəgnəʊz]	analysieren, diagnostizieren
fault [fɔ:lt]	Fehler, Defekt
to **provide sth** [prə'vaɪd]	etw (an)bieten, liefern
advice [əd'vaɪs]	Rat, Beratung
to **solve** [sɒlv]	lösen
in person [ɪn 'pɜ:sn]	persönlich
organization chart [ˌɔ:gənaɪ'zeɪʃn tʃɑ:t]	Organigramm
CEO (Chief Executive Officer) [ˌsi: i: 'əʊ / ˌtʃi:f ɪg'zekjətɪv ɒfɪsə]	Vorstandsvorsitzende/r, Geschäftsführer/in
CTO (Chief Technology Officer) [ˌsi: ti: 'əʊ / ˌtʃi:f tek'nɒlədʒi ɒfɪsə]	Technische/r Leiter/in
IT Operations Manager [aɪ ti: ɒpəˌreɪʃnz 'mænɪdʒə]	IT-Betriebsleiter/in
brief [bri:f]	kurz, knapp *T*
insight ['ɪnsaɪt]	Einblick *T*
title ['taɪtl]	Titel, Bezeichnung *T*
to **oversee** [ˌəʊvə'si:]	beaufsichtigen, überwachen *T*
branch [brɑ:ntʃ]	Zweig, Sparte *T*
goal [gəʊl]	Ziel *T*
to **report to sb** [rɪ'pɔ:t tə]	jdm unterstellt sein *T*
CIO (Chief Information Officer) [ˌsi: aɪ 'əʊ / ˌtʃi:f ɪnfə'meɪʃn ɒfɪsə]	IT-Leiter/in, Leitende/r Referent/in für Information *T*
direction [də'rekʃn]	Ausrichtung *T*
leader ['li:də]	Führungspersönlichkeit *T*
to **be glad** [bi 'glæd]	sich freuen *T*
data processing [ˌdeɪtə 'prəʊsesɪŋ]	Datenverarbeitung *T*
in broad terms [ɪn ˌbrɔ:d 'tɜ:mz]	im weitesten Sinn, im Allgemeinen *T*
in-depth [ˌɪn 'depθ]	gründlich *T*
understanding [ˌʌndə'stændɪŋ]	Verständnis, Kenntnisse *T*
front line manager [frʌnt ˌlaɪn 'mænɪdʒə]	leitende/r Angestellte/r *T*
quality assurance (QA) ['kwɒləti əʃʊərəns / kju: 'eɪ]	Qualitätssicherung *T*
executive level [ɪg'zekjətɪv levl]	Vorstandsebene *T*
talk [tɔ:k]	Vortrag *T*
to **have a close look** [həv ə ˌkləʊs 'lʊk]	sich etwas genau anschauen *T*

page 15

position [pə'zɪʃn]	Stellung, Position
to **swap** [swɒp]	tauschen
to **take place** [teɪk 'pleɪs]	stattfinden
to **draw** [drɔ:]	zeichnen
to **explain** [ɪk'spleɪn]	erklären, erläutern

page 16

to **abbreviate** [ə'bri:vieɪt]	abkürzen
to **nickname** ['nɪkneɪm]	(mit einem Spitznamen) nennen
corporate ['kɔ:pərət]	Unternehmens-
consulting [kən'sʌltɪŋ]	Beratung
continuous [kən'tɪnjuəs]	kontinuierlich, ununterbrochen
to **date back to** [ˌdeɪt 'bæk tə]	zurückgehen in
century ['sentʃəri]	Jahrhundert
to **manufacture** [ˌmænju'fæktʃə]	herstellen
to **range from ... to ...** ['reɪndʒ frəm tə]	sich von ... bis ... erstrecken
mainframe computer [ˌmeɪnfreɪm kəm'pju:tə]	Großrechner
employer [ɪm'plɔɪə]	Arbeitgeber/in
despite [dɪ'spaɪt]	trotz
total revenue [ˌtəʊtl 'revənju:]	Gesamterlös, Gesamtumsatz
profitable ['prɒfɪtəbl]	profitabel
patent ['peɪtnt, 'pætnt]	Patent
...-based [beɪst]	mit Sitz in ...
engineer [ˌendʒɪ'nɪə]	Ingenieur/in
consultant [kən'sʌltənt]	Berater/in
laboratory [lə'bɒrətri]	(Forschungs-)Labor
to **earn** [ɜ:n]	gewinnen
Nobel Prize [nəʊˌbel 'praɪz]	Nobelpreis
medal ['medl]	Orden, Medaille
maker ['meɪkə]	Hersteller/in

semiconductor [ˌsemikən'dʌktə]	Halbleiter
sales [seɪlz]	Verkauf, Vertrieb
to **pioneer** [ˌpaɪə'nɪə]	entwickeln, zum ersten Mal einsetzen
operating model ['ɒpəreɪtɪŋ mɒdl]	Betriebs-/ Geschäftsmodell
parent company [ˌpeərənt 'kʌmpəni]	Muttergesellschaft
to **replicate** ['replɪkeɪt]	nachbilden, reproduzieren
set [set]	Reihe, Satz, Menge, Klasse
process ['prəʊses]	Ablauf, Vorgang, Prozess
shared [ʃeəd]	gemeinsam genutzt
broad [brɔːd]	weit
to **distribute** [dɪ'strɪbjuːt]	verteilen, verbreiten, streuen
to **carry sth out** [ˌkæri 'aʊt]	etw durch-/ ausführen
highly skilled [ˌhaɪli 'skɪld]	hochqualifiziert
workforce ['wɜːkfɔːs]	Belegschaft, Personal
common ['kɒmən]	gemeinsam
shift [ʃɪft]	Schritt, Veränderung
integrated ['ɪntɪgreɪtɪd]	integriert
to **allow** [ə'laʊ]	gestatten, erlauben
to **refocus** [ˌriː'fəʊkəs]	sich neu konzentrieren
growth [grəʊθ]	Wachstum
to **serve sb** [sɜːv]	jdn bedienen, jdm dienen
client ['klaɪənt]	Kunde/-in
statement ['steɪtmənt]	Aussage, Behauptung
pioneer [ˌpaɪə'nɪə]	Pionier

Unit 2

page 17

to **summarize** ['sʌməraɪz]	zusammenfassen
column ['kɒləm]	*(Text:)* Spalte
pros and cons [ˌprəʊz ən 'kɒnz]	Für und Wider, Vor- und Nachteile
upgrade ['ʌpgreɪd]	Aktualisierung
satisfying ['sætɪsfaɪɪŋ]	befriedigend
to **recommend** [ˌrekə'mend]	empfehlen
pre-built [ˌpriː'bɪlt]	vorgefertigt

page 18

component [kəm'pəʊnənt]	Bauteil, Komponente
housing ['haʊzɪŋ]	Gehäuse
power supply unit ['paʊə səplaɪ juːnɪt]	Netzteil
memory ['meməri]	Arbeitsspeicher
drive [draɪv]	Laufwerk
hard drive [ˌhɑːd 'draɪv]	Festplatte
to **wonder** ['wʌndə]	sich fragen *T*
I was wondering if you ... [aɪ wəz 'wʌndərɪŋ ɪf juː]	Könnten Sie bitte ... *T*
word processing ['wɜːd prəʊsesɪŋ]	Textverarbeitung *T*
to **store** [stɔː]	*(Daten)* speichern *T*
mostly ['məʊstli]	hauptsächlich *T*
pretty ['prɪti]	ziemlich *T*
to **handle sth** ['hændl]	mit etw zurechtkommen *T*
occasionally [ə'keɪʒənəli]	gelegentlich *T*
powerful ['paʊəfl]	stark, leistungsfähig *T*
to **stick with sth** ['stɪk wɪð]	bei etw bleiben *T*
to **invest** [ɪn'vest]	investieren *T*
to **compromise on sth** ['kɒmprəmaɪz ɒn]	bei etw Kompromisse eingehen *T*
key [kiː]	Haupt- *T*
to **cut down on sth** [ˌkʌt 'daʊn ɒn]	etw bremsen, etw einschränken *T*
performance [pə'fɔːməns]	Leistung *T*
capable ['keɪpəbl]	fähig *T*
to **eat into sth** ['iːt ɪntə]	etw schmälern *T*
budget ['bʌdʒɪt]	Etat, Budget *T*
package ['pækɪdʒ]	(Software-)Paket *T*
core [kɔː]	Kern *T*
stable ['steɪbl]	stabil *T*
to **let sb down** [ˌlet 'daʊn]	jdn im Stich lassen *T*
energy saving ['enədʒi seɪvɪŋ]	energiesparend *T*
to **go for sth** ['gəʊ fə]	etw nehmen *T*
capability [ˌkeɪpə'bɪləti]	Fähigkeit *T*
to **save** [seɪv]	*(Daten)* sichern *T*
salesperson ['seɪlzpɜːsn]	Verkäufer/in

page 19

to express [ɪk'spres]	ausdrücken

page 21

screwdriver ['skruːdraɪvə]	Schraubendreher, -zieher
Phillips screwdriver [ˌfɪlɪps 'skruːdraɪvə]	Kreuzschlitz-schraubendreher
flat-head screwdriver [ˌflæt hed 'skruːdraɪvə]	Flachkopf-schraubendreher
pliers ['plaɪəz]	Zange
extreme(ly) [ɪk'striːmli]	äußerst
delicate ['delɪkət]	empfindlich
to **handle** ['hændl]	handhaben, behandeln, anfassen
with care [wɪð 'keə]	vorsichtig

edge [edʒ]	Ecke, Kante, Rand
to avoid [ə'vɔɪd]	vermeiden
damage ['dæmɪdʒ]	Beschädigung, Schaden
to beware of sth [bɪ'weər əv]	sich vor etw in Acht nehmen
sharp [ʃɑːp]	scharf
case [keɪs]	Gehäuse
solder pin ['səʊldə pɪn]	Lötstift
harmless ['hɑːmləs]	harmlos
knife [naɪf]	Messer
cut [kʌt]	Schnitt, Schnitt-verletzung
cable ['keɪbl]	Kabel
connector [kə'nektə]	Steckverbindung, Stecker, Buchse
generally ['dʒenrəli]	im Allgemeinen
alignment system [ə'laɪnmənt sɪstəm]	Ausrichtungssystem
to prevent [prɪ'vent]	verhindern
incorrect [ˌɪnkə'rekt]	falsch
connection [kə'nekʃn]	Verbindung
to line up [ˌlaɪn 'ʌp]	ausrichten
firm [fɜːm]	fest
even ['iːvn]	gleichmäßig
pressure ['preʃə]	Druck
excessive [ɪk'sesɪv]	zu viel
force [fɔːs]	Kraft, Gewalt
sensitive ['sensətɪv]	empfindlich
signal pin ['sɪgnəl pɪn]	Kontaktstift
dust [dʌst]	Staub
to attempt [ə'tempt]	versuchen
liquid ['lɪkwɪd]	flüssig
detergent [dɪ'tɜːdʒənt]	Reinigungsmittel
cloth [klɒθ]	Tuch
can [kæn]	Dose
compressed air [kəm'prest eə]	Pressluft

page 22

meaning ['miːnɪŋ]	Bedeutung
expression [ɪk'spreʃn]	Ausdruck
to alter ['ɔːltə]	(ab)ändern
to dismantle [dɪs'mæntl]	ausbauen, demontieren
to remove [rɪ'muːv]	entfernen
power ['paʊə]	Strom
to turn sth on [ˌtɜːn 'ɒn]	etw einschalten
power supply ['pauə səplaɪ]	Stromversorgung
to disconnect [ˌdɪskə'nekt]	trennen, ausschalten
mains [meɪnz]	(Strom-)Netz
to switch sth on [ˌswɪtʃ 'ɒn]	etw einschalten
voltag e ['vəʊltɪdʒ]	(elektrische) Spannung
to connect [kə'nekt]	verbinden
static ['stætɪk]	elektrostatische Ladung
wrist band ['rɪst bænd]	Armband
carpeted ['kɑːpɪtɪd]	mit Teppichboden
clothing ['kləʊðɪŋ]	Kleidung
to create [kri'eɪt]	erzeugen
further ['fɜːðə]	weitere/r/s

page 23

to skim read ['skɪm riːd]	querlesen, überfliegen
to scan [skæn]	überfliegen
to highlight ['haɪlaɪt]	hervorheben

page 24

to lower ['ləʊə]	absenken, einlassen, schieben
socket ['sɒkɪt]	Fassung, Sockel
to lift [lɪft]	anheben
retention arm [rɪ'tenʃn ɑːm]	Haltearm
to compare [kəm'peə]	vergleichen
layout ['leɪaʊt]	Anordnung
to fit [fɪt]	passen
to align [ə'laɪn]	ausrichten
to insert [ɪn'sɜːt]	einstecken
at an angle [ət ən 'æŋgl]	verkantet
to bend [bend]	verbiegen
to lock [lɒk]	einrasten lassen
lever ['liːvə]	Hebel
to secure [sɪ'kjuə]	sichern
to place [pleɪs]	legen
surface ['sɜːfɪs]	Oberfläche
to protect [prə'tekt]	schützen
retention clip [rɪ'tenʃn klɪp]	Halteklammer
notch [nɒtʃ]	Kerbe, Nut
slot [slɒt]	Steckplatz
to apply [ə'plaɪ]	anwenden, ausüben
to slide [slaɪd]	schieben
to mount [maʊnt]	montieren, einbauen
step [step]	Schritt
port [pɔːt]	Anschluss
to disassemble [ˌdɪsə'sembl]	wieder ausein-anderbauen
to fix (a problem) [ˌfɪks ə 'prɒbləm]	(ein Problem) beheben
to fold [fəʊld]	biegen, falten
hole [həʊl]	Loch
backplane ['bækpleɪn]	Rückwandplatine
standoff ['stændɒf]	Abstandsbolzen
mounting hole ['maʊntɪŋ həʊl]	Montage-, Befestigungsloch
to screw [skruː]	schrauben
to tighten ['taɪtn]	*(Schraube)* anziehen
to over-tighten [ˌəʊvə'taɪtn]	*(Schraube)* zu fest anziehen
fan [fæn]	Ventilator

lead [li:d]	Leitung, Kabel
excess ['ekses]	überschüssig, zu viel(e)

page **26**

electric shock [ɪˌlektrɪk 'ʃɒk]	Stromschlag
threat [θret]	Bedrohung
technician [tek'nɪʃn]	Techniker/in
crucial ['kru:ʃl]	äußerst wichtig, unerlässlich, entscheidend
to **suffer sth** ['sʌfə]	etw erleiden
to **treat** [tri:t]	behandeln
emergency [ɪ'mɜ:dʒənsi]	Notfall
to **occur** [ə'kɜ:]	auftreten
heart failure ['hɑ:t feɪljə]	Herzversagen
burn [bɜ:n]	Verbrennung
heart rhythm problems ['hɑ:t rɪðəm prɒbləmz]	Herzrhythmusstörungen
respiratory failure [reˌspɪrətri 'feɪljə]	Atemstillstand
muscle ['mʌsl]	Muskel
pain [peɪn]	Schmerz(en)
cramp [kræmp]	Krampf
unconsciousness [ʌn'kɒnʃəsnəs]	Bewusstlosigkeit
medical ['medɪkl]	medizinisch
colleague ['kɒli:g]	Kollege/-in
source [sɔ:s]	Quelle
electrical source [ɪˌlektrɪkl 'sɔ:s]	Stromquelle
current ['kʌrənt]	Strom
to **pass through** ['pɑ:s θru:]	hindurchgehen, -fließen
to **turn sth off** [ˌtɜ:n 'ɒf]	etw ausschalten
non-conducting [ˌnɒn kən'dʌktɪŋ]	nicht leitend
cardboard ['kɑ:dbɔ:d]	Pappe
circulation [ˌsɜ:kjə'leɪʃn]	Kreislauf
breathing ['bri:ðɪŋ]	Atmung, Atmen
coughing ['kɒfɪŋ]	Husten
movement ['mu:vmənt]	Bewegung
absent ['æbsənt]	nicht vorhanden
cardiopulmonary resuscitation [kɑ:diəʊ ˌpʌlmənəri ˌrɪsʌsɪ'teiʃn]	Herz-Lungen-Wiederbelebung
to **position** [pə'zɪʃn]	platzieren
slightly ['slaɪtli]	etwas, geringfügig, ein wenig
to **raise** [reɪz]	erhöhen
immediate [ɪ'mi:diət]	unmittelbar
blanket ['blæŋkɪt]	Decke
to **appear** [ə'pɪə]	scheinen
to **beat** [bi:t]	schlagen
first aid [ˌfɜ:st 'eɪd]	Erste Hilfe
instructions [ɪn'strʌkʃnz]	Anweisungen

Unit 3

page **27**

relation [rɪ'leɪʃn]	Beziehung
helpline ['helplaɪn]	Hotline
careful(ly) ['keəfəli]	sorgfältig, gut

page **28**

to **set sth up** [ˌset 'ʌp]	etw einrichten
to **be based in** [bi 'beɪst ɪn]	seinen Sitz haben in
requirement [rɪ'kwaɪəmənt]	Bedürfnis, Anforderung
head [hed]	Chef/in, Leiter/in
to **hold** [həʊld]	*(Telefon:)* am Apparat bleiben
to **put sb through** [ˌpʊt 'θru:]	*(Telefon:)* jdn durchstellen
extension [ɪk'stenʃn]	*(Telefon:)* Anschluss, Durchwahl
busy ['bɪzi]	*(Telefon:)* besetzt
surname ['sɜ:neɪm]	Nachname
country code ['kʌntri kəʊd]	Ländervorwahl
to **return a call** [rɪˌtɜ:n ə 'kɔ:l]	zurückrufen
pleasure ['pleʒə]	Vergnügen
My pleasure. [maɪ 'pleʒə]	Gern geschehen.

page **29**

equivalent [ɪ'kwɪvələnt]	Entsprechung
caller ['kɔ:lə]	Anrufer/in
to **take action** [ˌteɪk 'ækʃn]	Maßnahmen ergreifen
to **be available** [bi ə'veɪləbl]	*(Telefon:)* zu sprechen sein

page **30**

interior decorator [ɪnˌtɪəriə 'dekəreɪtə]	Innenarchitekt/in, Raumausstatter/in
advertising agency ['ædvətaɪzɪŋ eɪdʒənsi]	Werbeagentur
to **be busy** [bi 'bɪzi]	viel zu tun haben
to **be convenient** [bi kən'vi:niənt]	passen, günstig sein
space [speɪs]	(freier) Platz *T*
to **interview sb** ['ɪntəvju:]	mit jdm ein Vorstellungsgespräch führen *T*
to **sort** [sɔ:t]	sortieren
to **suggest** [sə'dʒest]	vorschlagen
to **reject** [rɪ'dʒekt]	ablehnen
suggestion [sə'dʒestʃən]	Vorschlag
to **accept** [ək'sept]	annehmen, akzeptieren

page 31

to **define** [dɪ'faɪn]	definieren
to **require** [rɪ'kwaɪə]	benötigen, erfordern
to **work sth out** [ˌwɜːk 'aʊt]	etw herausfinden
first name ['fɜːst neɪm]	Vorname *T*
by trade [baɪ 'treɪd]	gelernt, von Beruf *T*
tight [taɪt]	knapp *T*
to **begin with** [tə bɪ'gɪn wɪð]	zunächst (einmal) *T*
administrative staff [ədˌmɪnɪstrətɪv 'stɑːf]	Verwaltungspersonal *T*
advert(isement) ['ædvɜːt/ əd'vɜːtɪsmənt]	Anzeige, Werbespot *T*
feature ['fiːtʃə]	Merkmal, Eigenschaft, Besonderheit *T*
to **elaborate** [ɪ'læbəreɪt]	ins Detail gehen, näher ausführen *T*
speed [spiːd]	Geschwindigkeit *T*
to **upgrade** [ˌʌp'greɪd]	aufrüsten *T*
customized ['kʌstəmaɪzd]	individuell angepasst *T*
to **cut costs** [kʌt 'kɒsts]	Kosten senken *T*
range [reɪndʒ]	Produktlinie, Angebot *T*
to **draw sth up** [ˌdrɔː 'ʌp]	etw ausarbeiten, aufstellen *T*
specification [ˌspesɪfɪ'keɪʃn]	technische Daten/ Anforderungen *T*
to **pass sth on** [ˌpɑːs 'ɒn]	etw weiterreichen/ -leiten *T*

page 32

business trip ['bɪznəs trɪp]	Geschäftsreise
entry ['entri]	Eintrag
contractor [kən'træktə]	Dienstleister, beauftragte Firma
dentist ['dentɪst]	Zahnarzt/-ärztin
interview ['ɪntəvjuː]	Vorstellungsgespräch
current ['kʌrənt]	aktuell, laufend
need [niːd]	Bedarf
leaving party ['liːvɪŋ pɑːti]	Abschiedsparty

page 34

in terms of [ɪn 'tɜːmz əv]	was ... anbelangt
to **waste** [weɪst]	vergeuden, verschwenden
solution [sə'luːʃn]	Lösung
to **make sense** [meɪk 'sens]	sinnvoll sein
set-up ['setʌp]	System
to **afford sth** [ə'fɔːd]	sich etw leisten (können)
to **benefit** ['benɪfɪt]	profitieren
experience [ɪk'spɪəriəns]	Erfahrung
honest ['ɒnɪst]	ehrlich
whether ['weðə]	ob
to **meet sb's needs** [ˌmiːt sʌmbədiz 'niːdz]	jds Bedürfnissen entsprechen
schedule ['ʃedjuːl]	(Zeit-)Plan
to **suit** [suːt]	passen
to **continue to do sth** [kən'tɪnjuː]	etw weiter(hin) tun
in progress [ɪn 'prəʊgres]	im Gang
down-time ['daʊntaɪm]	Ausfallzeit, Stillstand
award [ə'wɔːd]	Preis, Auszeichung
award-winning [ə'wɔːd wɪnɪŋ]	preisgekrönt
after-sales service ['ɑːftəseɪlz sɜːvɪs]	Kundendienst
efficient(ly) [ɪ'fɪʃntli]	effizient
to **sort sth out** [ˌsɔːt 'aʊt]	etw klären, in Ordnung bringen
certain ['sɜːtn]	bestimmt
suitable ['suːtəbl]	passend, geeignet

page 35

unified ['juːnɪfaɪd]	einheitlich
to **report** [rɪ'pɔːt]	berichten
to **acquire** [ə'kwaɪə]	akquirieren
to **hold onto sb** [ˌhəʊld 'ɒntə]	jdn festhalten, *hier:* binden
complicated ['kɒmplɪkeɪtɪd]	kompliziert
direction [də'rekʃn]	Richtung
to **introduce** [ˌɪntrə'djuːs]	einführen
relationship [rɪ'leɪʃnʃɪp]	Beziehung
to **maintain** [meɪn'teɪn]	aufrechterhalten
flow [fləʊ]	Fluss
to **respond** [rɪ'spɒnd]	reagieren
swift(ly) ['swɪftli]	schnell
according to [ə'kɔːdɪŋ tə]	nach, zufolge, gemäß
to **realize sth** ['rɪəlaɪz]	etw begreifen, sich einer Sache bewusst werden
constant(ly) ['kɒnstəntli]	ständig, dauernd
to **fight** [faɪt]	kämpfen
to **put** [pʊt]	formulieren, sagen
to **collect** [kə'lekt]	sammeln, zusammentragen
to **feed sth back** [ˌfiːd 'bæk]	etw zurückführen, rückmelden
to **analyze** ['ænəlaɪz]	analysieren
to **monitor** ['mɒnɪtə]	dokumentieren
preference ['prefrəns]	Vorliebe, Wunsch

appropriate [ə'prəʊpriət]	entsprechend, passend
for instance [fə'rɪnstəns]	zum Beispiel
to **emphasize** ['emfəsaɪz]	betonen
to **target sb** ['tɑːɡɪt]	jdn als Zielgruppe ins Visier nehmen
customer lead ['kʌstəmə liːd]	Kundenkontakt, Kundendaten
sales force ['seɪlz fɔːs]	Vertriebspersonal
in the long run [ɪn ðə lɒŋ 'rʌn]	auf lange Sicht
to **select** [sɪ'lekt]	auswählen
to **purchase** ['pɜːtʃəs]	kaufen
to **implement** ['ɪmplɪmənt]	einführen, umsetzen
to **be paid handsomely for sth** [bi ˌpeɪd 'hænsəmli fə]	sich etw gut bezahlen lassen
to **support** [sə'pɔːt]	unterstützen, helfen
to **deploy** [dɪ'plɔɪ]	nutzen, einsetzen

page **36**

headline ['hedlaɪn]	Überschrift
comprehension [ˌkɒmprɪ'henʃn]	Verständnis, Verstehen

Unit 4

page **37**

to **customize** ['kʌstəmaɪz]	individuell anpassen
error ['erə]	Fehler
database ['deɪtəbeɪs]	Datenbank
encryption [ɪn'krɪpʃn]	Verschlüsselung
editor ['edɪtə]	Bearbeitungsprogramm
spreadsheet ['spredʃiːt]	Tabellenkalkulationsprogramm
word processor ['wɜːd prəʊsesə]	Textverarbeitungsprogramm
confidential [ˌkɒnfɪ'denʃl]	vertraulich
calculation [ˌkælkju'leɪʃn]	Berechnung
research [rɪ'sɜːtʃ]	Nachforschung(en), Recherche

page **38**

stage [steɪdʒ]	Phase, Abschnitt
to **review** [rɪ'vjuː]	überprüfen, bewerten
to **log on** [ˌlɒɡ 'ɒn]	sich einloggen
straightforward [ˌstreɪt'fɔːwəd]	einfach *T*
instructions [ɪn'strʌkʃnz]	Anleitung *T*
procedure [prə'siːdʒə]	Verfahren, Vorgehen *T*
to **consider** [kən'sɪdə]	in Erwägung ziehen
to **enable sb to do sth** [ɪ'neɪbl tə duː]	jdm ermöglichen, etw zu tun, jdn in die Lage versetzen, etw zu tun
to **pause sth** [pɔːz]	etw anhalten
to **resume sth** [rɪ'zjuːm]	etw wiederaufnehmen
deletion [dɪ'liːʃn]	Löschung *(von Daten)*
temporary ['temprəri]	provisorisch, vorübergehend
approximately [ə'prɒksɪmətli]	ungefähr, zirka
to **launch** [lɔːntʃ]	starten
mirror ['mɪrə]	Spiegelserver
close to ['kləʊs tə]	nahe bei
to **display** [dɪ'spleɪ]	*(auf dem Bildschirm)* anzeigen
to **note** [nəʊt]	darauf hinweisen
to **continue** [kən'tɪnjuː]	fortfahren
to **perform** [pə'fɔːm]	*(Tätigkeit)* ausführen

page **39**

to **confirm** [kən'fɜːm]	bestätigen
to **agree** [ə'ɡriː]	zustimmen
terms and conditions [ˌtɜːmz ən kən'dɪʃnz]	(Nutzungs-)Bedingungen
progress bar ['prəʊɡres bɑː]	Ladebalken, Fortschrittsbalken

page **40**

to **navigate** ['nævɪɡeɪt]	navigieren
to **enter** ['entə]	(Daten) eingeben
folder ['fəʊldə]	Ordner
wizard ['wɪzəd]	Zauberer, Hexenmeister
prompt [prɒmpt]	Aufforderung
licence ['laɪsns]	Lizenz
licence agreement ['laɪsns əɡriːmənt]	Lizenzvereinbarung
condition [kən'dɪʃn]	Bedingung
type [taɪp]	Schrift, Type
default [dɪ'fɔːlt]	Standard
to **deselect** [ˌdiːsɪ'lekt]	deaktivieren
tick [tɪk]	Häkchen
to **view** [vjuː]	ansehen
to **edit** ['edɪt]	bearbeiten
to **change one's mind** [ˌtʃeɪndʒ wʌnz 'maɪnd]	seine Meinung ändern
tedious ['tiːdiəs]	lästig, mühsam
to **reassociate** [ˌriːə'səʊʃiət]	erneut zuweisen
once [wʌns]	sobald
progress ['prəʊɡres]	Fortgang
effort ['efət]	Mühe, Anstregung
on one's part [ˌɒn wʌnz 'pɑːt]	von jds Seite

page 41

to encounter [ɪn'kaʊntə]	begegnen
setting ['setɪŋ]	Einstellung
to stick to sth ['stɪk tə]	an etw festhalten, bei etw bleiben *T*
major ['meɪdʒə]	groß *T*
basically ['beɪsɪkli]	grundsätzlich *T*
to recognize ['rekəgnaɪz]	erkennen *T*
to modify ['mɒdɪfaɪ]	modifizieren *T*
button ['bʌtn]	Knopf *T*

page 42

to uninstall [ˌʌnɪn'stɔːl]	deinstallieren
to corrupt [kə'rʌpt]	beschädigen
pirate ['paɪrət]	Pirat
to freeze [friːz]	erstarren, stehenbleiben
to be due to sth [bi 'djuː tə]	an etw liegen

page 43

to research [rɪ'sɜːtʃ]	Nachforschungen anstellen, recherchieren
likely ['laɪkli]	wahrscheinlich
insufficient [ˌɪnsə'fɪʃnt]	unzureichend
directory [də'rektəri]	Verzeichnis
invalid [ɪn'vælɪd]	ungültig
to press [pres]	drücken
to type [taɪp]	tippen, eintippen
specification [ˌspesɪfɪ'keɪʃn]	Angabe
to specify ['spesɪfaɪ]	(genau) angeben
to detect [dɪ'tekt]	erkennen, feststellen
attached to [ə'tætʃt tə]	verbunden mit

page 44

failure ['feɪljə]	Defekt, Versagen
to fail to do sth [ˌfeɪl tə 'duː]	etw nicht tun können
malicious [mə'lɪʃəs]	schädlich
to refresh [rɪ'freʃ]	auffrischen
word spider ['wɜːd spaɪdə]	Wortnetz

page 45

to refuse [rɪ'fjuːz]	sich weigern
valuable ['væljuəbl]	wertvoll
to close down [ˌkləʊz 'daʊn]	schließen
screensaver ['skriːnseɪvə]	Bildschirmschoner
to interfere with sth [ˌɪntə'fɪə wɪð]	etw stören, etw beeinträchtigen
incomplete [ˌɪnkəm'pliːt]	unvollständig
to result [rɪ'zʌlt]	resultieren
apparently [ə'pærəntli]	anscheinend
to trust [trʌst]	trauen, vertrauen
to disable [dɪs'eɪbl]	deaktivieren
to refer to sth [rɪ'fɜː tə]	sich auf etw beziehen
particularly [pə'tɪkjələli]	insbesondere
to require [rɪ'kwaɪə]	erfordern
additional [ə'dɪʃənl]	zusätzlich, Zusatz-
to come with sth ['kʌm wɪð]	mit etw geliefert werden
to wipe [waɪp]	(komplett) löschen
from scratch [frəm 'skrætʃ]	(ganz) von vorn

page 46

to ensure [ɪn'ʃʊə]	gewährleisten, sicherstellen
section ['sekʃn]	Teil, Abschnitt
close [kləʊs]	genau, sorgfältig
potential [pə'tenʃl]	potenziell
to mediate ['miːdieɪt]	vermitteln

Unit 5

page 47

flow chart ['fləʊ tʃɑːt]	Flussdiagramm

page 48

careful ['keəfl]	vorsichtig, *hier:* Vorsicht!
unnecessary [ʌn'nesəsəri]	unnötig
registry ['redʒɪstri]	eine Datenbank zur Speicherung von Konfigurationsdaten
to boost [buːst]	steigern
speaker ['spiːkə]	Lautsprecher
plug [plʌg]	Stecker
socket ['sɒkɪt]	Buchse
loose [luːs]	locker, lose
faulty ['fɔːlti]	defekt
defective [dɪ'fektɪv]	schadhaft, defekt
to accumulate [ə'kjuːmjəleɪt]	sich ansammeln
to switch off [ˌswɪtʃ 'ɒf]	(sich) ausschalten
in order to [ɪn 'ɔːdə tə]	um ... zu
to be sensitive to sth [bi 'sensətɪv tə]	auf etw empfindlich reagieren
radiation [ˌreɪdi'eɪʃn]	Strahlung
microwave ['maɪkrəweɪv]	Mikrowelle
dishwasher ['dɪʃwɒʃə]	Spülmaschine
equipment [ɪ'kwɪpmənt]	Geräte

noise [nɔɪz]	Lärm, Geräusch(e)
high-pitch [ˌhaɪ ˈpɪtʃ]	hochfrequent
to **go mad** [gəʊ ˈmæd]	spinnen *T*
to **shut down** [ˌʃʌt ˈdaʊn]	herunterfahren *T*
on one's own [ɒn wʌnz ˈəʊn]	selbstständig *T*
(for) ages [fər ˈeɪdʒɪz]	ewig *T*
fuzzy [ˈfʌzi]	unscharf, verschwommen *T*

page 49

cartridge [ˈkɑːtrɪdʒ]	Patrone, Kartusche
pile [paɪl]	Stapel
wire [ˈwaɪə]	Draht
power cord [ˈpaʊə kɔːd]	Stromkabel

page 50

to **adjust** [əˈdʒʌst]	einstellen, regulieren, anpassen
outlet [ˈaʊtlet]	Anschluss
to **plug** [plʌg]	(Stecker) einstecken
to **unplug** [ˌʌnˈplʌg]	(Stecker) herausziehen
volume [ˈvɒljuːm]	Lautstärke
jack [dʒæk]	Buchse
to **mute** [mjuːt]	stummschalten
to **resolve** [rɪˈzɒlv]	lösen

page 51

(the) gist [dʒɪst]	das Wesentliche
secure [sɪˈkjuə]	sicher
brightness [ˈbraɪtnəs]	Helligkeit
control [kənˈtrəʊl]	Regler
key [kiː]	Taste
to hit [hɪt]	drücken *T*
to **give it a go** [ˌgɪv ɪt ə ˈgəʊ]	es versuchen *T*
embarrassing [ɪmˈbærəsɪŋ]	peinlich *T*
Never mind . [ˌnevə ˈmaɪnd]	Macht nichts. *T*
silly [ˈsɪli]	dumm, albern *T*
I haven't got a clue. [aɪ ˌhævənt gɒt ə ˈkluː]	Ich habe keinen blassen Schimmer. *T*
straight away [streɪt əˈweɪ]	sofort *T*

page 52

to **direct sb** [dəˈrekt]	jdn anleiten

page 53

contract [ˈkɒntrækt]	Vertrag
to **provide for sth** [prəˈvaɪd fə]	etw vorsehen, etw regeln
servicing [ˈsɜːvɪsɪŋ]	Wartung, Instandhaltung
to **reduce** [rɪˈdjuːs]	verringern
width [wɪdθ]	Breite

page 54

Hold on. [ˌhəʊld ˈɒn]	Einen Moment.
to **paste** [peɪst]	einfügen
conversation [ˌkɒnvəˈseɪʃn]	Gespräch, Unterhaltung *P*
extract [ˈekstrækt]	Auszug, Ausschnitt *P*
erratic(ally) [ɪˈrætɪkli]	ungleichmäßig, wirr *P*
to leak [liːk]	austreten, auslaufen *P*
regarding [rɪˈgɑːdɪŋ]	bezüglich, betreffend

page 55

agreement [əˈgriːmənt]	Vereinbarung
hereafter [ˌhɪərˈɑːftə]	im Folgenden
period [ˈpɪəriəd]	Zeitraum, Laufzeit
through [θruː]	bis
to **agree** [əˈgriː]	vereinbaren
to **lay out** [ˌleɪ ˈaʊt]	darlegen
manual [ˈmænjuəl]	Handbuch
contents [ˈkɒntents]	Inhalt
to **outline** [ˈaʊtlaɪn]	umreißen, darstellen
primary [ˈpraɪməri]	Haupt-
means [miːnz]	Mittel
confirmation [ˌkɒnfəˈmeɪʃn]	Bestätigung
to guarantee [ˌgærənˈtiː]	garantieren
timely [ˈtaɪmli]	rechtzeitig
excluding [ɪkˈskluːdɪŋ]	außer
public holiday [ˌpʌblɪk ˈhɒlədeɪ]	gesetzlicher Feiertag
representative [ˌreprɪˈzentətɪv]	Vertreter/in
present [ˈpreznt]	anwesend
on-site [ˌɒn ˈsaɪt]	vor Ort
approved [əˈpruːvd]	zugelassen, genehmigt
to be deemed [bi ˈdiːmd]	erachtet werden
eligible [ˈelɪdʒəbl]	geeignet
to **inspect** [ɪnˈspekt]	prüfen
prior to [ˈpraɪə tə]	vor
commencement [kəˈmensmənt]	(Vertrags-)Beginn
to **be subject to** [bi ˈsʌbdʒekt tə]	unterliegen, vorbehaltlich gelten
acceptance [əkˈseptəns]	Zustimmung
obligation [ˌɒblɪˈgeɪʃn]	Verpflichtung
malfunction [ˌmælˈfʌŋkʃn]	Ausfall, Versagen, Störung
improper use [ɪmˌprɒpə ˈjuːs]	unsachgemäßer Gebrauch
natural disaster [ˌnætʃrəl dɪˈzɑːstə]	Naturkatastrophe

strike [straɪk]	Streik
riot ['raɪət]	Aufstand, Unruhe(n)
war [wɔː]	Krieg
nuclear disaster [ˌnjuːkliə dɪ'zɑːstə]	Reaktorkatastrophe
neglect [nɪ'glekt]	Fahrlässigkeit
transit ['trænzɪt]	Transport
failure ['feɪljə]	Versäumnis
to **hold sb responsible** [ˌhəʊld rɪ'spɒnsəbl]	jdn haftbar machen, jdn verantwortlich machen
delay [dɪ'leɪ]	Verzögerung
beyond [bɪ'jɒnd]	jenseits, über ... hinaus
reasonable ['riːznəbl]	vernünftig, zumutbar
stationery ['steɪʃənri]	Büromaterial
duly ['djuːli]	ordnungsgemäß
to **note** [nəʊt]	vermerken
archival [ɑː'kaɪvl]	Archiv-
purpose ['pɜːpəs]	Zweck
worn [wɔːn]	abgenutzt
verification [ˌverɪfɪ'keɪʃn]	Nachweis, Überprüfung
charge [tʃɑːdʒ]	Gebühr, Preis
in effect [ɪn ɪ'fekt]	in Kraft, gültig
alteration [ˌɔːltə'reɪʃn]	Änderung
in writing [ɪn 'raɪtɪŋ]	schriftlich, in Schriftform
classified ['klæsɪfaɪd]	geheim
coverage ['kʌvərɪdʒ]	Deckung, Erfassung
consumable item [kənˌsjuːməbl 'aɪtəm]	Verbrauchsartikel
to **utilize** ['juːtəlaɪz]	nutzen
to **cover** ['kʌvə]	(vertraglich) erfassen, abdecken, decken
evidence ['evɪdəns]	Beweis(e), Nachweis

page **56**

to **drop** [drɒp]	fallen lassen
grateful ['greɪtfl]	dankbar
to **play up** [ˌpleɪ 'ʌp]	Ärger machen
unusual [ʌn'juːʒʊəl]	ungewöhnlich
prepared [prɪ'peəd]	bereit, willens

Unit 6

page **57**

acceptable [ək'septəbl]	akzeptabel
policy ['pɒləsi]	Linie, Vorgehensweise, Politik
acceptable use policy (AUP) [əkˌseptəbl 'juːs 'pɒləsi]	allgemeine Nutzungsbedingungen
risky ['rɪski]	riskant
aside from [ə'saɪd frəm]	abgesehen von
briefly ['briːfli]	kurz, schnell
lunch break ['lʌntʃ breɪk]	Mittagspause
to **keep in touch** [ˌkiːp ɪn 'tʌtʃ]	in Kontakt bleiben
attack [ə'tæk]	Angriff
engineering [ˌendʒɪ'nɪərɪŋ]	Maschinenbau

page **58**

secretary ['sekrətri]	Sekretär/in
to **act up** [ˌækt 'ʌp]	verrückt spielen
I'm not bothered about ... [aɪm nɒt 'bɒðəd əbaʊt]	Es macht mir nichts aus, dass ...
concerned [kən'sɜːnd]	besorgt
to spread [spred]	sich ausbreiten, sich verbreiten

page **59**

to **respect** [rɪ'spekt]	beachten, respektieren
physically ['fɪzɪkli]	physisch
to **destroy** [dɪ'strɔɪ]	zerstören

page **60**

to **execute** ['eksɪkjuːt]	ausführen
to **hijack** ['haɪdʒæk]	kapern, entführen
to **infect** [ɪn'fekt]	infizieren
to **self-replicate** [ˌself 'replɪkeɪt]	sich reproduzieren
to **note** [nəʊt]	zur Kenntnis nehmen
to **be considered sth** [bi kən'sɪdəd]	als etw gelten
legitimate [lɪ'dʒɪtɪmət]	rechtmäßig, seriös
up front [ˌʌp 'frʌnt]	offen, im Voraus
remote [rɪ'məʊt]	entfernt
command [kə'mɑːnd]	Befehl
permission [pə'mɪʃn]	Erlaubnis
to **redirect** [ˌriːdə'rekt]	umleiten
query ['kwɪəri]	(Such-)Anfrage
popular ['pɒpjələ]	beliebt
search engine ['sɜːtʃ endʒɪn]	Suchmaschine
ability [ə'bɪləti]	Fähigkeit
joke [dʒəʊk]	Witz, Scherz
to **replicate oneself** ['replɪkeɪt]	sich reproduzieren
to **tend to** ['tend tə]	dazu neigen
worm [wɜːm]	Wurm
technique [tek'niːk]	Methode, Technik
to **discover** [dɪ'skʌvə]	entdecken
to **default to sth** [dɪ'fɔːlt tə]	etw *(eine Webseite)* standardmäßig aufrufen
to **get rid of sth** [ˌget 'rɪd əv]	etw loswerden

page 61

spread [spred]	Ausbreitung, Verbreitung
to **stop sth in its tracks** [ˌstɒp ɪn ɪts 'træks]	etw stoppen, aufhalten *T*
to **affect** [ə'fekt]	betreffen, befallen *T*
route [ruːt]	Weg, Route *T*
to **evade** [ɪ'veɪd]	vermeiden, sich entziehen *T*
attempt [ə'tempt]	Versuch *T*
specialist ['speʃəlɪst]	Spezial- *T*
code of conduct [ˌkəʊd əv 'kɒndʌkt]	Verhaltensregeln *T*

page 62

to **worry about sth** ['wʌri əbaʊt]	sich um etw Sorgen machen
daily ['deɪli]	täglich
trojan ['trəʊdʒən]	Trojaner
to **be related to sth** [bi rɪ'leɪtɪd tə]	mit etw zu tun haben

page 63

to **give your opinion** [ˌgɪv jɔːr ə'pɪniən]	seine Meinung äußern
up to a point [ˌʌp tu ə 'pɔɪnt]	bis zu einem gewissen Grad/Punkt
to **an extent** [tu ən ɪk'stent]	bis zu einem gewissen Maß
to **disagree** [ˌdɪsə'griː]	nicht zustimmen, anderer Meinung sein
doubt [daʊt]	Zweifel
to **state** [steɪt]	erklären, angeben, sagen
unacceptable [ˌʌnək'septəbl]	nicht akzeptabel
explicitly [ɪk'splɪsɪtli]	ausdrücklich *P*
to **forbid** [fə'bɪd]	verbieten P
to **argue your case** [ˌɑːgjuː jɔː 'keɪs]	Argumente (dafür) anführen P
to **ban** [bæn]	verbieten P
which have risk attached to them [wɪtʃ ˌhəv ə 'rɪsk ətætʃt tə ðəm]	die risikobehaftet sind

page 64

intentional(ly) [ɪn'tenʃənəli]	absichtlich, vorsätzlich
resource [rɪ'sɔːs]	Ressourcen
strict(ly) ['strɪktli]	streng
privacy ['prɪvəsi]	Privatsphäre
to **harass** ['hærəs]	belästigen
to **harm** [hɑːm]	schaden, verletzen
to **offend** [ə'fend]	beleidigen
to **insult** [ɪn'sʌlt]	beleidigen
to **bypass** ['baɪpɑːs]	umgehen
to **put sth at risk** [ˌpʊt ət 'rɪsk]	etw aufs Spiel setzen, etw gefährden
to **belong to** [bɪ'lɒŋ tə]	gehören
responsibly [rɪ'spɒnsəbli]	verantwortungsbewusst
ownership right ['əʊnəʃɪp raɪt]	Eigentumsrecht
to **abide by sth** [ə'baɪd baɪ]	sich an etw halten
law [lɔː]	Gesetz
polite [pə'laɪt]	höflich
to **appreciate sth** [ə'priːʃieɪt]	sich einer Sache bewusst sein
view [vjuː]	Ansicht
swearing ['sweərɪŋ]	Fluchen

page 65

rule [ruːl]	Vorschrift, Regel
violent ['vaɪələnt]	gewalttätig
racist ['reɪsɪst]	rassistisch
inappropriate [ˌɪnə'prəʊpriət]	unangemessen
to **access sth** ['ækses]	auf etw zugreifen
unlawful [ˌʌn'lɔːfl]	ungesetzlich
obscene [əb'siːn]	obszön
abusive [ə'bjuːsɪv]	beleidigend, gewalttätig
to **permit** [pə'mɪt]	erlauben, gestatten
spillage ['spɪlɪdʒ]	Verschütten, Verschüttetes
wary ['weəri]	misstrauisch
to **reveal** [rɪ'viːl]	preisgeben, verraten
to **rearrange** [ˌriːə'reɪndʒ]	neu anordnen

page 66

to **hire** ['haɪə]	beauftragen, anstellen
flaw [flɔː]	Mangel, Lücke
to **face** [feɪs]	vor etw stehen
charge [tʃɑːdʒ]	Anklage
to **face sth** [feɪs]	vor etw stehen, sich etw gegenüber sehen
to **point out** [ˌpɔɪnt 'aʊt]	darauf hinweisen
to **pave the way** [ˌpeɪv ðə 'weɪ]	den Weg bereiten/ebnen
to **steal** [stiːl]	stehlen
to **come clean** [ˌkʌm 'kliːn]	auspacken, die Wahrheit sagen
antics ['æntɪks]	Streiche
outfit ['aʊtfɪt]	Unternehmen
unwanted [ˌʌn'wɒntɪd]	unerwünscht
to **leave sth in one's wake** [ˌliːv ɪn wʌnz 'weɪk]	etw zürücklassen, etw hinterlassen

to **claim responsibility** [ˌkleɪm rɪspɒnsəˈbɪləti]	sich für etw verantwortlich erklären
to **investigate sb** [ɪnˈvestɪgeɪt]	gegen jdn ermitteln
case [keɪs]	Fall
court [kɔːt]	Gericht
to **admit** [ədˈmɪt]	zugeben, eingestehen
to **lay the ground for sth** [ˌleɪ ðə ˈgraʊnd fə]	die Grundlage für etw bilden
ethical(ly) [ˈeθɪkli]	moralisch
to **reward** [rɪˈwɔːd]	belohnen
guideline [ˈgaɪdlaɪn]	Richtlinie, Hinweis

Unit 7

page 67

to **participate** [pɑːˈtɪsɪpeɪt]	teilnehmen
venue [ˈvenjuː]	(Veranstaltungs-) Ort
industry [ˈɪndəstri]	Branche, Industrie
retailer [ˈriːteɪlə]	Einzelhändler/in
passionate [ˈpæʃənət]	leidenschaftlich
trade [treɪd]	Branche
trade visitor [ˈtreɪd vɪzɪtə]	Fachbesucher/in
focus [ˈfəʊkəs]	Schwerpunkt
vendor [ˈvendə]	Anbieter/in, Lieferant/in
operator [ˈɒpəreɪtə]	Betreiber/in
trader [ˈtreɪdə]	Händler/in
environmentally-friendly [ɪnvaɪrənˌmentəli ˈfrendli]	umweltfreundlich
throughout [θruːˈaʊt]	in ganz
steadily [ˈstedɪli]	kontinuierlich, stetig
seller [ˈselə]	Verkäufer/in, Anbieter/in
travel agency [ˈtrævl eɪdʒənsi]	Reisebüro
to **achieve** [əˈtʃiːv]	erreichen

page 68

to **attend sth** [əˈtend]	an etw teilnehmen
exhibitor [ɪgˈzɪbɪtə]	Aussteller/in
to **exhibit** [ɪgˈzɪbɪt]	ausstellen
to **display** [dɪˈspleɪ]	ausstellen, vorführen
to **accelerate** [əkˈseləreɪt]	beschleunigen
exhibition [ˌeksɪˈbɪʃn]	Ausstellung, Messe
wireless [ˈwaɪələs]	drahtlos, Funk-
square metre [ˈskweə miːtə]	Quadratmeter
exhibition space [ˌeksɪˈbɪʃn speɪs]	Ausstellungsfläche
attendee [əˌtenˈdiː]	Teilnehmer/in
professional visitor [prəˌfeʃənl ˈvɪzɪtə]	Fachbesucher
to **represent** [ˌreprɪˈzent]	repräsentieren, vertreten
variety [vəˈraɪəti]	Vielzahl, Vielfalt
thorough [ˈθʌrə]	gründlich
comprehensive [ˌkɒmprɪˈhensɪv]	umfassend
coverage [ˈkʌvərɪdʒ]	*(Medien:)* Berichterstattung
event [ɪˈvent]	Veranstaltung
government [ˈgʌvənmənt]	Regierung, staatliche Stellen, öffentliche Verwaltung
community [kəˈmjuːnəti]	Gemeinschaft
official [əˈfɪʃl]	Beamte/r
keynote (speech) [ˈkiːnəʊt spiːtʃ]	Haupt-/ Eröffnungsvortrag
panel [ˈpænl]	Gremium
to **announce** [əˈnaʊns]	ankündigen
nationwide [ˈneɪʃnwaɪd]	landesweit
to **extend sth** [ɪkˈstend]	etw verbreiten
distributor [dɪˈstrɪbjətə]	(Zwischen-, Vertriebs-)Händler/in
to **be eager to do sth** [bi ˈiːgə tə duː]	etw unbedingt tun wollen, es kaum abwarten können, etw zu tun
objective [əbˈdʒektɪv]	Ziel
partnership [ˈpɑːtnəʃɪp]	Beteiligung, Teilhaberschaft
billing [ˈbɪlɪŋ]	Abrechnung, Rechnungsstellung

page 69

booth [buːð]	(Messe-)Stand
to **increase** [ɪnˈkriːs]	steigern
huge [hjuːdʒ]	riesengroß

page 70

agenda [əˈdʒendə]	Tagesordnung
to **link** [lɪŋk]	verbinden
item [ˈaɪtəm]	Punkt
chairperson [ˈtʃeəpɜːsn]	Vorsitzende/r, Leiter/in
minutes [ˈmɪnɪts]	Protokoll
participant [pɑːˈtɪsɪpənt]	Teilnehmer/in
AOB (Any Other Business) [ˌeɪ əʊ ˈbiː / ˌeni ʌðə ˈbɪznəs]	Sonstiges
affair [əˈfeə]	Angelegenheit
participation [pɑːˌtɪsɪˈpeɪʃn]	Teilnahme
copy [ˈkɒpi]	Exemplar
to **take minutes** [ˌteɪk ˈmɪnɪts]	Protokoll führen

to **chair** [tʃeə]	leiten

page 71

aim [eɪm]	Ziel
to **call a meeting** [ˌkɔːl ə 'miːtɪŋ]	eine Sitzung einberufen
vehicle ['viːəkl]	Mittel, Medium *T*
to **enhance** [ɪn'hɑːns]	verbessern, fördern *T*
visibility [ˌvɪzə'bɪləti]	Bekanntheit *T*
to **establish** [ɪ'stæblɪʃ]	herstellen, festigen *T*
to **conquer** ['kɒŋkə]	erobern *T*
to **observe** [əb'zɜːv]	beobachten *T*
competitor [kəm'petɪtə]	Konkurrent/in *T*
to **appeal to sb** [ə'piːl tə]	jdn ansprechen, jdm gefallen *T*
therefore ['ðeəfɔː]	deshalb, also *T*
to **adapt to sth** [ə'dæpt tə]	sich an etw anpassen *T*
first and foremost [ˌfɜːst ən 'fɔːməʊst]	zuallererst, an erster Stelle *T*
measurable ['meʒərəbl]	messbar *T*
to **confuse** [kən'fjuːz]	verwirren, durcheinander bringen *T*
equally ['iːkwəli]	gleichermaßen, genauso *T*
to **pick** [pɪk]	auswählen, aussuchen *T*
exposure to sth [ɪk'spəʊʒə tə]	Ausgesetzt sein *T*
competition [ˌkɒmpə'tɪʃn]	Konkurrenz, Konkurrenten *T*
accommodation [əˌkɒmə'deɪʃn]	Unterkunft *T*
expenses [ɪk'spensɪz]	Kosten *T*
to **provide hospitality to sb** [prəˌvaɪd ˌhɒspɪ'tæləti tə]	jdn bewirten *T*
to **match sth** [mætʃ]	mit etw übereinstimmen *T*
next to ['nekst tə]	neben *T*
to **follow up** [ˌfɒləʊ 'ʌp]	nachfassen, verfolgen *T*
to **close** [kləʊz]	*(Vortrag:)* zum Schluss kommen *T*
intention [ɪn'tenʃn]	Absicht *T*
to **establish** [ɪ'stæblɪʃ]	etablieren *T*
in particular [ɪn pə'tɪkjələ]	insbesondere *T*
to **watch out for sth** [ˌwɒtʃ 'aʊt fə]	auf etw achten, auf etw aufpassen *T*
competitive [kəm'petətɪv]	*(Markt:)* umkämpft *T*
expertise [ˌekspɜː'tiːz]	Fachwissen *T*
to **realize** ['rɪəlaɪz]	verwirklichen, umsetzen *T*
degree [dɪ'griː]	Grad *T*
distinction [dɪ'stɪŋkʃn]	Unterscheidung *T*
to **conclude** [kən'kluːd]	abschließen *T*
essential [ɪ'senʃl]	wesentlich, unabdingbar, notwendig *T*
afterwards ['ɑːftəwədz]	hinterher, danach *T*

page 72

to **signal** ['sɪgnəl]	weisen, anzeigen
similarity [ˌsɪmə'lærəti]	Gemeinsamkeit, Ähnlichkeit

page 73

to **act as sth** ['ækt əz]	als etw fungieren
audience ['ɔːdiəns]	Publikum
mark [mɑːk]	Note
delivery [dɪ'lɪvəri]	Vortrag
cross-cultural [ˌkrɒs'kʌltʃərəl]	kulturübergreifend
awareness [ə'weənəs]	Bewusstsein
to **brainstorm** ['breɪnstɔːm]	Ideen sammeln
to **pour** [pɔː]	(ein)gießen *T*
unfortunately [ʌn'fɔːtʃənətli]	leider *T*
stereotype ['steriətaɪp]	Klischee *T*
rainy ['reɪni]	regnerisch *T*
coincidence [kəʊ'ɪnsɪdəns]	Zufall *T*
impression [ɪm'preʃn]	Eindruck *T*
to **enjoy sth** [ɪn'dʒɔɪ]	etw mögen *T*
at some point [ət ˌsʌm 'pɔɪnt]	irgendwann *T*

page 74

to **structure** ['strʌktʃə]	strukturieren
to **compile** [kəm'paɪl]	zusammenstellen

page 75

appearance [ə'pɪərəns]	Erscheinungsbild, Auftreten
subconscious(ly) [ˌsʌb'kɒnʃəsli]	unterbewusst
to **affect** [ə'fekt]	beeinflussen
to **go with your gut** [ˌgəʊ wɪð jɔː 'gʌt]	dem Bauchgefühl folgen
speech [spiːtʃ]	Rede, Vortrag
however [haʊ'evə]	wie auch immer
credibility [ˌkredə'bɪləti]	Glaubhaftigkeit
to **gesture** ['dʒestʃə]	Handbewegungen machen
brain [breɪn]	Gehirn
drooping ['druːpɪŋ]	*(Schultern:)* hängend
bowed [baʊd]	*(Kopf:)* gesenkt
chemical ['kemɪkl]	Chemikalie
bloodstream ['blʌdstriːm]	Blutkreislauf
attribute ['ætrɪbjuːt]	Eigenschaft, Attribut

relaxed [rɪ'lækst]	locker, entspannt
posture ['pɒstʃə]	Haltung
authentic [ɔː'θentɪk]	authentisch
to **imagine sth** [ɪ'mædʒɪn]	sich etw vorstellen
lion ['laɪən]	Löwe
jungle ['dʒʌŋgl]	Dschungel
territory ['terətri]	Territorium
graceful(ly) ['greɪsfli]	elegant
confidence ['kɒnfɪdəns]	Selbstvertrauen
stability [stə'bɪləti]	Stabilität
purposeful ['pɜːpəsfl]	zielstrebig
stride [straɪd]	Schritt
to **swing** [swɪŋ]	schwingen
to **convey** [kən'veɪ]	vermitteln
banquet hall ['bæŋkwɪt hɔːl]	Bankettsaal
to **get stuck** [ˌget 'stʌk]	eingeklemmt sein, festsitzen
row [rəʊ]	Reihe
back row [bæk 'rəʊ]	letzte Reihe
to **stir sb up** [ˌstɜːr 'ʌp]	jdn aufrütteln, aufscheuchen
entranced ['entrɑːnst]	gebannt
transition [træn'zɪʃn]	Übergang
to **pause** [pɔːz]	innehalten, pausieren
to **address sth** [ə'dres]	sich einer Sache widmen
silently ['saɪləntli]	schweigend, lautlos
intimate ['ɪntɪmət]	intim, vertraulich
fearful ['fɪəfl]	ängstlich
to **draw up** [ˌdrɔː 'ʌp]	hochziehen
to **arch** [ɑːtʃ]	sich wölben
to **hunch** [hʌntʃ]	sich krümmen, sich beugen
to **curve in** [ˌkɜːv 'ɪn]	*(Schultern)* einziehen
chest [tʃest]	Brust
to **shorten** ['ʃɔːtn]	sich verkürzen
tight [taɪt]	fest
to grow tight [ˌgrəʊ 'taɪt]	*(Muskel:)* sich verspannen
to **take breaths** [ˌteɪk 'breθs]	einatmen
relaxation [ˌriːlæk'seɪʃn]	Entspannung
gesture ['dʒestʃə]	Geste
animated ['ænɪmeɪtɪd]	lebhaft
to retain [rɪ'teɪn]	behalten
to **appeal to sth** [ə'piːl tə]	sich an etw richten, etw ansprechen
vital ['vaɪtl]	unerlässlich
to **be proven to be** [bi ˌpruːvn tə biː]	etw nachweislich sein
skilled [skɪld]	kompetent

page **76**

etiquette ['etɪket]	Etikette, Regeln

Unit 8

page **77**

to **handle sth** ['hændl]	mit etw umgehen
supplies [sə'plaɪz]	Bedarf
in total [ɪn 'təʊtl]	insgesamt *T*
to **equal** ['iːkwəl]	gleich sein *T*
value added tax (VAT) [ˌvæljuː 'ædɪd tæks / ˌviː eɪ 'tiː]	Mehrwertsteuer *T*
inclusive of [ɪn'kluːsɪv əf]	inklusive, einschließlich *T*
in stock [ɪn 'stɒk]	auf Lager, vorrätig *T*
underscore [ˌʌndə'skɔː]	Unterstrich *T*
in lower case [ɪn ˌləʊə 'keɪs]	kleingeschrieben *T*
to come [kʌm]	*(Waren:)* geliefert werden *T*
accompanying [ə'kʌmpəniɪŋ]	begleitend, Begleit- *T*
warranty ['wɒrənti]	Garantie, Gewährleistung *T*

page **78**

in bold [ɪn 'bəʊld]	fettgedruckt

page **80**

to **hesitate** ['hezɪteɪt]	zögern
within [wɪ'ðɪn]	innerhalb
subtotal ['sʌbtəʊtl]	Zwischensumme

page **81**

invoice ['ɪnvɔɪs]	Rechnung

page **82**

bill [bɪl]	Rechnung
to **bring sth up** [ˌbrɪŋ 'ʌp]	etw ansprechen
to **forgo** [fɔː'gəʊ]	auf etw verzichten
to **appreciate sth** [ə'priːʃieɪt]	etw zu schätzen wissen
distinct [dɪ'stɪŋkt]	deutlich
to **raise sth** [reɪz]	etw ansprechen
to **be surprised** [bi sə'praɪzd]	sich wundern
to **waive sth** [weɪv]	auf etw verzichten
to **quote** [kwəʊt]	einen Kostenvoranschlag machen, *(Preis:)* nennen
to **settle** ['setl]	*(Rechnung:)* begleichen, bezahlen
to **clarify** ['klærəfaɪ]	klären
separately ['seprətli]	separat, extra
in advance [ɪn əd'vɑːns]	im Voraus
response [rɪ'spɒns]	Reaktion, Antwort

page **83**

to **reply** [rɪ'plaɪ]	antworten

to **amend** [ə'mend]	(ab)ändern
apology [ə'pɒlədʒi]	Entschuldigung
to **make up for sth** [ˌmeɪk 'ʌp fə]	etw wiedergutmachen
inconvenience [ˌɪnkən'viːniəns]	Unannehmlichkeiten
first off [ˌfɜːst 'ɒf]	zuallererst
oversight ['əʊvəsaɪt]	Versehen
to **get in touch with sb** [ˌget ɪn 'tʌtʃ wɪð]	sich mit jdm in Verbindung setzen
regards [rɪ'gɑːdz]	*(Brief:)* Mit freundlichen Grüßen
appropriate(ly) [ə'prəʊpriətli]	angemessen
tone [təʊn]	Ton
formality [fɔː'mæləti]	Förmlichkeit

page **84**

occasion [ə'keɪʒn]	Gelegenheit
term [tɜːm]	Begriff
to **disregard** [ˌdɪsrɪ'gɑːd]	ignorieren
addition [ə'dɪʃn]	Zusatz, Hinzufügung
revised [rɪ'vaɪzd]	überarbeitet, neu
given that ['gɪvn ðət]	unter der Voraussetzung, dass
to **anticipate** [æn'tɪsɪpeɪt]	erwarten
Yours sincerely [ˌjɔːz sɪn'sɪəli]	*(Brief:)* Mit freundlichen Grüßen

page **85**

strength [streŋθ]	Stärke
to **encourage sb to do sth** [ɪnˌkʌrɪdʒ tə 'duː]	jdn dazu bringen, etw zu tun
to **indicate** ['ɪndɪkeɪt]	darauf hindeuten
model ['mɒdl]	Muster, Vorbild

page **86**

angry ['æŋgri]	verärgert, wütend
even if ['iːvn ɪf]	selbst wenn
argument ['ɑːgjumənt]	Streit
to **calm sb down** [ˌkɑːm 'daʊn]	jdn beruhigen
behaviour [bɪ'heɪvjə]	Verhalten
heat [hiːt]	Hitze
anger ['æŋgə]	Ärger, Wut
to **argue** ['ɑːgjuː]	streiten
to **argue back** [ˌɑːgjuː 'bæk]	widersprechen
satisfactory [ˌsætɪs'fæktəri]	befriedigend
opportunity [ˌɒpə'tjuːnəti]	Gelegenheit
patient ['peɪʃnt]	geduldig
impatient [ɪm'peɪʃnt]	ungeduldig
to **glance** [glɑːns]	(kurz) blicken
to **stay with sth** ['steɪ wɪð]	bei etw bleiben
to **adopt sth** [ə'dɒpt]	etw einnehmen, annehmen
attitude ['ætɪtjuːd]	Einstellung, Haltung
frame [freɪm]	Rahmen
frame of mind [ˌfreɪm əv 'maɪnd]	*etwa:* Einstellung
to **be sucked in by sth** [bi ˌsʌkt 'ɪn baɪ]	sich von etw anstecken lassen
upset [ˌʌp'set]	verärgert

Unit 9

page **87**

topology [tə'pɒlədʒi]	Topologie, Netzstruktur
owner ['əʊnə]	Inhaber/in, Eigentümer/in
to **network** ['netwɜːk]	vernetzen
destination [ˌdestɪ'neɪʃn]	Ziel, Bestimmungsort
distributed [dɪ'strɪbjuːtɪd]	verteilt
hub [hʌb]	Netzknoten
interconnection [ˌɪntəkə'nekʃn]	Querverbindung, Zusammenschaltung
physical ['fɪzɪkl]	physisch
transmission [træns'mɪʃn]	Übertragung
approach [ə'prəʊtʃ]	Ansatz, Herangehensweise
limited ['lɪmɪtɪd]	begrenzt
to operate ['ɒpəreɪt]	bedienen
to **perform** [pə'fɔːm]	Leistung bringen, funktionieren
node [nəʊd]	Knotenpunkt
to **handle** ['hændl]	bedienen
to **fail** [feɪl]	ausfallen
entire [ɪn'taɪə]	ganze/r/s
to **affect** [ə'fekt]	beeinträchtigen
suited to ['suːtɪd tə]	geeignet für

page **88**

confused [kən'fjuːzd]	verwirrt
to **classify** ['klæsɪfaɪ]	einteilen, klassifizieren
path [pɑːθ]	Weg, Pfad
dual ['djuːəl]	Doppel-
to **flow** [fləʊ]	fließen
star [stɑː]	Stern
state of the art [ˌsteɪt əv ði 'ɑːt]	Stand der Technik

page **89**

to **fill sb in** [ˌfɪl 'ɪn]	jdn über etw informieren
to **assure** [ə'ʃʊə]	zusichern, versichern
to **manage** ['mænɪdʒ]	es schaffen

to **meet a deadline** [ˌmiːt ə 'dedlaɪn]	einen Termin einhalten
various ['veəriəs]	verschiedene
to **convince** [kən'vɪns]	überzeugen
to **arrange for sth** [ə'reɪndʒ fə]	etw besorgen, für etw sorgen
operational [ˌɒpə'reɪʃənl]	betriebsbereit
to **put sb in charge of sth** [ˌpʊt ɪn 'tʃɑːdʒ əv]	jdm die Verantwortung für etw übertragen
to **get onto sth** [ˌget 'ɒntə]	mit etw anfangen
subcontractor [ˌsʌbkən'træktə]	Subunternehmer/in
to **lay** [leɪ]	verlegen
quotation [kwəʊ'teɪʃn]	Angebot, Kostenvoranschlag
to **bear sth in mind** [ˌbeər ɪn 'maɪnd]	an etw denken
to **catch up** [ˌkætʃ 'ʌp]	(Neuigkeiten) austauschen

page **90**

labour ['leɪbə]	Arbeit
estimated ['estɪmeɪtɪd]	geschätzt
in the meantime [ɪn ðə 'miːntaɪm]	in der Zwischenzeit

page **91**

troubleshoot ['trʌblʃuːt]	Fehlersuche/-behebung
provisional [prə'vɪʒənl]	vorläufig, provisorisch
go-ahead ['gəʊ əhed]	grünes Licht *T*
to **bring sb up to speed** [brɪŋ ˌʌp tə 'spiːd]	jdn auf den neuesten Stand bringen *T*
unforeseen [ˌʌnfɔː'siːn]	unvorhergesehen *T*
to **criticize** ['krɪtɪsaɪz]	kritisieren *T*
reputation [ˌrepju'teɪʃn]	Ruf *T*
to **suffer** ['sʌfə]	leiden, Schaden nehmen *T*
to **smooth things over** [ˌsmuːð θɪŋz 'əʊvə]	die Dinge wieder ins Lot bringen *T*

page **92**

to **soften** ['sɒfn]	(ab)mildern

page **93**

to **worry** ['wʌri]	sich Sorgen machen
to **miss** [mɪs]	*(Termin:)* nicht einhalten
to **misunderstand** [ˌmɪsʌndə'stænd]	missverstehen, falsch verstehen
to **come across** [ˌkʌm ə'krɒs]	begegnen, treffen auf
to **forecast** ['fɔːkɑːst]	vorhersagen, voraussagen

page **94**

progress report ['prəʊgres rɪpɔːt]	Arbeitsbericht, Zwischenbericht

page **95**

to **hit** [hɪt]	treffen auf, stoßen auf
smooth(ly) ['smuːðli]	glatt
concerns [kən'sɜːnz]	Bedenken
strict [strɪkt]	streng, strikt
snag [snæg]	Haken, Schwierigkeiten
ultimately ['ʌltɪmətli]	letztendlich
to **give criticism** [ˌgɪv 'krɪtɪsɪzəm]	Kritik üben

page **96**

issue tracking ['ɪʃuː trækɪŋ]	Problemverfolgung
scheduling ['ʃedjuːlɪŋ]	Terminplanung, Disposition
project portfolio ['prɒdʒekt pɔːtfəʊliəʊ]	Projektportfolio
to **feature** ['fiːtʃə]	haben, aufweisen
progress ['prəʊgres]	Fortschritte
timeline ['taɪmlaɪn]	Zeitschiene
to **keep track of sth** [ˌkiːp 'træk əv]	den Überblick über etw behalten
to **maximize** ['mæksɪmaɪz]	maximieren
efficiency [ɪ'fɪʃnsi]	Effizienz
to **rank** [ræŋk]	einstufen

Unit 10

page **97**

to **apply for sth** [ə'plaɪ fə]	sich für etw bewerben
job advert(isement) ['dʒɒb ædvɜːt]	Stellenanzeige
CV (curriculum vitae) [ˌsiː 'viː / kəˌrɪkjələm 'viːtaɪ]	Lebenslauf
covering letter [ˌkʌvərɪŋ 'letə]	Anschreiben, Begleitschreiben
speech bubble ['spiːtʃ bʌbl]	Sprechblase
freedom ['friːdəm]	Freiheit
responsibility [rɪˌspɒnsə'bɪləti]	Verantwortung
pay [peɪ]	Bezahlung
promotion [prə'məʊʃn]	Beförderung
praise [preɪz]	Lob
pleasant ['pleznt]	angenehm
newly ['njuːli]	vor kurzem

to qualify ['kwɒlɪfaɪ] einen Abschluss machen
contract of employment [ˌkɒntrækt əv ɪm'plɔɪmənt] Arbeitsvertrag
candidate ['kændɪdət] Bewerber/in
application [ˌæplɪ'keɪʃn] Bewerbung
employment [ɪm'plɔɪmənt] Anstellung, Einstellung

page 98

salary ['sæləri] Gehalt
per annum [pər 'ænəm] pro Jahr
to seek [si:k] suchen
permanent ['pɜ:mənənt] *(Anstellung:)* fest
production facility [prə'dʌkʃn fəsɪləti] Produktionsstätte, Werk
to possess [pə'zes] besitzen, verfügen über
environment [ɪn'vaɪrənmənt] Umgebung
to think on one's feet [ˌθɪŋk ɒn wʌnz 'fi:t] schnell reagieren
to liaise with sb [li'eɪz wɪð] mit jdm zusammenarbeiten
qualification [ˌkwɒlɪfɪ'keɪʃn] Abschluss, Qualifikation
accredited [ə'kredɪtɪd] anerkannt
to demonstrate ['demənstreɪt] unter Beweis stellen
to assess [ə'ses] beurteilen, einschätzen
with a view to [wɪð ə 'vju: tə] mit Blick auf
driving licence ['draɪvɪŋ laɪsns] Führerschein
oral ['ɔ:rəl] mündlich
closing date ['kləʊzɪŋ deɪt] Einsendeschluss
referee [ˌrefə'ri:] Referenz
regardless [rɪ'gɑ:dləs] ungeachtet
gender ['dʒendə] Geschlecht

page 99

vocational [vəʊ'keɪʃənl] Berufs-
vocational training [vəʊˌkeɪʃənl 'treɪnɪŋ] Berufsausbildung
vocational school [vəʊˌkeɪʃənl 'sku:l] Berufsschule
primary school *(BE)* ['praɪməri sku:l] Grundschule
elementary school *(AE)* [ˌelɪ'mentri sku:l] Grundschule
GCSE [ˌdʒi: si: es 'i:] *brit. Schulabschlussprüfung für 16-Jährige,* Sekundarbschluss
A levels *(BE)* ['eɪ levlz] *brit. Schulabschlussprüfung für 17- und 18-Jährige,* Abitur
High School Diploma *(AE)* [ˌhaɪ sku:l dɪ'pləʊmə] *amerikan. Schulabschlussprüfung für 17- und 18-Jährige,* Abitur
apprenticeship [ə'prentɪʃɪp] Lehre, Ausbildung
comprehensive school [ˌkɒmprɪ'hensɪv sku:l] Gesamtschule
grammar school *(BE)* ['græmə sku:l] Gymnasium
to attend [ə'tend] *(Schule etc.)* besuchen
educational [ˌedʒu'keɪʃənl] Bildungs-, Lern-
institution [ˌɪnstɪ'tju:ʃn] Einrichtung, Institution
entrance ['entrəns] Zugang
to train [treɪn] ausbilden
to produce [prə'dju:s] *(Dokument etc.)* vorlegen
unless [ən'les] außer (wenn)
to sign [saɪn] unterschreiben
to date [tə 'deɪt] datieren
to insist on sth [ɪn'sɪst ɒn] auf etw bestehen
date of birth [ˌdeɪt əv 'bɜ:θ] Geburtsdatum
to provide [prə'vaɪd] *(Adresse etc.)* angeben
reverse [rɪ'vɜ:s] umgekehrt
to exceed [ɪk'si:d] überschreiten
to space sth out [ˌspeɪs 'aʊt] *(Text)* spationieren
to enclose [ɪn'kləʊz] *(Brief:)* beifügen, beilegen
dos and dont's [ˌdu:z ən 'dəʊnts] *Dinge, die man tun und lassen sollte*

page 100

outline ['aʊtlaɪn] Entwurf
improvement [ɪm'pru:vmənt] Verbesserung

page 101

line [laɪn] *(Text:)* Zeile
qualified ['kwɒlɪfaɪd] qualifiziert
to advertise ['ædvətaɪz] *(Stelle)* ausschreiben
to gain [geɪn] erwerben
to equip sb for sth [ɪ'kwɪp fə] jdn auf etw vorbereiten
to consider [kən'sɪdə] halten für
hard-working [ˌhɑ:d 'wɜ:kɪŋ] fleißig
reliable [rɪ'laɪəbl] zuverlässig, verlässlich
workload ['wɜ:kləʊd] Arbeitspensum

collaborative [kə'læbərətɪv]	gemeinschaftlich
moreover [mɔːr'əʊvə]	darüber hinaus
to **be keen to do sth** [bi ˌkiːn tə 'duː]	sehr daran interessiert sein, etw zu tun
to **provide** [prə'vaɪd]	bieten
to **fulfil** [fʊl'fɪl]	erfüllen

page 102

to **broaden** ['brɔːdn]	erweitern, ausbauen *T*
impressive [ɪm'presɪv]	beeindruckend *T*
pleased [pliːzd]	zufrieden, froh *T*

page 103

gap [gæp]	Lücke
to **aim** [eɪm]	zielen, darauf abzielen

page 104

weakness ['wiːknəs]	Schwäche
lecturer ['lektʃərə]	Dozent/in

page 105

to **enrol** [ɪn'rəʊl]	sich einschreiben
to **enter sth** ['entə]	in etw eintreten
member ['membə]	Mitglied
practitioner [præk'tɪʃənə]	Fachmann/-frau
guidance ['gaɪdəns]	Beratung
coherent [kəʊ'hɪərənt]	schlüssig, klar
manner ['mænə]	Art (und Weise)
to **consist of** [kən'sɪst əv]	bestehen aus
individual [ˌɪndɪ'vɪdʒuəl]	Einzelperson
independent(ly) [ˌɪndɪ'pendəntli]	selbstständig
on behalf of sb [ɒn bɪ'hɑːf əv]	in jds Auftrag/Namen
supplement ['sʌplmənt]	Ergänzung
associated [ə'səʊʃieɪtɪd]	verbunden
principal ['prɪnsəpl]	wichtig, hauptsächlich
citizen ['sɪtɪzn]	Bürger/in
accessible [ək'sesəbl]	(leicht) zugänglich
to **promote** [prə'məʊt]	fördern
link [lɪŋk]	Verbindung
continuing [kən'tɪnjuːɪŋ]	anhaltend, kontinuierlich
adequate ['ædɪkwət]	angemessen

page 106

to **judge** [dʒʌdʒ]	beurteilen

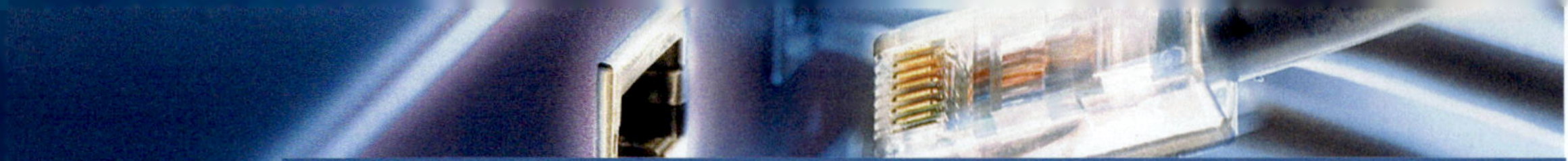

Alphabetical word list

Diese Liste enthält alle Wörte in alphabetischer Reihenfolge. Hier sind jedoch die Wörter, die zum Grundwortschatz gehören, sowie internationale Wörter wie *software*, *hacker* und *virus* nicht aufgeführt. Die Zahl nach dem Stichwort bezieht sich auf die Seite, auf der das Wort zum ersten mal erscheint.

P = das Wort befindet sich in den *Partner files*
T = das Wort befindet sich im *Transcript*

A

to **abbreviate** *16* abkürzen
to **abide by sth** *64* sich an etw halten
ability *60* Fähigkeit
abroad *8* im Ausland
absent *26* nicht vorhanden
abusive *65* beleidigend, gewalttätig
to **accelerate** *68* beschleunigen
to **accept** *30* annehmen, akzeptieren
acceptable *57* akzeptabel
acceptable use policy (AUP) *57* allgemeine Nutzungsbedingungen
acceptance *55* Zustimmung
access *8* Zugang
to **access sth** *65* auf etw zugreifen
accessible *105* (leicht) zugänglich
accommodation *71T* Unterkunft
accompanying *77T* begleitend, Begleit-
according to *35* nach, zufolge, gemäß
accredited *98* anerkannt
to **accumulate** *48* sich ansammeln
to **achieve** *67* erreichen
to **acquire** *35* akquirieren
to **act as sth** *73* als etw fungieren
to **act up** *58* verrückt spielen
action, to **take ~** *29* Maßnahmen ergreifen
to **adapt to sth** *71T* sich an etw anpassen
addition *84* Zusatz, Hinzufügung
additional *45* zusätzlich, Zusatz-
to **address sth** *75* sich einer Sache widmen
adequate *105* angemessen
to **adjust** *50* einstellen, regulieren, anpassen
administration *13* Verwaltung
administrative staff *31T* Verwaltungspersonal
to **admit** *66* zugeben, eingestehen
to **adopt sth** *86* etw einnehmen, annehmen
advance, in ~ *82* im Voraus
to **advertise** *101* *(Stelle)* ausschreiben
advert(isement) *31T* Anzeige, Werbespot
advertising agency *30* Werbeagentur
advice *14* Rat, Beratung
to **advise sb** *13* jdn beraten
affair *70* Angelegenheit
to **affect** *61T* betreffen, befallen; *75* beeinflussen; *87* beeinträchtigen
to **afford sth** *34* sich etw leisten (können)
afraid, I'm ~ *12* leider
after-sales service *34* Kundendienst
afterwards *71T* hinterher, danach
agenda *70* Tagesordnung
(for) ages *48T* ewig
to **agree** *39* zustimmen; *55* vereinbaren
agreement *55* Vereinbarung
aim *71* Ziel
to **aim** *103* zielen, darauf abzielen
A levels *(BE)* *99* *brit. Schulabschlussprüfung für 17- und 18-Jährige*, Abitur
to **align** *24* ausrichten
alignment system *21* Ausrichtungssystem
to **allow** *16* gestatten, erlauben
to **alter** *22* (ab)ändern
alteration *55* Änderung
to **amend** *83* (ab)ändern
to **analyze** *35* analysieren
anger *86* Ärger, Wut
angle, at an ~ *24* verkantet
angry *86* verärgert, wütend
animated *75* lebhaft
to **announce** *68* ankündigen
annual *8* jährlich, Jahres-
annum, per ~ *98* pro Jahr
to **anticipate** *84* erwarten
antics *66* Streiche
AOB (Any Other Business) *70* Sonstiges
apology *83* Entschuldigung
apparently *45* anscheinend
to **appeal to sb** *71T* jdn ansprechen, jdm gefallen
to **appeal to sth** *75* sich an etw richten, etw ansprechen
to **appear** *26* scheinen
appearance *75* Erscheinungsbild, Auftreten
application *12* Anwendung; *97* Bewerbung
to **apply** *24* anwenden, ausüben
to **apply for sth** *97* sich für etw bewerben
to **appreciate sth** *64* sich einer Sache bewusst sein; *82* etw zu schätzen wissen
apprenticeship *99* Lehre, Ausbildung
approach *87* Ansatz, Herangehensweise
appropriate *35* entsprechend, passend
appropriate(ly) *83* angemessen
approved *55* zugelassen, genehmigt
approximately *38* ungefähr, zirka
to **arch** *75* sich wölben
archival *55* Archiv-

to **argue** *86* streiten
to **argue back** *86* widersprechen
to **argue your case** *63P* Argumente (dafür) anführen
argument *86* Streit
to **arrange** *12* arrangieren, *(Termin)* ausmachen
to **arrange for sth** *89* etw besorgen, für etw sorgen
aside from *57* abgesehen von
to **assemble** *7* montieren, zusammenbauen
to **assess** *98* beurteilen, einschätzen
associated *105* verbunden
assurance, quality ~ (QA) *14T* Qualitätssicherung
to **assure** *89* zusichern, versichern
attached to *43* verbunden mit
attached to, which have risk ~ them *63P* die risikobehaftet sind
attack *57* Angriff
attempt *61T* Versuch
to **attempt** *21* versuchen
to **attend** *99* *(Schule etc.)* besuchen
to **attend sth** *68* an etw teilnehmen
attendee *68* Teilnehmer/in
attitude *86* Einstellung, Haltung
attribute *75* Eigenschaft, Attribut
audience *73* Publikum
authentic *75* authentisch
automotive *8* Automobil-
available, to be ~ *29* *(Telefon:)* zu sprechen sein
to **avoid** *21* vermeiden
award *34* Preis, Auszeichnung
award-winning *34* preisgekrönt
awareness *73* Bewusstsein

B

back row *75* letzte Reihe
backplane *24* Rückwandplatine
to **ban** *63P* verbieten
banquet hall *75* Bankettsaal
...-based *16* mit Sitz in ...
based, to be ~ in *28* seinen Sitz haben in
basically *41T* grundsätzlich
to **bear sth in mind** *89* an etw denken
to **beat** *26* schlagen
begin, to ~ with *31T* zunächst (einmal)
behalf, on ~ of sb *105* in jds Auftrag/Namen
behaviour *86* Verhalten
to **belong to** *64* gehören
to **bend** *24* verbiegen
to **benefit** *34* profitieren
to **benefit sb** *12* jdm zugute kommen, jdm nützen
to **beware of sth** *21* sich vor etw in Acht nehmen
beyond *55* jenseits, über ... hinaus
bill *82* Rechnung
billing *68* Abrechnung, Rechnungsstellung
birth, date of ~ *99* Geburtsdatum
blanket *26* Decke
bloodstream *75* Blutkreislauf
bold, in ~ *78* fettgedruckt
to **boost** *48* steigern
booth *69* (Messe-)Stand
bother, I'm not ~ed about ... *58* Es macht mir nichts aus, dass ...
bowed *75* *(Kopf:)* gesenkt
brain *75* Gehirn
to **brainstorm** *73* Ideen sammeln
branch *14T* Zweig, Sparte
breath, to take ~s *75* einatmen
breathing *26* Atmung, Atmen
brief *14T* kurz, knapp
briefly *57* kurz, schnell
brightness *51* Helligkeit
to **bring sth up** *82* etw ansprechen
to **bring sb up to speed** *91T* jdn auf den neuesten Stand bringen
broad *16* weit
broad, in ~ terms *14T* im weitesten Sinn, im Allgemeinen
to **broaden** *14* sich erweitern; *102T* erweitern, ausbauen
brochure *12* Prospekt, Broschüre
budget *18T* Etat, Budget
burn *26* Verbrennung
business trip *32* Geschäftsreise
busy *28* *(Telefon:)* besetzt
busy, to be ~ *30* viel zu tun haben
button *41T* Knopf
to **bypass** *64* umgehen

C

cable *21* Kabel
calculation *37* Berechnung
call, to be on ~ *13* Bereitschaftsdienst haben
to **call a meeting** *71* eine Sitzung einberufen
caller *29* Anrufer/in
to **calm sb down** *86* jdn beruhigen
can *21* Dose
candidate *97* Bewerber/in
canteen *12* Kantine
capability *18T* Fähigkeit
capable *18T* fähig
cardboard *26* Pappe
cardiopulmonary resuscitation *26* Herz-Lungen-Wiederbelebung
care, with ~ *21* vorsichtig
care, to take ~ of sb *13* sich um jdn kümmern
careful *48* vorsichtig, *hier:* Vorsicht!
careful(ly) *27* sorgfältig, gut
carpeted *22* mit Teppichboden
to **carry sth out** *16* etw durch-/ausführen
cartridge *49* Patrone, Kartusche
case *21* Gehäuse; *66* Fall
case, in lower ~ *77T* kleingeschrieben
to **catch up** *89* (Neuigkeiten) austauschen
century *16* Jahrhundert
CEO (Chief Executive Officer) *14* Vorstandsvorsitzende/r, Geschäftsführer/in
certain *34* bestimmt
to **chair** *70* leiten
chairperson *70* Vorsitzende/r, Leiter/in
to **change one's mind** *40* seine Meinung ändern
charge *55* Gebühr, Preis; *66* Anklage
charge, to be in ~ of sth *13* etw leiten, für etw verantwortlich sein

charge, to put sb in ~ of sth *89* jdm die Verantwortung für etw übertragen
chemical *75* Chemikalie
chest *75* Brust
CIO (Chief Information Officer) *14T* IT-Leiter/in, Leitende/r Referent/in für Information
circulation *26* Kreislauf
citizen *105* Bürger/in
to claim responsibility *66* sich für etw verantwortlich erklären
to clarify *82* klären
classified *55* geheim
to classify *88* einteilen, klassifizieren
client *16* Kunde/-in
close *46* genau, sorgfältig
close, to have a ~ look *14T* sich etwas genau anschauen
close to *38* nahe bei
to close *71T* *(Vortrag:)* zum Schluss kommen
to close down *45* schließen
closing date *98* Einsendeschluss
cloth *21* Tuch
clothing *22* Kleidung
clue, I haven't got a ~. *51T* Ich habe keinen blassen Schimmer.
code of conduct *61T* Verhaltensregeln
coherent *105* schlüssig, klar
coincidence *73T* Zufall
collaborative *101* gemeinschaftlich
colleague *26* Kollege/-in
to collect *35* sammeln, zusammentragen
column *17* *(Text:)* Spalte
to come (with sth) *45* *(Waren:)* (mit etw) geliefert werden
to come across *93* begegnen, treffen auf
to come clean *66* auspacken, die Wahrheit sagen
command *60* Befehl
commencement *55* (Vertrags-) Beginn
commercial *7* geschäftlich, Geschäfts-
common *16* gemeinsam
community *68* Gemeinschaft
company *7* Unternehmen
to compare *24* vergleichen
competition *71T* Konkurrenz, Konkurrenten
competitive *71T* *(Markt:)* umkämpft
competitor *71T* Konkurrent/in
to compile *74* zusammenstellen
complaint *12* Reklamation, Beschwerde
complicated *35* kompliziert
component *18* Bauteil, Komponente
comprehension *36* Verständnis, Verstehen
comprehensive *68* umfassend
comprehensive school *99* Gesamtschule
compressed air *21* Pressluft
to compromise on sth *18T* bei etw Kompromisse eingehen
to concentrate on sth *8* sich auf etw konzentrieren
concerned *58* besorgt
concerned, to be ~ with sth *8* mit etw beschäftigt sein, mit etw zu tun haben
concerns *95* Bedenken
to conclude *71T* abschließen
condition *40* Bedingung
confidence *75* Selbstvertrauen
confidential *37* vertraulich
to confirm *39* bestätigen
confirmation *55* Bestätigung
to confuse *71T* verwirren, durcheinander bringen
confused *88* verwirrt
to connect *22* verbinden
connection *21* Verbindung
connector *21* Steckverbindung, Stecker, Buchse
to conquer *71T* erobern
to consider *38* in Erwägung ziehen; *101* halten für
considered, to be ~ sth *60* als etw gelten
to consist of *105* bestehen aus
constant(ly) *35* ständig, dauernd
consultant *16* Berater/in
consulting *16* Beratung
consumable item *55* Verbrauchsartikel
contents *55* Inhalt
contest *13* Wettbewerb
to continue *38* fortfahren
to continue to do sth *34* etw weiter(hin) tun
continuing *105* anhaltend, kontinuierlich
continuous *16* kontinuierlich, ununterbrochen
contract *53* Vertrag
contract of employment *97* Arbeitsvertrag
contractor *32* Dienstleister, beauftragte Firma
control *51* Regler
convenient, to be ~ *30* passen, günstig sein
conversation *54P* Gespräch, Unterhaltung
to convey *75* vermitteln
to convince *89* überzeugen
copy *70* Exemplar
core *18T* Kern
corporate *16* Unternehmens-
to corrupt *42* beschädigen
coughing *26* Husten
country code *28* Ländervorwahl
court *66* Gericht
to cover *55* (vertraglich) erfassen, abdecken, decken
coverage *55* Deckung, Erfassung; *68* *(Medien:)* Berichterstattung
covering letter *97* Anschreiben, Begleitschreiben
cramp *26* Krampf
to create *22* erzeugen
creative *13* kreativ
credibility *75* Glaubhaftigkeit
criticism, to give ~ *95* Kritik üben
to criticize *91T* kritisieren
cross-cultural *73* kulturübergreifend
crucial *26* äußerst wichtig, unerlässlich, entscheidend
CTO (Chief Technology Officer) *14* Technische/r Leiter/in
current *26* Strom; *32* aktuell, laufend
currently *12* gegenwärtig, im Moment
to curve in *75* *(Schultern)* einziehen
customer *7* Kunde/-in
customer lead *35* Kundenkontakt, Kundendaten
customer service *12* Kundendienst
to customize *37* individuell anpassen

customized *31T* individuell angepasst
cut *21* Schnitt, Schnittverletzung
to **cut costs** *31T* Kosten senken
to **cut down on sth** *18T* etw bremsen, etw einschränken
CV (curriculum vitae) *97* Lebenslauf

D

daily *62* Täglich
damage *21* Beschädigung, Schaden
database *37* Datenbank
data processing *14T* Datenverarbeitung
to **date** *99* datieren
to **date back to** *16* zurückgehen in
date of birth *99* Geburtsdatum
day-to-day *12* Alltags-
deadline, to **meet a ~** *89* einen Termin einhalten
to **deal with sth** *12* etw bearbeiten, sich mit etw befassen, mit etw zu tun haben
deemed, to **be ~** *55* erachtet werden
default *40* Standard
to **default to sth** *60* etw *(eine Webseite)* standardmäßig aufrufen
defective *48* schadhaft, defekt
to **define** *31* definieren
degree *71T* Grad
delay *55* Verzögerung
deletion *38* Löschung *(von Daten)*
delicate *21* empfindlich
delivery *73* Vortrag
to **demonstrate** *12* vorführen; *98* unter Beweis stellen
dentist *32* Zahnarzt/-ärztin
department *7* Abteilung
depending on *14* je nach, abhängig von
to **deploy** *35* nutzen, einsetzen
to **deselect** *40* deaktivieren
to **design** *7* entwerfen, konstruieren, *(Software:)* entwickeln
designer *7* *(Software:)* Entwickler/in
despite *16* Trotz
destination *87* Ziel, Bestimmungsort
to **destroy** *59* zerstören
details *13* Angaben, Einzelheiten
to **detect** *43* erkennen, feststellen
detergent *21* Reinigungsmittel
to **determine** *8* bestimmen
to develop *9* entwickeln
development *12* Entwicklung
device *13* Gerät
to **diagnose** *14* analysieren, diagnostizieren
to **direct sb** *52* jdn anleiten
direction *14T* Ausrichtung; *35* Richtung
directory *43* Verzeichnis
to **disable** *45* deaktivieren
to **disagree** *63* nicht zustimmen, anderer Meinung sein
to **disassemble** *24* wieder auseinanderbauen
disaster, natural ~ *55* Naturkatastrophe
to **disconnect** *22* trennen, ausschalten
discount *9* Rabatt, Preisnachlass
to **discover** *60* entdecken
to **discuss sth** *7* über etw sprechen, etw erörtern
to **dismantle** *22* ausbauen, demontieren
dishwasher *48* Spülmaschine
to **display** *38* (auf dem Bildschirm) anzeigen; *68* ausstellen, vorführen
to **disregard** *84* ignorieren
distinct *82* deutlich
distinction *71T* Unterscheidung
to **distribute** *16* verteilen, verbreiten, streuen
distributed *87* verteilt
distributor *68* (Zwischen-, Vertriebs-)Händler/in
to **divide** *12* Teilen, aufteilen
dos and don'ts *99* *Dinge, die man tun und lassen sollte*
doubt *63* Zweifel
down-time *34* Ausfallzeit, Stillstand
to **draw** *15* zeichnen
to **draw sth up** *31T* etw ausarbeiten, aufstellen
to **draw up** *75* hochziehen
drive *18* Laufwerk
driving licence *98* Führerschein
drooping *75* *(Schultern:)* hängend
to **drop** *56* fallen lassen
dual *88* Doppel-
due to, to **be ~ sth** *42* an etw liegen
duly *55* ordnungsgemäß
dust *21* Staub
duties *13* Aufgaben

E

eager, to **be ~ to do sth** *68* etw unbedingt tun wollen, es kaum abwarten können, etw zu tun
to **earn** *16* gewinnen
to **eat into sth** *18T* etw schmälern
edge *21* Ecke, Kante, Rand
to **edit** *40* bearbeiten
editor *37* Bearbeitungsprogramm
educational *99* Bildungs-, Lern-
effect, in ~ *55* in Kraft, gültig
efficiency *96* Effizienz
efficient(ly) *34* effizient
effort *40* Mühe, Anstregung
to **elaborate** *31T* ins Detail gehen, näher ausführen
electric shock *26* Stromschlag
electrical source *26* Stromquelle
elementary school (AE) *99* Grundschule
eligible *55* geeignet
embarrassing *51T* peinlich
emergency *26* Notfall
to **emphasize** *35* betonen
employee *8* Beschäftigte/r, Angestellte/r
employer *16* Arbeitgeber/in
employment *97* Anstellung, Einstellung
employment, contract of ~ *97* Arbeitsvertrag
to enable sb to do sth *38* jdm ermöglichen, etw zu tun, jdn in die Lage versetzen, etw zu tun
to **enclose** *99* *(Brief:)* beifügen, beilegen
to **encounter** *41* begegnen
to **encourage sb to do sth** *85* jdn dazu bringen, etw zu tun
encryption *37* Verschlüsselung

energy saving *18T* energiesparend
engineer *16* Ingenieur/in
engineering *57* Maschinenbau
to **enhance** *71T* verbessern, fördern
to **enjoy sth** *73T* etw mögen
to **enrol** *105* sich einschreiben
entire *87* ganze/r/s
to **ensure** *46* gewährleisten, sicherstellen
to **enter** *40* *(Daten)* eingeben
to **enter sth** *105* in etw eintreten
entrance *99* Zugang
entranced *75* gebannt
entry *32* Eintrag
environment *14* Umfeld; *98* Umgebung
environmentally-friendly *67* umweltfreundlich
to **equal** *77T* gleich sein
equally *71T* gleichermaßen, genauso
to **equip sb for sth** *101* jdn auf etw vorbereiten
equipment *48* Geräte
equivalent *29* Entsprechung
erratic(ally) *54P* ungleichmäßig, wirr
error *37* Fehler
especially *10T* besonders
essential *71T* wesentlich, unabdingbar, notwendig
to **establish** *71T* herstellen, festigen, etablieren
estimated *90* geschätzt
ethical(ly) *66* moralisch
etiquette *76* Etikette, Regeln
to evade *61T* vermeiden, sich entziehen
even *21* gleichmäßig
even if *86* selbst wenn
event *68* Veranstaltung
evidence *55* Beweis(e), Nachweis
to **exceed** *99* überschreiten
excess *24* überschüssig, zu viel(e)
excessive *21* zu viel
excluding *55* außer
to **execute** *60* ausführen
executive level *14T* Vorstandsebene
to **exhibit** *68* ausstellen
exhibition *68* Ausstellung, Messe
exhibition space *68* Ausstellungsfläche
exhibitor *68* Aussteller/in
to **expand** *9* expandieren, sich vergrößern
expenses *71T* Kosten
experience *34* Erfahrung
experiment *13* Versuch, Experiment
expertise *71T* Fachwissen
to **explain** *15* erklären, erläutern
explanation *8* Erklärung, Erläuterung
explicitly *63P* ausdrücklich
to **explore** *7* erkunden, erforschen
exposure to sth *71T* Ausgesetzt sein
to **express** *19* ausdrücken
expression *22* Ausdruck
to **extend sth** *68* etw verbreiten
extension *28* *(Telefon:)* Anschluss, Durchwahl
extent, to an ~ *63* bis zu einem gewissen Maß
extract *54P* Auszug, Ausschnitt
extreme(ly) *21* äußerst

F

to **face** *66* vor etw stehen
to **face sth** *66* vor etw stehen, sich etw gegenüber sehen
to **fail** *87* ausfallen
to **fail to do sth** *44* etw nicht tun können
failure *44* Defekt, Versagen; *55* Versäumnis
fan *24* Ventilator
fault *14* Fehler, Defekt
faulty *48* defekt
fearful *75* ängstlich
feature *31T* Merkmal, Eigenschaft, Besonderheit
to **feature** *96* haben, aufweisen
to **feed sth back** *35* etw zurückführen, rückmelden
feet, to **think on one's ~** *98* schnell reagieren
to **fight** *35* kämpfen
to **fill sb in** *89* jdn über etw informieren
finance *12* Finanzabteilung
findings *11* Ergebnisse
firm *21* fest
firmly *8* fest, bestimmt
first aid *26* Erste Hilfe
first and foremost *71T* zuallererst, an erster Stelle
first name *31T* Vorname
first off *83* zuallererst
to **fit** *24* passen
to **fix (a problem)** *24* *(ein Problem)* beheben
fixed *8* Festnetz-
fixed hours *13* feste Arbeitszeiten
flat-head screwdriver *21* Flachkopfschraubendreher
flaw *66* Mangel, Lücke
flexitime *13* Gleitzeit
to **flow** *88* fließen
flow *35* Fluss
flow chart *47* Flussdiagramm
focus *67* Schwerpunkt
to **focus on sth** *8* sich auf etw konzentrieren
to **fold** *24* biegen, falten
folder *40* Ordner
to **follow up** *71T* nachfassen, verfolgen
to **forbid** *63P* verbieten
force *21* Kraft, Gewalt
to **forecast** *93* vorhersagen, voraussagen
to **forgo** *82* auf etw verzichten
formality *83* Förmlichkeit
frame *86* Rahmen
frame of mind *86* *etwa:* Einstellung
freedom *97* Freiheit
to **freeze** *42* erstarren, stehenbleiben
front line manager *14T* leitende/r Angestellte/r
front, up ~ *60* offen, im Voraus
to **fulfil** *101* erfüllen
full-colour *12* Farb-
further *22* weitere/r/s
fuzzy *48T* unscharf, verschwommen

G

to **gain** *101* erwerben
gap *103* Lücke
GCSE *99* *brit. Schulabschlussprüfung für 16-Jährige,* Sekundarabschluss
gender *98* Geschlecht
generally *21* im Allgemeinen
to **generate** *8* (Umsätze usw.) erzielen
gesture *75* Geste

to **gesture** *75* Handbewegungen machen
to **get in touch with sb** *83* sich mit jdm in Verbindung setzen
to **get onto sth** *89* mit etw anfangen
to **get rid of sth** *60* etw loswerden
to **get stuck** *75* eingeklemmt sein, festsitzen
(the) gist *51* das Wesentliche
to **give it a go** *51T* es versuchen
given that *84* unter der Voraussetzung, dass
glad, to **be ~** *14T* sich freuen
to **glance** *86* (kurz) blicken
to **go for sth** *18T* etw nehmen
to **go with your gut** *75* dem Bauchgefühl folgen
go-ahead *91T* grünes Licht
goal *14T* Ziel
good value for money *9* günstige/preiswerte Produkte/Dienstleistungen
government *68* Regierung, staatliche Stellen, öffentliche Verwaltung
graceful(ly) *75* elegant
grammar school *(BE)* *99* Gymnasium
grateful *56* dankbar
grid *8* Gitter
to **grow tight** *75* *(Muskel:)* sich verspannen
growth *16* Wachstum
to **guarantee** *55* garantieren
guidance *105* Beratung
guide *12* (Reise-)Führer/in
guideline *66* Richtlinie, Hinweis
gut, to go with your ~ *75* dem Bauchgefühl folgen

H

to **handle** *18T* mit etw zu rechtkommen; *21* handhaben, behandeln, anfassen; *77* mit etw umgehen; *87* bedienen
handsome, to **be paid ~ly for sth** *35* sich etw gut bezahlen lassen
hard drive *18* Festplatte
hard-working *101* fleißig
harmless *21* harmlos
to **harass** *64* belästigen
to **harm** *64* schaden, verletzen
head *28* Chef/in, Leiter/in
headline *36* Überschrift
headquarters *8* Zentrale
health care *8* Gesundheitswesen
heart failure *26* Herzversagen
heart rhythm problems *26* Herzrhythmusstörungen
heat *86* Hitze
helpline *27* Hotline
hereafter *55* im Folgenden
to **hesitate** *80* zögern
High School Diploma *(AE)* *99* *amerikan. Schulabschlussprüfung für 17- und 18-Jährige,* Abitur
to **highlight** *23* hervorheben
highly skilled *16* hochqualifiziert
high-pitch *48* hochfrequent
to **hijack** *60* kapern, entführen
to **hire** *66* beauftragen, anstellen
to **hit** *51T* drücken; *95* Treffen auf, stoßen auf
to **hold** *28* *(Telefon:)* am Apparat bleiben
to **hold onto sb** *35* jdn festhalten, *hier:* binden
to **hold sb responsible** *55* jdn haftbar machen, jdn verantwortlich machen
Hold on. *54* Einen Moment.
hole *24* Loch
honest *34* ehrlich
hospitality, to **provide ~ to sb** *71T* jdn bewirten
household *12* Haushalt
housing *18* Gehäuse
however *75* wie auch immer
hub *87* Netzknoten
huge *69* riesengroß
human resources (HR) *12* Personal(abteilung)
to **hunch** *75* sich krümmen, sich beugen

I

to **identify** *11* herausfinden, feststellen, nennen
to **imagine sth** *75* sich etw vorstellen
immediate *26* unmittel-bar
impatient *86* ungeduldig
to **implement** *35* einführen, umsetzen
impression *73T* Eindruck
impressive *102T* beeindruckend
improper use *55* unsachgemäßer Gebrauch
improvement *100* Verbesserung
inappropriate *65* unangemessen
to **include** *7* einschließen, einbeziehen, umfassen
including *8* einschließlich, inklusive
inclusive of *77T* inklusive, einschließlich
income *8* Einkommen, Einkünfte
incomplete *45* unvollständig
inconvenience *83* Unannehmlichkeiten
incorrect *21* falsch
to **increase** *69* steigern
independent(ly) *105* selbstständig
in-depth *14T* gründlich
to **indicate** *85* darauf hindeuten
individual *105* Einzelperson
industrial *7* industriell, Industrie-
industry *67* Branche, Industrie
to **infect** *60* infizieren
innovative *12* innovativ
to **insert** *24* einstecken
insight *14T* Einblick
to **insist on sth** *99* auf etw bestehen
to **inspect** *55* prüfen
instance, for ~ *35* zum Beispiel
institution *99* Einrichtung, Institution
instructions *26* Anweisungen; *38T* Anleitung
insufficient *43* unzureichend
to **insult** *64* beleidigen
integrated *16* integriert
intention *71T* Absicht
intentional(ly) *64* absichtlich, vorsätzlich
interconnection *87* Querverbindung, Zusammenschaltung
to **interfere with sth** *45* etw stören, etw beeinträchtigen
interior decorator *30* Innenarchitekt/in, Raumausstatter/in
intern *11* Praktikant/in
interview *32* Vorstellungsgespräch

to interview sb *30T* mit jdm ein Vorstellungsgespräch führen
intimate *75* intim, vertraulich
to introduce *35* einführen
invalid *43* ungültig
to invest *18T* investieren
to investigate sb *66* gegen jdn ermitteln
invoice *81* Rechnung
issue *14* Frage, Problem
issue tracking *96* Problemverfolgung
IT Operations Manager *14* IT-Betriebsleiter/in
item *70* Punkt

J

jack *50* Buchse
job advert(isement) *97* Stellenanzeige
joke *60* Witz, Scherz
to judge *106* beurteilen
jungle *75* Dschungel

K

keen, to be ~ to do sth *101* sehr daran interessiert sein, etw zu tun
to keep in touch *57* in Kontakt bleiben
to keep track of sth *96* den Überblick über etw behalten
key *18T* Haupt-; *51* Taste
keynote (speech) *68* Haupt-/Eröffnungsvortrag
knife *21* Messer

L

to label *12* etikettieren
laboratory *16* (Forschungs-)Labor
labour *90* Arbeit
latest *12* neueste/r/s
to launch *38* starten
law *64* Gesetz
to lay *89* verlegen
to lay out *55* darlegen
to lay the ground for sth *66* die Grundlage für etw bilden
layout *24* Anordnung
lead *24* Leitung, Kabel
lead, customer ~ *35* Kundenkontakt, Kundendaten
leader *14T* Führungspersönlichkeit
to leak *54P* austreten, auslaufen
to leave sb with sb *10T* jdn mit jdm allein lassen
to leave sth in one's wake *66* etw zurücklassen, etw hinterlassen
leaving party *32* Abschiedsparty
lecturer *104* Dozent/in
legitimate *60* rechtmäßig, seriös
to let sb down *18T* jdn im Stich lassen
lever *24* Hebel
to liaise with sb *98* mit jdm zusammenarbeiten
licence *40* Lizenz
licence agreement *40* Lizenzvereinbarung
to lift *24* anheben
likely *43* wahrscheinlich
limited *87* begrenzt
line *101* *(Text:)* Zeile
to line up *21* ausrichten
link *105* Verbindung
to link *70* verbinden
lion *75* Löwe
liquid *21* flüssig
located *7* gelegen
to lock *24* einrasten lassen
to log on *38* sich einloggen
loose *48* locker, lose
to lower *24* absenken, einlassen, schieben
lunch break *57* Mittagspause

M

mad, to go ~ *48T* spinnen
main *7* Haupt-
mainframe computer *16* Großrechner
mainly *7* hauptsächlich
mains *22* (Strom-)Netz
to maintain *14* betreuen, instandhalten, warten; *35* aufrechterhalten
major *41T* groß
to make sense *34* sinnvoll sein
to make sure *13* sicherstellen, gewährleisten, sich vergewissern
to make up for sth *83* etw wiedergutmachen
maker *16* Hersteller/in
malfunction *55* Ausfall, Versagen, Störung
malicious *44* schädlich
to manage *89* es schaffen
manner *105* Art (und Weise)
manual *55* Handbuch
to manufacture *16* herstellen
mark *73* Note
market *8* Markt
to match sth *71T* mit etw übereinstimmen
to maximize *96* maximieren
meaning *22* Bedeutung
means *55* Mittel
meantime, in the ~ *90* in der Zwischenzeit
measurable *71T* messbar
medal *16* Orden, Medaille
to mediate *46* vermitteln
medical *26* medizinisch
to meet a deadline *89* einen Termin einhalten
to meet sb's needs *34* jds Bedürfnissen entsprechen
member *105* Mitglied
memory *18* Arbeitsspeicher
to mention *12* erwähnen
microwave *48* Mikrowelle
mind, to bear sth in ~ *89* an etw denken
mind, to change one's ~ *40* seine Meinung ändern
mind, frame of ~ *86* *etwa:* Einstellung
to mind *10T* etw dagegen haben
mind, Never ~. *51T* Macht nichts.
minutes *70* Protokoll
minutes, to take ~ *70* Protokoll führen
mirror *38* Spiegelserver
to miss *93* *(Termin:)* nicht einhalten
to misunderstand *93* missverstehen, falsch verstehen
model *85* Muster, Vorbild
to modify *41T* modifizieren
to monitor *14* überwachen; *35* dokumentieren
moreover *101* darüber hinaus
mostly *18T* hauptsächlich
motor vehicle *8* Kraftfahrzeug
to mount *24* montieren, einbauen
mounting hole *24* Montage-, Befestigungsloch
movement *26* Bewegung
muscle *26* Muskel
to mute *50* stummschalten

N

name, first ~ *31T* Vorname
nationwide *68* landesweit
natural disaster *55* Naturkatastrophe
to **navigate** *40* navigieren
need *32* Bedarf
neglect *55* Fahrlässigkeit
network *8* Netzwerk
to **network** *87* vernetzen
newly *97* vor kurzem
next to *71T* neben
to **nickname** *16* *(mit einem Spitznamen)* nennen
Nobel Prize *16* Nobelpreis
node *87* Knotenpunkt
noise *48* Lärm, Geräusch(e)
non-conducting *26* nicht leitend
notch *24* Kerbe, Nut
to **note** *38* darauf hinweisen; *55* vermerken; *60* zur Kenntnis nehmen
nuclear disaster *55* Reaktorkatastrophe

O

objective *68* Ziel
obligation *55* Verpflichtung
obscene *65* obszön
to **observe** *71T* beobachten
occasion *84* Gelegenheit
occasionally *18T* gelegentlich
to **occur** *26* auftreten
to **offend** *64* beleidigen
official *68* Beamte/r
once *40* sobald
to **operate** *87* bedienen
operating model *16* Betriebs-/Geschäftsmodell
operational *89* betriebsbereit
operator *67* Betreiber/in
opinion, to give your ~ *63* seine Meinung äußern
opportunity *86* Gelegenheit
oral *98* mündlich
order *11* Reihenfolge; *12* Auftrag, Bestellung
order, in ~ to *48* um ... zu
order processing *12* Auftragsbearbeitung
organization chart *14* Organigramm
outfit *66* Unternehmen
outlet *50* Anschluss
outline *100* Entwurf
to **outline** *55* umreißen, darstellen
to **oversee** *14T* beaufsichtigen, überwachen
oversight *83* Versehen
to **over-tighten** *24* *(Schraube)* zu fest anziehen
overtime *13* Überstunden
own, on one's ~ *48T* selbstständig
owner *87* Inhaber/in, Eigentümer/in
ownership right *64* Eigentumsrecht

P

to **pack** *12* packen, verpacken
package *18T* (Software-)Paket
pain *26* Schmerz(en)
panel *68* Gremium
parent company *16* Muttergesellschaft
part, on one's ~ *40* von jds Seite
participant *70* Teilnehmer/in
to **participate** *67* teilnehmen
participation *70* Teilnahme
particular, in ~ *71T* insbesondere
particularly *45* insbesondere
partnership *68* Beteiligung, Teilhaberschaft
to **pass sth on** *31T* etw weiterreichen/-leiten
to **pass through** *26* hindurchgehen, -fließen
passionate *67* leidenschaftlich
to **paste** *54* einfügen
patent *16* Patent
path *88* Weg, Pfad
patient *86* geduldig
to **pause** *75* innehalten, pausieren
to **pause sth** *38* etw anhalten
to **pave the way** *66* den Weg bereiten/ebnen
pay *97* Bezahlung
per annum *98* pro Jahr
to **perform** *38* *(Tätigkeit)* ausführen; Leistung bringen, funktionieren
performance *18T* Leistung
period *55* Zeitraum, Laufzeit
peripheral *14* Peripheriegerät
permanent *98* *(Anstellung:)* fest
permission *60* Erlaubnis
to **permit** *65* erlauben, gestatten
person, in ~ *14* persönlich
Phillips screwdriver *21* Kreuzschlitzschraubendreher
physical(ly) *59* physisch
to **pick** *71T* auswählen, aussuchen
pile *49* Stapel
pioneer *16* Pionier
to **pioneer** *16* entwickeln, zum ersten Mal einsetzen
pirate *42* Pirat
to **place** *24* legen
to **place (an order)** *12* *(einen Auftrag)* erteilen
placement *10T* Praktikum
to **play up** *56* Ärger machen
pleasant *97* angenehm
pleased *102T* zufrieden, froh
Pleased to meet you. *10T* Nett, Sie kennen zu lernen.
pleasure *28* Vergnügen
pleasure, My ~. *28* Gern geschehen.
pliers *21* Zange
plug *48* Stecker
to **plug** *50* (Stecker) einstecken
point, at some ~ *73T* irgendwann
point, up to a ~ *63* bis zu einem gewissen Grad/Punkt
to **point out** *66* darauf hinweisen
policy *57* Linie, Vorgehensweise, Politik
polite *64* höflich
popular *60* beliebt
port *24* Anschluss
position *15* Stellung, Position
to **position** *26* platzieren
to **possess** *98* besitzen, verfügen über
posture *75* Haltung
potential *46* potenziell
to **pour** *73T* (ein)gießen
power *22* Strom
power cord *49* Stromkabel
power supply *22* Stromversorgung
power supply unit *18* Netzteil
powerful *18T* stark, leistungsfähig
practitioner *105* Fachmann/-frau
praise *97* Lob
pre-built *17* vorgefertigt
preference *35* Vorliebe, Wunsch
prepared *56* bereit, willens

presence *12* Präsenz, Anwesenheit
present *55* anwesend
to **press** *43* drücken
pressure *21* Druck
pretty *18T* ziemlich
to **prevent** *21* verhindern
primary *55* Haupt-
primary school *(BE)* *99* Grundschule
principal *105* wichtig, hauptsächlich
principle *8* Prinzip
prior to *55* vor
privacy *64* Privatsphäre
procedure *38T* Verfahren, Vorgehen
process *16* Ablauf, Vorgang, Prozess
to **produce** *99* *(Dokument etc.)* vorlegen
production facility *98* Produktionsstätte, Werk
professional visitor *68* Fachbesucher
profile *7* Porträt, Profil
profitable *16* profitabel
progress *40* Fortgang; *96* Fortschritte
progress, in ~ *34* im Gang
progress bar *39* Ladebalken, Fortschrittsbalken
progress report *94* Arbeitsbericht, Zwischenbericht
project portfolio *96* Projektportfolio
to promote sth *13* für etw Werbung machen; *105* etw fördern
promotion *97* Beförderung
promotional *12* Werbe-
prompt *40* Aufforderung
pros and cons *17* Für und Wider, Vor- und Nachteile
proven, to **be ~ to be** *75* etw nachweislich sein
to **provide** *14* (an)bieten, liefern; *99* *(Adresse etc.)* angeben
to **provide sb with sth** *8* jdn mit etw versorgen, jdm etw bieten
to **provide for sth** *53* etw vorsehen, etw regeln
to **provide hospitality to sb** *71T* jdn bewirten
provisional *91* vorläufig, provisorisch

to **protect** *24* schützen
public holiday *55* gesetzlicher Feiertag
to **purchase** *35* kaufen
purpose *55* Zweck
purposeful *75* zielstrebig
to **put** *35* formulieren, sagen
to **put sb in charge of sth** *89* jdm die Verantwortung für etw übertragen
to **put sb through** *28* *(Telefon:)* jdn durchstellen
to **put sth at risk** *64* etw aufs Spiel setzen, etw gefährden

Q

qualification *98* Abschluss, Qualifikation
qualified *101* qualifiziert
to **qualify** *97* einen Abschluss machen
quality assurance (QA) *14T* Qualitätssicherung
query *60* (Such-)Anfrage
quotation *89* Angebot, Kostenvoranschlag
to **quote** *82* einen Kostenvoranschlag machen, *(Preis:)* nennen

R

racist *65* rassistisch
radiation *48* Strahlung
radio station *11* Radiosender
rainy *73T* regnerisch
to **raise** *26* erhöhen
to **raise sth** *82* etw ansprechen
range *31T* Produktlinie, Angebot
to **range from ... to ...** *16* sich von ... bis ... erstrecken
to **rank** *96* einstufen
rapidly *9* rasch, schnell
to **realize** *71T* verwirklichen, umsetzen
to **realize sth** *35* etw begreifen, sich einer Sache bewusst werden
to **rearrange** *65* neu anordnen
reasonable *55* vernünftig, zumutbar
to **reassociate** *40* erneut zuweisen
recent, in ~ years *14* in den letzten Jahren
reception *10* Empfang
receptionist *10* Empfangsmitarbeiter/in

to **recognize** *41T* erkennen
to **recommend** *17* empfehlen
to **recruit** *9* *(Personal)* einstellen
to **redirect** *60* umleiten
to **reduce** *53* verringern
to **refer to sth** *45* sich auf etw beziehen
referee *98* Referenz
to **refocus** *16* sich neu konzentrieren
to **refresh** *44* auffrischen
to **refuse** *45* sich weigern
regarding *54* bezüglich, betreffend
regardless *98* ungeachtet
regards *83* *(Brief:)* Mit freundlichen Grüßen
registry *48* eine Datenbank zur Speicherung von Konfigurationsdaten
to **reject** *30* ablehnen
related *14* bezogen (auf)
related, to **be ~ to sth** *62* mit etw zu tun haben
relation *27* Beziehung
relationship *35* Beziehung
relaxation *75* Entspannung
relaxed *75* locker, entspannt
reliable *101* zuverlässig, verlässlich
remaining *9* übrige/r/s
remote *60* entfernt
removable *14* austauschbar, Wechsel-
to **remove** *22* entfernen
to **replicate** *16* nachbilden, reproduzieren
to **reply** *83* antworten
to **report** *35* berichten
to **report to sb** *14T* jdm unterstellt sein
to **represent** *68* repräsentieren, vertreten
representative *55* Vertreter/in
reputation *91T* Ruf
request *12* Bitte, Wunsch, Anfrage
to **require** *31* benötigen, erfordern
requirement *28* Bedürfnis, Anforderung
research *12* Forschung; *37* Nachforschung(en), Recherche
to **research** *43* Nachforschungen anstellen, recherchieren
to **resolve** *50* lösen

resource *64* Ressourcen
to **respect** *59* beachten, respektieren
respiratory failure *26* Atemstillstand
to **respond** *35* reagieren
response *82* Reaktion, Antwort
responsibility *13* Zuständigkeit, Aufgabenbereich; *97* Verantwortung
responsible *12* verantwortlich, zuständig
responsible, to hold sb ~ *55* jdn haftbar machen, jdn verantwortlich machen
responsibly *64* verantwortungsbewusst
result *12* Ergebnis, Resultat
to **result** *45* resultieren
to **resume sth** *38* etw wiederaufnehmen
resuscitation, cardiopulmonary ~ *26* Herz-Lungen-Wiederbelebung
retailer *67* Einzelhändler/in
to **retain** *75* behalten
retention arm *24* Haltearm
retention clip *24* Halteklammer
to **return a call** *28* zurückrufen
to **reveal** *65* preisgeben, verraten
revenue *8* Einkünfte, Einnahmen, Umsatz
revenue, total ~ *16* Gesamterlös, Gesamtumsatz
reverse *99* umgekehrt
to **review** *38* überprüfen, bewerten
revised *84* überarbeitet, neu
to **reward** *66* belohnen
rid, to get ~ of sth *60* etw loswerden
riot *55* Aufstand, Unruhe(n)
risk, to put sth at ~ *64* etw aufs Spiel setzen, etw gefährden
risk, which have ~ attached to them *63P* die risikobehaftet sind
risky *57* riskant
role *14* Rolle
route *61T* Weg, Route
row *75* Reihe
rule *65* Vorschrift, Regel
run, in the long ~ *35* auf lange Sicht

S

salary *98* Gehalt
sales *16* Verkauf, Vertrieb
sales force *35* Vertriebspersonal
salesperson *18* Verkäufer/in
satisfactory *86* befriedigend
satisfying *17* befriedigend
to **save** *18T* (Daten) sichern
to **scan** *23* überfliegen
schedule *34* (Zeit-)Plan
scheduling *96* Terminplanung, Disposition
scratch, from ~ *45* (ganz) von vorn
screensaver *45* Bildschirmschoner
to **screw** *24* schrauben
screwdriver *21* Schraubendreher, -zieher
screwdriver, flat-head ~ *21* Flachkopfschraubendreher
screwdriver, Phillips ~ *21* Kreuzschlitzschraubendreher
search engine *60* Suchmaschine
secretary *58* Sekretär/in
section *46* Teil, Abschnitt
secure *51* sicher
to **secure** *24* sichern
security *14* Sicherheit
to **seek** *98* suchen
to **select** *35* auswählen
to **self-replicate** *60* sich reproduzieren
seller *67* Verkäufer/in, Anbieter/in
semiconductor *16* Halbleiter
sense, to make ~ *34* sinnvoll sein
sensitive *21* empfindlich
sensitive, to be ~ to sth *48* auf etw empfindlich reagieren
separately *82* separat, extra
to **serve sb** *16* jdn bedienen, jdm dienen
servicing *53* Wartung, Instandhaltung
session *12* Runde, Sitzung
set *16* Reihe, Satz, Menge, Klasse
to **set sth up** *28* etw einrichten
setting *41* Einstellung
to **settle** *82* *(Rechnung)* begleichen, bezahlen
set-up *34* System
several *8* einige, mehrere
shared *16* gemeinsam genutzt
sharp *21* scharf
shift *13* Schicht; *16* Schritt, Veränderung
to **ship** *12* versenden
to **shorten** *75* sich verkürzen
to **show sb around** *12* jdn herumführen
to **shut down** *48T* herunterfahren
to **sign** *99* unterschreiben
to **signal** *72* weisen, anzeigen
signal pin *21* Kontaktstift
silently *75* schweigend, lautlos
silly *51T* dumm, albern
similarity *72* Gemeinsamkeit, Ähnlichkeit
sincerely, Yours ~ *84* *(Brief:)* Mit freundlichen Grüßen
site, on ~ *13* vor Ort
skilled *75* kompetent
to **skim read** *23* querlesen, überfliegen
to **slide** *24* schieben
slightly *26* etwas, geringfügig, ein wenig
slot *24* Steckplatz
to **smooth things over** *91T* die Dinge wieder ins Lot bringen
smooth(ly) *95* glatt
snag *95* Haken, Schwierigkeiten
socket *24* Fassung, Sockel; *48* Buchse
to **soften** *92* (ab)mildern
solder pin *21* Lötstift
solution *34* Lösung
to **solve** *14* lösen
to **sort** *30* sortieren
to **sort sth out** *34* etw klären, in Ordnung bringen
source *26* Quelle
space *30T* (freier) Platz
to **space sth out** *99* *(Text)* spationieren
speaker *48* Lautsprecher
specialist *7* Spezialist/-in, Fachmann/-frau
specialist *61T* Spezial-
to **specialize in sth** *7* sich auf etw spezialisieren
specific *14* konkret, speziell, bestimmt, spezifisch
specification *31T* technische Daten/Anforderungen; *43* Angabe
to **specify** *43* (genau) angeben
speech *75* Rede, Vortrag
speech bubble *97* Sprechblase

speed *31T* Geschwindigkeit
speed, to bring sb up to ~ *91T* jdn auf den neuesten Stand bringen
spillage *65* Verschütten, Verschüttetes
to **spread** *58* sich ausbreiten, sich verbreiten
spread *61* Ausbreitung, Verbreitung
spreadsheet *37* Tabellenkalkulationsprogramm
square metre *68* Quadratmeter
stability *75* Stabilität
stable *18T* stabil
staff *9* Personal
stage *38* Phase, Abschnitt
standoff *24* Abstandsbolzen
star *88* Stern
to **state** *63* erklären, angeben, sagen
state of the art *88* Stand der Technik
statement *16* Aussage, Behauptung
static *22* elektrostatische Ladung
stationery *55* Büromaterial
stay *10* Aufenthalt
to **stay with sth** *86* bei etw bleiben
steadily *67* kontinuierlich, stetig
to **steal** *66* stehlen
step *24* Schritt
stereotype *73T* Klischee
to **stick to sth** *41T* an etw festhalten, bei etw bleiben
to **stick with sth** *18T* bei etw bleiben
to **stir sb up** *75* jdn aufrütteln, aufscheuchen
stock, in ~ *77T* auf Lager, vorrätig
to **stop sth in its tracks** *61T* etw stoppen, aufhalten
storage *14* *(Daten:)* Speicherung
to **store** *18T* *(Daten)* speichern
straight away *51T* sofort
straightforward *38T* einfach
strength *85* Stärke
strict(ly) *64* streng, strikt
stride *75* Schritt
strike *55* Streik
stuck, to **get ~** *75* eingeklemmt sein, festsitzen
subconscious(ly) *75* unterbewusst
subcontractor *89* Subunternehmer/in
subject, to **be ~ to** *55* unterliegen, vorbehaltlich gelten
subsidiary *8* Niederlassung
subtotal *80* Zwischensumme
suck, to be ~ed in by sth *86* sich von etw anstecken lassen
to **suffer** *91T* leiden, Schaden nehmen
to **suffer sth** *26* etw erleiden
to **suggest** *30* vorschlagen
suggestion *30* Vorschlag
suitable *34* passend, geeignet
to **suit** *34* passen
suited to *87* geeignet für
to **summarize** *17* zusammenfassen
supplement *105* Ergänzung
supplier *13* Lieferant/in
supplies *77* Bedarf
to **supply** *8* liefern, anbieten
support *9* Unterstützung, Hilfe
to **support** *35* unterstützen, helfen
sure, to **make ~** *13* sicherstellen, gewährleisten, sich vergewissern
surface *24* Oberfläche
surname *28* Nachname
surprised, to **be ~** *82* sich wundern
to **swap** *15* Tauschen
swearing *64* Fluchen
swift(ly) *35* schnell
to **swing** *75* schwingen
to **switch off** *48* (sich) ausschalten
to **switch sth on** *22* etw einschalten

T

to **take action** *29* Maßnahmen ergreifen
to **take breaths** *75* einatmen
to **take care of sb** *13* sich um jdn kümmern
to **take minutes** *70* Protokoll führen
to **take place** *15* stattfinden
talk *14T* Vortrag
to **target sb** *35* jdn als Zielgruppe ins Visier nehmen
technician *26* Techniker/in
technique *60* Methode, Technik
tedious *40* lästig, müh-sam
temporary *38* provisorisch, vorübergehend
to **tend to** *60* dazu neigen
term *84* Begriff
term, in ~s of *34* was ... anbelangt
terms and conditions *39* (Nutzungs-)Bedingungen
territory *75* Territorium
therefore *71T* deshalb, also
to **think on one's feet** *98* schnell reagieren
thorough *68* gründlich
threat *26* Bedrohung
through *55* bis
throughout *67* in ganz
tick *40* Häkchen
tight *31T* knapp; *75* fest
tight, to grow ~ *75* *(Muskel:)* sich verspannen
to **tighten** *24* *(Schraube)* anziehen
time, on ~ *13* pünktlich
timeline *96* Zeitschiene
timely *55* rechtzeitig
timetable *11* Zeitplan, Stundenplan
title *14T* Titel, Bezeichnung
tone *83* Ton
topology *87* Topologie, Netzstruktur
total, in ~ *77T* insgesamt
total revenue *16* Gesamterlös, Gesamtumsatz
touch, to **get in ~ with sb** *83* sich mit jdm in Verbindung setzen
touch, to **keep in ~** *57* in Kontakt bleiben
tour *11* Rundgang; *12* Reise, Tour
track, to keep ~ of sth *96* den Überblick über etw behalten
track, to stop sth in its ~s *61T* etw stoppen, aufhalten
trade *67* Branche
trade, by ~ *31T* gelernt, von Beruf
trade fair *12* (Handels-)Messe
trade visitor *67* Fachbesucher/in
trader *67* Händler/in
to **train** *99* ausbilden
training *13* Schulung, Ausbildung

Textquellen

S.16, shortened and adapted from http://www.linkedin.com/companies/ibm
S. 26, modified from http://www.mayoclinic.com/health/first-aid-electrical-shock/FA00051
S. 40, modified from www.OpenOffice.org
S. 50, flow chart from http://it.ccri.edu/helpdesk/pc-troubleshooting.shtml
S. 59, modified from http://www.bleepingcomputer.com/tutorials/tutorial101.html
S. 66, modified from http://www.newser.com/story/74888/iphone-hacker-gets-job-writing-apps.html and http://www.fudzilla.com/home/news/latest/twitter-hacker-gets-job
S. 75, shortened and adapted from http://www.pattiwood.net/article.asp?PageID=2331
S. 88, modified from http://www.buzzle.com/articles/types-of-network-topologies.html
and http://www.buzzle.com/articles/advantages-and-disadvantages-of-different-network-topologies.html
S. 105, modified from www.europass.ie/europass/

Bildquellen

RF-Fotos

Alamy: S. 7/4/Epcot Images, S. 18/8/Jan Hanus;
Getty Images: S. 7/2/Fuse;
IStockphoto: S. 7/1/Andrew Howe, S. 18/4/Clayton Hansen, S. 63/Diane Diederich, S.71/Mark Stay;
Shutterstock: S. 7/2/Julien Bastide, S. 13/1/Dean Mitchell, S. 13/2/Kamira, S. 13/3/Yuri Arcurs, S. 13/4/Studio Johann2000, S. 18/1/Oleksiy Mark, S. 18/2/Jim Guy, S. 18/3/ipixs, S. 18/5/Kayros Studio "Be Happy!", S. 18/6/Garsya, S. 18/7/Studio 37, S. 27/wavebreak-media ltd, S. 37/1/Losevsky Pavel, S. 37/2/3/crisovao, S. 37/4/Elena Elisseeva, S. 48/Monika Wisniewska, S. 58/StockLite, S. 97/Franck Boston

RM-Fotos

Alamy: S. 12/Cultura RM;
Corbis: S. 14/Creasource

Cartoons

Oxford Designers & Illustrators: S. 21/1/2/3/4, S. 23/1/2/3/4, S. 26/1/2, S. 35, S. 47/1/2/3, S. 76/1/2/3/4